Horror:
A Literary History

Horror:
A Literary History

Edited by Xavier Aldana Reyes

This book is dedicated to my sister, Alexandra Aldana Reyes.
Amor hermano desde tierra hermana.

First published in 2016 by
The British Library
96 Euston Road
London NW1 2DB

Text copyright © the Authors, 2016
Illustrations © the British Library Board and other named copyright holders

Cataloguing in Publication Data
A catalogue record for this book is available from the British Library

ISBN 978 0 7123 5607 7

Jacket design by Rawshock Design
Typeset by IDSUK (DataConnection) Ltd
Printed in Estonia by Greif Ltd

Acknowledgements

I would like to thank Rob Davies and Miranda Harrison for their interest, editorial help and general support of this project. It has been an absolute pleasure working with them and the British Library.

I would also like to thank the six contributors, Dale Townshend, Agnieszka Soltysik Monnet, Royce Mahawatte, Roger Luckhurst, Bernice M. Murphy and Steffen Hantke, for sharing their expertise and for their timeliness, patience and understanding. It is safe to say that a job of this scope is best done in good company.

I would also like to thank David McWilliam and Keith O'Sullivan for additional reviewing help.

Finally, I would like to thank my family and partner for their continued support and love.

Frontispiece: *The Empty House*, Algernon Blackwood, 1906. Front cover of edition published by Eveleigh Nash, 1906.

Contents

List of Contributors

Xavier Aldana Reyes is Senior Lecturer in English Literature and Film at Manchester Metropolitan University. His books include *Body Gothic: Corporeal Transgression in Contemporary Literature and Horror Film* (University of Wales Press, 2014), *Digital Horror: Haunted Technologies, Network Panic and the Found Footage Phenomenon* (co-edited with Linnie Blake; I.B. Tauris, 2015) and *Horror Film and Affect: Towards a Corporeal Model of Viewership* (Routledge, 2016). His work has appeared in international peer-reviewed journals such as *Horror Studies* and *Gothic Studies*. Xavier is the editor of the Horror Studies series at the University of Wales Press.

Steffen Hantke has written on contemporary literature, film and culture. He is the author of *Conspiracy and Paranoia in Contemporary Literature* (Peter Lang, 1994), as well as editor of *Horror*, a special issue of *Paradoxa* (2002), *Horror: Creating and Marketing Fear* (University Press of Mississippi, 2004), *Caligari's Heirs: The German Cinema of Fear after 1945* (Scarecrow Press, 2007) and *American Horror Film: The Genre at the Turn of the Millennium* (University Press of Mississippi, 2010). His essays and reviews have appeared in *Science Fiction Studies*, *Critique*, *Story Telling*, *Literature/Film Quarterly* and other journals.

Roger Luckhurst is Professor of Modern and Contemporary Literature at Birkbeck College, University of London. He is the author of *The Mummy's Curse: The True History of a Dark Fantasy* (Oxford University Press, 2012) and *Zombies: A Cultural History* (Reaktion, 2015), and has edited several Gothic works for the Oxford World's Classics series.

Royce Mahawatte is Lecturer in Cultural Studies at Central Saint Martins, University of the Arts (London), and obtained his doctorate from the University of Oxford. He is the author of *George Eliot and the Gothic Novel* (University of Wales Press, 2013) and has chapters in the collections *Queering the Gothic* (Manchester University Press, 2009), and *More Dirty Looks: Gender, Pornography and Power* (British Film Institute, 2003). His research interests are Victorian fiction, the Gothic and the literary and cultural study of fashion and the body.

Bernice M. Murphy is Lecturer in Popular Literature at the School of English, Trinity College, the University of Dublin. Her recent publications include *The Highway Horror Film* (Palgrave, 2014) and *The Rural Gothic in American Popular Culture: Backwoods Horror and Terror in the Wilderness* (Palgrave, 2013). She is currently writing *Key Concepts in Contemporary Popular Fiction* for Edinburgh University Press, and (with Elizabeth McCarthy) editing a collection entitled *Lost Souls: Essays on Gothic Horror's Forgotten Personages* for McFarland. Along with Elizabeth McCarthy, she co-founded and co-edited the online *Irish Journal of Gothic and Horror Studies* from 2006 to 2012. She has written many articles and book chapters on horror fiction and film.

Agnieszka Soltysik Monnet is Professor of American Literature and Culture at the University of Lausanne in Switzerland. She is the author of *The Poetics and Politics of the American Gothic: Gender and Slavery in Nineteenth Century American Literature* (Ashgate, 2010) and the editor of several collections of essays, including *The Gothic in Contemporary Literature and Popular Culture* (with Justin Edwards; Routledge, 2012). She is also the co-editor of a special issue of *Gothic Studies* (with Marie Lienart; Manchester University Press) on 'The Gothic in an Age of Terror(ism)'.

Dale Townshend is Senior Lecturer in Gothic and Romantic Studies at the University of Stirling, Scotland. His recent publications include *The Gothic World* (with Glennis Byron; Routledge, 2014), *Ann Radcliffe, Romanticism and the Gothic* (with Angela Wright; Cambridge University Press, 2014), *Terror and Wonder: The Gothic Imagination* (British Library Publishing, 2014) and *Romantic Gothic: An Edinburgh Companion* (with Angela Wright; Edinburgh University Press, 2014). As the holder of an AHRC Leadership Fellowship, he is currently completing a book entitled *Gothic Antiquity: History, Romance and the Architectural Imagination, 1760–1840*.

Introduction:
What, Why and When Is Horror Fiction?

Xavier Aldana Reyes

What Is Horror Fiction?

In some respects, defining horror is easy enough. Deriving, etymologic-
ally, from the Latin verb *horrere*, to tremble or shudder (or, of hair, to
stand on end), horror is normally used in fiction to refer to texts or narratives that aim to generate fear, shock or disgust (or a combination of
these), alongside associated emotional states such as dread or suspense.
Although this is not necessarily a requisite, horror is also thought to
revolve around supernatural phenomena or fantastic events. Where the
latter focus on the speculative aspects of supernatural phenomena, horror uses them to secure a reaction. Widely read and published – and
not like other genres that rely more heavily on specific historical and
locational coordinates, such as the Western or science fiction – horror is
largely defined by its affective pretences. Horror takes its name, in other
words, from the effects that it seeks to elicit in its readers. Since these
are, arguably, best conjured up over short and intense fictional stretches,
the genre is strongly associated with the short story format and, in the
late twentieth and twenty-first centuries, with cinema, where the horror experience rarely lasts longer than 90 minutes. A largely constant
stream of blockbusters since the 1970s, alongside changes in publishing
trends and fan practices, has meant that horror is now, in fact, more
readily associated with the film industry than with the literary one. Yet

horror has also manifested in other media, from graphic novels to video games, where it has produced a string of successes since the release of the first *Resident Evil* instalment in 1996.

An eminently transmedial, transhistorical and marketable genre, horror's characters and trends escape the confines of given texts and become part of the broader zeitgeist. Dracula costumes, themselves a palimpsestic result of the cinematic appropriation of Bram Stoker's novel of 1897, may be worn to Hallowe'en parties, and the unnameable, out-of-space creatures of H. P. Lovecraft's Cthulhu mythos may be interacted with, almost a century later, in a video game such as *Call of Cthulhu: Dark Corners of the Earth* (2005). Heavily intertextual and referential, often intentionally formulaic, horror texts can be easily identified by the enticing or daring messages that often address the potential reader from the lurid covers of books or from film posters. Horror, in short, tends to propose an entertaining and scary ride.

In other respects, defining the intricacies of horror can be a somewhat trickier affair than first appears. Although we may readily associate the genre with specific characters or creatures – including spiritual visitations, mad scientists, monsters from the deep, bloodsucking aristocrats, perverse serial killers, the undead, lycanthropes, mutations of the atom age – and settings – such as the old dark house, a castle or similar haunted building, the cursed landscape, the slaughterhouse, the freak show parade, the ruined abbey, the cemetery, the basement or the underground tunnel, the unfathomable sea – these alone are not sufficient to guarantee generic allegiance. The works of Terry Pratchett, full of every conceivable supernatural character, are a good example: at no point is his fantasy work, full of self-referential humour, in danger of being taken for horror (not even for comedy horror); the tone of the fiction, witty and satirical, is diametrically opposed to horror's suspenseful, heart-wrenching, disturbing and confrontational exercises. For this very reason, horror can appear virtually anywhere: the prospect of someone's horrific death or an impending sense of doom can materialise in the most mundane of situations. This is why novels that may largely belong to other genres, such as J. G. Ballard's dystopian science fiction works, the visceral crime procedurals of Tess Gerritsen or Chuck Palahniuk's neoliberal nightmares, teeter on the brink of the horrific. Because fear is itself a rather vague emotion which may be caused by anything that poses a sense of threat (see Aldana Reyes 2016), the feelings connected to horror, and necessarily its catalysts, are also up for debate. For some, horror must be, at least in part, 'disgusting' (Cavarero 2009: 8); for others, however, 'grossing out' readers is only one – the easiest and less complex – of the ways in which horror can affect readers (see King 1991: 40).

When conflated with the weird, which itself could be considered a melange of horror, science fiction and fantasy elements, horror may be defined by the terrifying moment of sublimity experienced as human consciousness is faced with its insignificant position in a vast cosmos. Here the unnameable, the thing we cannot understand or put into words, becomes the source of fear. The horror produced by ghosts, those presences which should not be there and remind us of the past or the afterlife, are similar in essence. However, when graphically inclined, horror can be a lot more materially specific: it can stand in for the weakening process of identification behind the vulnerability of the victim, so that when knives slash fictional stomachs we may suffer for our own safety and for that of the characters. Equally visceral is the gnawed and putrid body of the shuffling zombie, who, in its abjection, foregrounds the eminent corruptibility and transience of life. In fictions of transformation, the moment of horror can stem from the deathly nature of a werewolf or a Mr Hyde, and yet the encounter with our 'other', be it primal or unconscious, offers a different type of horror experience.

While 'horror' as a more general word – although never in the sense of 'real' horror experienced in day-to-day life, which can be even more difficult to pin down – may designate a product's appeal to channel some form of fear, the specificities of horror are chiefly determined by the medium through which it is experienced. Hence horror films rely on moving images and the use of cinematography: a given editing style, camera angles, post-production effects and, aurally, the use of stingers, loud bangs and a host of other techniques can be the direct consequences of feelings of fear, ranging from the jump scare (or startle) to dread or the encounter with images that may be 'too much'. Horror fiction, like all other forms of literature, relies on a non-indexical engagement with the world. Unlike cinema, which cannot help but show us images, fiction forces us to process information. This defines horror fiction and distinguishes it from other species of fictional horror. Horror fiction may more readily disturb the minds of readers by engaging with their imagination. For this reason, a significant number of horror stories leave their monsters relatively unexplained or vague; as we have learnt, suggestion is often enough to ignite fearful feelings. Horror has to work harder to create a sense of atmosphere, as it uses words (sometimes illustrations), but it can also, equally, get by on very little – just what may be needed in order to disconcert or disturb, in fact. It is this creative and imaginative potential that, for this writer, makes horror such a personal experience. In this light, horror fiction may be best understood as the literature that actively, and predominantly, seeks to create a pervasive feeling of unease and which, consistently, although not necessarily always successfully, attempts to arouse the emotions and sensations we would normally ascribe to feeling under threat.

Why Is Horror Fiction?

The issue of what horror can do is intricately woven into the question of what it may be. Horror can, naturally, be understood as more than a genre of fiction that subscribes to certain thematic concerns or specific affective drives. For some, many of them academics who study the genre, horror is also a '*phobic* cultural form' (Jones 2014: xi), that is, a product of a given time and socio-cultural and psychological make-up that changes and moulds according to shifts in power and historically contingent anxieties. This means that horror acts as a form of cathartic entertainment: it both probes our deepest fears and allows us to fantasise about their dangers from the vantage point of fiction. A good example is the slew of late twentieth- and early twenty-first-century horror narratives, most recently David Cronenberg's *Consumed* (2014), where digital technologies are either connected to evil or perversion, or else the mediator of misfortune. Inevitably these texts explore, among other things, the real cost of technology and the detrimental effects of social networking and instant information communication systems on human relationships. In other words, they serve to investigate the darker side of our gadget-obsessed, hyper-connected capitalist consumer culture. For

an older example, the colonial, orientalist nightmares of *fin-de-siècle* horror landmarks – such as Rudyard Kipling's short story 'The Mark of the
Beast' (1890) or Richard Marsh's novel *The Beetle* (1897) – may be read
as fictional negotiations of prevalent concerns surrounding degeneration and the fall of the British Empire around the turn of the century.

According to this pragmatic view of horror, the genre, by delving
into what is repressed by society, including the traumas we bury in the
most inscrutable recesses of our minds, is brilliantly placed to undertake
cultural work that reflects our darkest, forgotten and best left unspoken
fears. Such an approach also legitimises the use and value of horror: the
genre is more than frivolous entertainment, more than the sum of its
chills and thrills. It can take on serious work and may – more successfully than social realism, constrained as it is by specific generic and taste
demands – allow for veritable insights into the nature of taboo areas
that otherwise remain outside the remit of the acceptable. As a number
of the contributors to this volume show, this capacity for horror to
encapsulate an era, its unspoken worries and aspirations, makes its study
particularly rewarding. This is, quite logically, not tantamount to affirm-
ing that all horror constitutes an enlightening piece of social critique.
After all, the casual reader is likely to pick up a horror novel because he
or she wishes to be entertained and, perhaps, pleasantly horrified. We
can propose, however, that the best horror, or at least the horror that
has been retrospectively recuperated as the richest, is the one that manages to contain social and historical preoccupations within a narrative
that may be experienced very differently by its initial, or non-scholarly
trained, readers.

Acknowledging the social and political work of horror is, therefore, only half the story. Partially this is the case because there is a gap
between what critics or casual readers see in horror and the experience
of its fans, for whom horror may be more than a pastime; it may even
determine a lifestyle. Although this book is not concerned with fan
practices, it is important to acknowledge that, for horror fans, pleasures
may be as varied as recognising formulas and scenarios, discovering
texts that do something new with them, relishing favourite writers for
their craftsmanship or developing empathic, even sympathetic, connections with given characters. Although I am aware that there are dangers

in assuming any essentialist position (see Hills 2005: 3), it is still important to note that fandom can lead to reactions which re-appropriate fear and may even turn it into a source of comfort.

The gamut of experiences that horror allows for is, in many respects, as wide as that of any other genre (see Tudor 1997). For this reason, it is not necessary to legitimise the existence of horror over that of any other type of fiction (or vice versa), although it might be interesting briefly to consider, as many have done, what the appeal could be of a genre that aims to horrify and scare, and should instinctively draw us away or repel us. Part of the attraction of horror derives from its transgressive nature – from the fact that it can deal in matters often left out of other genres or considered too extreme, maybe even harmful. Sex, graphic violence and murder feature in plenty of the novels by Stephen King or Clive Barker, to name only two of the titans of late twentieth-century horror. These excessive proclivities, by no means necessary but, equally, not uncommon, have led to a questioning of horror's usefulness, as fiction that may not help to build character and could pose a 'real' threat to young readers or to those who may not be fully discerning and could seek to replicate the acts in such works. Although culturally we have moved past the moral outrage of the 1980s 'video nasties' scandal, horror is still perceived to lead to perverse pleasures. Arguably horror may be understood as a fictional indulgence in fantasies of violence, and our fascination with it seen as a form of sublimation of repressed desires. If we accept this line of thinking, then horror has the benefit of, at least, being one of the most honest of genres.

To the degree that horror fiction channels social fears, it also allows for a representation of how we should respond to and manage them: are fear and evil to be embraced or else contained, where they cannot be eradicated? While there may be a conservative or reactionary streak to horror fiction, insofar as it sometimes restores the status quo and expels the transgressive, it is equally possible to conceive of horror as attractive and capable of holding our fascination because it enables readers to interrogate the limits of what is socially acceptable, the boundaries imposed by decorum and 'good taste'. According to such a view, horror is not exciting because it is illicit, but because it dares go where other sanctioned literature does not. This can be equally true of its creative landscapes. The supernatural in horror, especially in the weird, can be of cosmic proportions and, on occasion, ventures far into the realms of the unknown. In the same way that taboos are ever-changing, conventional and socially prescribed, horror continues to adapt itself to suit the needs of readers who seek it out for its promise of radical otherness. Obviously not all horror is bold, and formulaic fixes are as much a part of the trade as wild leaps of the imagination, but in all cases horror affords an extreme experience: it constitutes a thought exercise, requiring projection into the situations of characters and enabling visceral impressions. This also helps explain why the genre is as old as human beings. Readers of horror like to harness this primeval emotion of fear and render it safe for consumption.

When Is Horror Fiction?

This particular history of horror begins, like many others (Tymn 1981; Jones 2002; Wisker 2005; Bloom 2007), with the development and rise of Gothic fiction in the eighteenth century, via the graveyard poetry that influenced it. Such a decision may appear contentious for a number of reasons. To begin with, horror does not become a recognisable genre in fiction, or indeed in film, until the twentieth century. If this collection is happy to embrace the Gothic, itself a particular form of 'literature of terror' (Punter 1980) that spoke directly to the Enlightenment and its investment in scientific reason, then why not begin with revenge tragedy – or, as Dale Townshend's consideration of William Shakespeare's influence on Gothic writers in chapter 1 suggests, with the plays of the Bard? After all, there are plenty of horrific moments in *Titus Andronicus* (1588–93?), if this should be a deciding factor, and monsters appear in plays such as *Macbeth* (1599–1606?) or *The Tempest* (1610–1?). As S. T. Joshi's *Unutterable Horror: A History of Supernatural Fiction* (2012) has shown, the supernatural in literature, especially the weird and its evil ramifications, can be traced back to the *Epic of Gilgamesh* (c. 2100 BC) and to a number of Greek and Latin texts. Prior to Joshi, Noël Carroll (1990: 13) had already suggested that horrific imagery could be found in Petronius's *Satyricon* (first century AD), Ovid's *Metamorphoses* (second century AD) or Apuleius's *The Golden Ass* (late second century AD). The poetry of Dante Alighieri and John Milton, among others, can also be seen as proto-horrific in places, and the Bible's 'Book of Revelation' has been the inspiration for a number of hellish horrors in Western literature.

On a practical note, the answer to these questions can be boiled down to a simple matter of spatial economy. A thorough history of horror would require a multi-volume approach and a bigger body of specialised scholars who could tease out the relevance of horrific imagery to each specific period and writer. Given that this book is intended for the casual and interested reader, it aims to act, first and foremost, as an introduction, and to provide a survey to periods in which horror, or some roughly approximate form of it, has played a distinctive role in fiction. The focus on more 'contemporary' times, from 1764 onwards, with a noticeable bias for the twentieth and twenty-first centuries, is intentional. It is a result of the desire to investigate the development of a self-conscious horror fiction that has, increasingly, been marketed and sold as a characteristic product.

The twentieth century has also produced the most significant number of horror texts. In fact, the industry boom of the 1980s was so substantial that to give this period the credit it deserves nearly an entire chapter becomes necessary. It could thus be argued that the privileging of the contemporary is also propelled by the need to showcase and explore the genre's gradual coalescence into what we now understand by the label 'horror'. Since our approach in this volume is one that endeavours to paint, in broad brush strokes, the development of horror fiction, the emphasis lies in establishing patterns in the publication of novels or across writers, and to highlight subgenres, movements or texts that have been relevant to its establishment.

The book, then, starts with the eighteenth-century Gothic tradition, as this is when horror fiction, in a different shape, under a different name and answering to different needs of its readers, began to consolidate into something resembling a genre (for more, see Townshend 2014). Although Gothic novels could be very formulaic, especially following the successes of Ann Radcliffe, the canon varies in its motifs, themes and approaches to our encounter with the source of fear. These divergences have sometimes been investigated productively as gender-specific subgenres (the Female Gothic) or as branches of the Gothic interested in national agendas (for example, the orientalist Gothic of William Beckford's *Vathek* 1786 novel). It is also possible, and I would argue beneficial, to see the numerous works that we now study under the umbrella term 'Gothic' as the beginnings of a wider crystallisation of horror fiction. Ann Radcliffe's own separation of terror from horror in her posthumous article 'On the Supernatural in Poetry' (1826, considered in chapter 1) and Edmund Burke's musings on terror in his *A Philosophical Enquiry into the Origin of Our Ideas of the Sublime and the Beautiful* (1757, also considered in chapter 1), although vague by our contemporary standards, also belie an early concern with theorisations of the horrific. Precisely because the term 'Gothic' is now applied more generally to non-realist literature, or to literature that draws on a set of images, figures and settings we readily associate with 'first wave Gothic', it is even more important that 'horror' is retrieved as a term. For one thing, it is more intuitive in its definition of texts that seek to generate fear and has the advantage, unlike the Gothic, of not being circumscribed by particular settings, characters or situations. As the Gothic becomes more intrinsically connected to aesthetics in the contemporary period – being used, for example, to describe art and fashion – it is even more crucial that a distinction be drawn between the Gothic, an artistic mode, and horror, an affective marker.

It is also necessary to say a word on the national focus of the book. The consideration of work from countries that have developed this genre under specific historical and cultural conditions, such as Japan or Mexico, lies outside our scope. To do otherwise would require, as with the pre-history of the genre, a far bigger and more exhaustive job. Our focus on Britain and America can thus be explained as the need to consider the literature of the two countries that have contributed most prevalently to the genre and which have influenced the work of writers worldwide. Both American and British works of horror are therefore considered alongside each other, together with dashes of other international horror where these have had a sizeable effect or impact. Chapter 1 focuses on the development of the Gothic in Britain and chapter 2 on its transplantation to America in the late 1790s and, more obviously, the nineteenth century. The work of early American writers, most notably that of Edgar Allan Poe, has been so fundamental to the genre that it begged for its own separate consideration. The rest of the chapters are presented in a roughly chronological fashion, with chapters 3 and 4 focusing mostly on the developments in horror in Britain, from the nineteenth-century penny dreadful and ghost story to the harnessing of the weird tale in the early twentieth century. This era is so central to the crystallisation of the aesthetic and conceptual preoccupations of the late eighteenth-century Gothic that some of the creatures to come out of it, such as Frankenstein's monster, Count Dracula or Mr Hyde, have been more seamlessly associated with the birth of the Gothic (and horror) than its predecessors (see Halberstam 1995; Frayling 1996). Chapters 5 and 6 turn to the twentieth century, more specifically to the evolution of horror as a discernible and distinct genre in its own right and to a peak in interest in the 1980s. Chapter 7 considers the noteworthy trends and writers to emerge from the genre's second period of overdrive in the twenty-first century.

In keeping with the introductory ethos underpinning the chapters, all of them include a selection of five to six texts entitled 'What to Read Next' that will serve as a next step for the interested reader. These texts have been chosen for their historical value, because we feel they captured the spirit of the period or simply because we think they are noteworthy and deserving of a wider readership. Although the chapters themselves have been kept jargon-free and low on ancillary critical material in order best to serve the purpose of a general survey, the book ends with a list of further critical reading for those who may want to learn more about horror fiction and the debates it has generated. Although not exhaustive, the list is indicative of major works in the area and should provide a good introduction to anyone seeking to research this genre in more depth.

References

Aldana Reyes, Xavier, *Horror Film and Affect: Towards a Corporeal Model of Viewership* (London and New York: Routledge, 2016).

Bloom, Clive, *Gothic Horror: A Guide for Students and Readers* (Basingstoke: Palgrave Macmillan, 2007).

Carroll, Noël, *The Philosophy of Horror: Or, Paradoxes of the Heart* (London and New York: Routledge, 1990).

Cavarero, Adriana, *Horrorism: Naming Contemporary Violence* (New York: Columbia University Press, 2009).

Frayling, Christopher, *Nightmare: Birth of Horror* (London: BBC Books, 1996).

Halberstam, Judith, *Skin Shows: Gothic Horror and the Technology of Monsters* (London and Durham, NC: Duke University Press, 1995).

Hills, Matt, *The Pleasures of Horror* (London: Continuum, 2005).

Jones, Darryl (ed.), *Horror Stories: Classic Tales from Hoffmann to Hodgson* (Oxford: Oxford University Press, 2014).

——, *Horror: A Thematic History in Fiction and Film* (London: Arnold, 2002).

Joshi, S. T., *Unutterable Horror: A History of Supernatural Fiction*, 2 vols (New York: Hippocampus Press, 2012).

King, Stephen, *Danse Macabre* (London: Hodder, 1991).

Punter, David, *The Literature of Terror: A History of Gothic Fictions from 1765 to the Present Day* (London: Longman, 1980).

Townshend, Dale (ed.), *Terror and Wonder: The Gothic Imagination* (London: British Library Publishing, 2014).

Tudor, Andrew, 'Why Horror? The Peculiar Pleasures of a Popular Genre', *Cultural Studies*, 11.3 (1997), 443–63.

Tymn, Marshall B., *Horror Literature: A Core Collection and Reference Guide* (London and New York: R. R. Bowker, 1981).

Wisker, Gina, *Horror Fiction: An Introduction* (New York: Continuum, 2005).

The Castle of Otranto, Horace Walpole, 1764. Theodore and Matilda, engraving. Plate 3 from edition published by C. F. Himbourg, 1794.

Chapter 1

Gothic and the Cultural Sources of Horror, 1740–1820

Dale Townshend

Horrible Romance

In 1827, an entry in the *Encyclopædia Londinensis; or, An Universal Dictionary of Arts, Sciences, and Literature* digressed to provide a definition of what it took to be a distinct subgenre within the broader category of 'Romance':

> There is another numerous and dull class of compositions, extending
> to some hundred volumes, with which we presume most persons who
> have inspected the old circulating libraries are sufficiently familiar; they
> might conveniently be called *horrible* romances. They are distinguished
> by perfect inattention to style, and considerable dependence upon for-
> mer publications: – A dark and wicked man, usually a knight, pursues
> with amorous ardour a lady, whose purity and transcendental virtue
> are continually displayed by her aversion to ravishment. The knight
> has dungeons deep, fortified castles, assassins, bandits, and sometimes
> a treacherous priest, at command. The lady is assisted by some lover as
> virtuous as herself, and, in the last emergencies, by a ghost. Mystery and
> horror are the ingredients of interest in these romances; and as these
> are the stimuli which most strongly affect the uninstructed, they have
> commonly had great popularity with young persons. Certainly the best
> of this terrific school are those of Mrs. Radcliffe, whose occasionally

powerful language, and deep feeling, gave them an excellence her predecessors were unacquainted with. In our time this species has taken a
new turn. The peculiar horrors of the German school has [*sic*] given it a
novel aspect by the assimilation of modern characters and supernatural
agents, and this preposterous union has not deprived them of interest.
Witness the *Vampires, Frankenstein*, &c. (Anon. 1827: 210)

The views expressed here in the third decade of the nineteenth century
were by no means exceptional. Dull, repetitive and conventional to the
point of being formulaic, 'horrible romance' was, as at least one earlier
commentator put it, the 'trash of the circulating library' (Anon. 1797:
347) and, for some, barely deserving of the appellation of 'literature'
at all. Consumed avidly by the young, these were the fictions of the
immature and uninformed mind, the fevered consumption of which,
for Samuel Taylor Coleridge in *Biographia Literaria* (1817), amounted
more to a 'sort of beggarly day-dreaming' than an active and produc-
tive act of 'reading' (Coleridge 1817: 49). Trafficking in the emotions of
mystery and horror, this was the writing of the supernatural, the spectral
and the ghostly that was perceived to have arisen in the wake of Horace
Walpole's *The Castle of Otranto* (1764), and later galvanised and rendered more 'horrid' by literary influences imported into Britain from
Germany. Presided over in the 1790s by Ann Radcliffe, this literary
'school' was revived in the nineteenth century by such fictions as John
Polidori's *The Vampyre: A Tale* (1819) and Mary Shelley's *Frankenstein; or,
The Modern Prometheus* (1818). The *Encyclopædia*'s attempt at isolating
the 'horrible romance' as a separate generic entity neatly encapsulates
many of the crucial factors at stake when attempting to chart the rise
of horror as a distinct literary subgenre in late eighteenth- and early
nineteenth-century Britain – not least of all the fact that, in 1827, horror, in its own terms, was yet to be generically formulated as such, and
was unthinkable outside of the broader 'Gothic' mode in literature in
which it first took shape.

Walpolean Horrors

Certainly *The Castle of Otranto*, a fiction self-consciously intended
by Horace Walpole as 'a new species of romance' (Walpole 2014: 13)

and the first novel in English to define itself as 'A Gothic Story' in a second edition of 1765, did much to bring the literature of horror into being. Initially offered to the reading public as the translation of a printed Italian story found in the library of an ancient Catholic family in the North of England, Walpole's narrative describes a series of strange and mysterious happenings that take place in and around the eponymous Castle of Otranto, Italy, during 'the darkest ages of [C]hristianity', that is, in or around the period between 1095 ('the æra of the first crusade') and 1243 ('the date of the last') (Walpole 2014: 5). In a desperate attempt to secure his tenuous and illegitimate claims to the Castle and principality of Otranto, Manfred, Walpole's villain, seeks to marry off his young, weak and sickly son, Conrad, to Isabella, daughter of Frederic, Marquis of Vicenza, the 'nearest of blood' to Otranto's 'last rightful lord', Alfonso the Good (57). Manfred's plans are thwarted, however, when, on the morning of Conrad and Isabella's intended marriage, a giant, feather-plumed helmet falls suddenly from the sky and violently crushes the groom-to-be to death beneath it. As Conrad's 'disfigured corpse' (19) is brought into view, the onlookers gathered in the castle's courtyard emit loud shrieks at the 'horror of the spectacle' (18). Manfred, however, utterly unmoved by the loss of his only son and heir, immediately turns to a more ghastly alternative: the securing of his wrongful rule of Otranto through marriage to his intended daughter-in-law. When confronted with the 'horrid measures' (26) of this quasi-incestuous proposition, Isabella is understandably overcome with 'fright and horror' (24). Escaping into the dark, labyrinthine vaults beneath the castle, she is pursued by the politically ambitious villain, each step of her flight pregnant with horrific potential: her blood 'curdle[s]' when she concludes that Manfred is about to seize her, while her mind is overcome by every 'suggestion that horror could inspire' (26). In a jarring transition to the present tense, Walpole's narrator exclaims that '[w]ords cannot paint the horror of the princess's situation' (27). The text thus sets in place a concern with the ineffable, with that which is both nameless and beyond the powers of verbal expression, that would become central to the literary representation of horror from 1764 onwards. So extreme is its experience that horror cannot adequately be rendered in words.

Hamlet (Act I, scene iv), depicting Hamlet, Horatio, Marcellus and the armour-suited ghost. Drawing by Henry Fuseli, published as a print by the Boydell Shakespeare Gallery, 29 September 1796.

The fugitive Isabella, however, is not the only character in *Otranto* to experience horror's extra-linguistic yet strikingly corporeal effects. When, in anticipation of the impending fall of Manfred's dynasty, the portrait of his grandfather that hangs in the castle mysteriously leaves its frame to glide forth as a ghost, Manfred, echoing the young Prince Hamlet following the shade of his murdered father on the battlements of Elsinore Castle in Shakespeare's play, is compelled to go after it in an attitude 'full of anxiety and horror' (25); later, when the increasingly guilt-ridden villain mistakenly recognises Theodore, the true and legitimate ruler of Otranto, as Alfonso the Good, his distant ancestor, he is overcome with the sensations of 'secret horror' (77). Morally undiscriminating in its effects, horror plagues the experiences of the virtuous characters in the narrative, too. Informing Theodore, the soon-to-be-restored legitimate heir of Otranto, of the acts of murder and usurpation that lurk in his familial past, Father Jerome has his son kneel before him as he paraphrases the lines of Hamlet's father's ghost in Shakespeare's play. 'I could a tale unfold whose lightest word / Would harrow up thy soul' (Shakespeare I.v.15–16) becomes 'Kneel, head-strong boy, while a father unfolds a tale of horror, that will expel every sentiment from thy soul, but sensations of sacred vengeance' (Walpole 2014: 87). When the otherwise morally noble Frederic, having been talked round to Manfred's incestuous plans, momentarily agrees to deliver Isabella, his daughter, to Manfred in exchange for the hand of Manfred's own daughter, Matilda, in marriage, the statue of Alfonso the Good in the nearby Church of Saint Nicholas haemorrhages three drops of blood from its nose. A more horrific source of admonition occurs shortly thereafter when Frederic is confronted with the spectre of 'the fleshless jaws and empty sockets of a skeleton, wrapt in a hermit's cowl' (98). In yet another allusion to the speech of the ghost in *Hamlet*, Frederic's responses appropriately betray horror's effects upon the body: his 'blood', we are told, 'froze in his veins' (98), and from this moment onwards his collusion with Manfred is brought to an abrupt end.

Replete with horrific description, imagery and effects though this 'Gothic Story' undoubtedly is, it is important to remember that, by his own admission, Walpole in *The Castle of Otranto* was more concerned with revivifying the prosaic turns of the eighteenth-century realist novel with the imaginative capacities of medieval romance than in crafting what we would today describe as a 'horror novel'. Furthermore, crucial to literary renditions of horror though it certainly was, *Otranto*, as the above synopsis suggests, looked back to the older tradition of the Shakespearean supernatural for the staging of its most blood-curdling effects. Indeed, as Walpole later justified it, his literary experiment was to a large extent intended as a defence of Shakespeare against the tide of vitriolic criticism that French critics such as Voltaire had directed towards the national English Bard. Labouring under the pressures of neoclassical aesthetics, the eighteenth-century French literary tradition habitually castigated Shakespeare for what it took to be his 'barbarism', a certain roughness and uncouthness, it was thought, that was a product of his plays' refusal to conform to the Aristotelian unities of time, space and action. Equally offensive to this measured, neoclassical aesthetic were Shakespeare's fanciful extremes, such as the use of the supernatural in *Hamlet* (1603), *Macbeth* (1611) and *Julius Caesar* (1599), or the preoccupation with the fairy realm in *A Midsummer Night's Dream* (1605). Walpole responds in *Otranto* with a defiant representation of the supernatural. However, his appropriation of Shakespeare is undertaken as much in a spirit of *self*-defence as one of British cultural nationalism. 'The result of all I have said,' Walpole declares towards the end of the second Preface, 'is to shelter my own daring under the cannon of the brightest genius this country, at least, has produced' (13).

Beyond the example of Walpole, writers of 'horrible' romance and drama in the late eighteenth century continuously looked back to the writings of Shakespeare and his contemporaries as models for their own aesthetic practice. As Thomas Gray put it in 'The Progress of Poesy: A Pindaric Ode' (1757), Nature had presented Shakespeare with the 'golden keys' capable of unlocking not only joy and sympathy, but also the sentiments of thrill, fear and horror:

> Thine too these golden keys, immortal Boy!
> This can unlock the gates of Joy;
> Of Horrour [*sic*] that, and thrilling Fears,
> Or ope the sacred source of sympathetic Tears. (Gray 1757: 10)

The sources of horror fiction in Britain thus lie not so much in *The Castle of Otranto* as in the earlier corpus of Elizabethan and Jacobean dramas to which many 'Gothic' writers from Walpole onwards continuously looked as the source of their plots, scenarios, epigraphs, character types and even linguistic choices.

Crucial to literary renditions of horror though it was, *The Castle of Otranto* also took little care to differentiate between horror, on the one hand, and the contrasting but related aesthetic of terror, on the other – two terms that, together with the broader category of the 'Gothic', structure our negotiation of the darker sides of literary history today. Indeed, as I shall elaborate below, the distinction between horror and terror, and, with that, the appreciation of horror as a discrete literary mode, postdates *The Castle of Otranto* by 60 years or more, an historical fact reflected not only in the nebulous definition of the 'horrible romance' offered in the *Encyclopædia Londinensis* in 1827, but also in Walpole's conflation of the effects of horror and terror throughout the narrative. It is 'Terror', Walpole's first Preface to *Otranto* confidently reminds its readers, that is 'the author's principal engine' in the tale, a quality that purportedly 'prevents the story from ever languishing' (Walpole 2014: 6). Consequently, even as it makes continuous reference to the characters' experience of horror, Walpole's narrative makes equally liberal use of the term 'terror' throughout: Isabella in the subterranean labyrinth experiences a 'new terror' (26) at Manfred's approach; Matilda is filled with 'terror and alarm' (37) at her father's machinations; and, with the arrival of Frederic at Otranto, Manfred himself is struck with 'terror' (56). Neither are the experiences of horror and terror in *Otranto* entirely unmarked by moments of what we would today describe as camp humour: Clara Reeve in *The Champion of Virtue* (1777), her own self-proclaimed 'Gothic Story' that was subsequently republished under the more familiar title of *The Old English Baron* in 1778, felt that the hyperbolic excesses of Walpole's fiction were more likely to inspire 'laughter' (Reeve 1777: vi) than fear. Verging always on the brink of humour, and with few distinctions between them, horror and terror are subsumed under the broader category of the 'Gothic' in Walpole's influential literary experiment of 1764–5.

With hindsight, it seems plausible to argue that, though it was yet to be theorised as a separate aesthetic category, horror received a more focused exploration and treatment in Walpole's *The Mysterious Mother* (1768), a Gothic tragedy that, though unperformed in its own day and circulated only among a small group of Walpole's friends, was eventually given a wider readership upon its publication in 1781. Set in a medieval castle in southern France, *The Mysterious Mother* relates the story of the Countess of Narbonne, the 'mysterious mother' of the play's title who, in a moment of passionate grief occasioned by the sudden death of her husband 16 years earlier, knowingly seduced her own son, Edmund, by stealthily insinuating herself into the place of his lover. Banishing Edmund, who remains entirely unaware of his mother's act of sexual substitution, from Narbonne shortly thereafter, the contrite Countess bears of this incestuous union a daughter, Adeliza. Giving the child no insight into her incestuous origins, the Countess raises Adeliza as if she were an orphan. Following a long absence from the realm, the exiled Edmund returns to Narbonne and, in a fatalistic turn of events, falls in

love with Adeliza, his own daughter-cum-sister; true to the inevitabil-
ities of the tragic mode, Adeliza returns her father-brother's affections.
Friar Benedict, a double-dealing Catholic priest, comes to learn of the
guilty secret that lurks in the Countess's dark past and, intent upon
securing her ruin in revenge for her abandoning of Catholicism in
favour of the new Protestant religion, knowingly officiates over the
incestuous marriage of father and daughter, half-brother and half-sister.
Devastation, suicide and tragic death ensue when all is finally revealed,
the curtain falling upon what Edmund's closing speech appropriately
refers to as 'this theatre of monstrous guilt!' (Walpole 2000:V.i.417).

As the Postscript to the published version of the play notes, Walpole
remained firmly of the opinion that its subject matter was too 'horrid'
ever to warrant production (Walpole 2000: 65). Though conceptualised
and written according to the two tragic principles of pity and terror that Aristotle had theorised in his *Poetics* (*c.* 335 BC), the drama in
Walpole's estimation compromised its own tragic effects by what he
took to be an excess of a third category, that of horror: 'its greatest fault',
the Postscript continues, 'is the horror which it must occasion in the
audience; particularly in the fairer, more tender, and less criminal part
of it' (Walpole 2000: 67). As in *The Castle of Otranto*, extreme horror for
Walpole lies, or at least ought to lie, beyond the limits of language and
dramatic representation. Paradoxically, though, Walpole makes continuous use of the term 'horror' throughout *The Mysterious Mother*. Upon
erroneously recognising her recently returned son as the ghost of her
late husband, for instance, the Countess swoons at what she describes
as 'this complicated scene of horrors' (Walpole 2000: II.i.270), identify-
ing the uncanny return of her original act of incestuous transgression
in the love between her two children as horror's ultimate source. In
Otranto Walpole had explored a similar sense of the generational perpetuation of parental misdeed through the biblical adage, '*the sins of
fathers are visited on their children to the third and fourth generation*' (Walpole
2014: 6; emphasis in original); in *The Mysterious Mother* this is figured
as an overbearing process of horrific accumulation. 'Horror on horror!'
(Walpole 2000: III.i.285), the Countess cries out, 'My children! horror!
horror!' (V.i.313): a dreadful combination of implacable fate and Catholic turpitude has brought down upon the house of Narbonne a 'pillar of

accumulated horrors!' (V.i.323). Here, too, Walpole's use of Shakespeare is prominent. 'I have supped full with horrors,' declares a defeated Macbeth in Act V, scene v of Shakespeare's Scottish play; in the words of the jealous Othello, 'On horror's head horrors accumulate' (Shakespeare: III.iii.375) in Walpole's tragic universe.

Supernumerary Horrors

Eighteenth-century poetic diction expressed this sense of horror piled upon horror to the point of saturation through the phrase 'supernumerary horrors', employing the adjective 'supernumerary' to suggest that which, according to the *Oxford English Dictionary*, 'is beyond or in excess of a usual, regular, stated, or prescribed number or amount'. The phrase 'supernumerary horrors' was first coined in an essay contributed by the English politician and man of letters, Joseph Addison, to the periodical *The Spectator* on Friday 6 July 1711. While recounting a visit to his fictionalised friend Sir Roger, whose house was once apparently haunted by the ghost of a suicide, Addison describes his evening walk to a ruined abbey nearby. As the superstitions of the local servants describe it, the abbey is haunted by the spirit of a headless black horse, while the ruin's deserted churchyard evokes in Addison thoughts of the return of revenants altogether more human in nature. Addison employs the phrase 'supernumerary horrors' to describe the psychological effects conjured up by the accumulation of sensory impressions of sound and sight within the darkened ruin:

> At the same time the walk of elms, with the croaking of the ravens, which from time to time are heard from the tops of them, looks exceeding solemn and venerable. These objects naturally raise seriousness and attention; and when night heightens the awfulness of the place, and pours out her *supernumerary horrors* upon every thing in it, I do not at all wonder that weak minds fill it with spectres and apparitions. (Addison 1809: 230–1; emphasis added).

While Addison, following Locke's argument in the fourth edition of his *An Essay Concerning Humane* [sic] *Understanding* (1690), partly dismisses the thoughts of ghosts and spectres that swarm in his mind in the churchyard as 'ridiculous horrors', he ends his essay with a quiet but telling affirmation of the spectral afterlife: '[a]t the same time I think a person who is thus terrified with the imagination of ghosts and spectres much more reasonable than one who, contrary to the reports of all historians sacred and profane, ancient and modern, and to the traditions of all nations, thinks the appearance of spirits fabulous and groundless' (Addison 1809: 232).

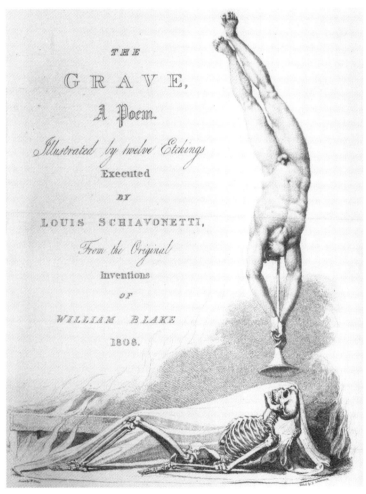

The Grave, Robert Blair, 1743. Titlepage. Engravings by Luigi Schiavonetti, based on designs by William Blake. Edition published by R. H. Cromek, 1808.

In what appears to be a deliberate allusion to Addison's essay, the so-called 'Graveyard' poet Robert Blair employed the phrase 'supernumerary horror' in his lengthy poem, *The Grave* (1743), in order to express the part-dizzying, part-claustrophobic heaping of horrors upon horrors *ad infinitum* that we find in Shakespeare and Horace Walpole. Here, by the light of a 'sickly Taper' that momentarily flickers in the gloomy night, the persona is made witness to an accretion of morbid horrors in a deserted churchyard, including skulls, coffins, epitaphs, worms, ghosts and ever-funereal yew trees:

> The sickly Taper
> By glimmering thro' thy low-brow'd misty Vaults,
> (Furr'd round with mouldy Damps, and ropy Slime,)
> Lets fall a supernumerary Horror,
> And only serves to make thy Night more irksome.
> Well do I know thee by thy trusty *Yew*,
> Chearless, unsocial Plant! that loves to dwell
> 'Midst Sculls and Coffins, Epitaphs and Worms:
> Where light-heel'd Ghosts, and visionary Shades,
> Beneath the wan cold Moon (as Fame reports)
> Embody'd, thick, perform their mystick Rounds.
> No other Merriment, Dull tree! is thine. (Blair 1743: 4)

As in Addison earlier, we see here, over two decades before the official 'rise' of the Gothic in Walpole's *The Castle of Otranto*, a clearly articulated sense of the paraphernalia of horror – an aesthetic characterised in the first half of the eighteenth century, as now, by a morbid fixation upon darkness, death and the relics of the corrupted and corruptible body, both spiritual and material. Together, Addison's essay of 1711 and Blair's *The Grave* influentially presage what we might term the 'spatiality' of horror in the eighteenth century, that is, horror's intimate associations with particular architectural spaces or particular constructions of physical place: ruined abbeys and castles, mouldy tombs, overgrown graveyards and other dark, marginal sites of death and dereliction.

Odes to Horror

In their preoccupations with the melancholy powers of darkness and death, Young, Blair and other graveyard poets of the 1740s initiated a poetic tradition that turned to the apostrophising of horror as the most powerful and effective of literary and psychological sentiments. Although it does not specifically mention horror, William Collins's influential 'Ode to Fear' (1747) sought actively to celebrate and invoke the emotion of Fear through images that are decidedly horrific: residing in the 'shadowy shapes' of the 'World unknown', Fear brings danger-ous 'Monsters' (Collins 1747: 5) and other hideous forms in its wake. Spatially, Fear in the poem occupies the same locations – the graveyard and the haunted ruin – as the 'supernumerary horrors' of Addison and Blair: as Collins's persona rhetorically enquires, 'Thou who such weary Lengths hast past, / Where wilt thou rest, mad Nymph, at last? / Say, wilt thou shroud in haunted Cell, / Where gloomy *Rape* and *Murder* dwell?' (Collins 1747: 8). The poem ends with the articulation of the persona's desire that he be possessed by the same Spirit of Fear that, though originating in the tragedies of Aeschylus and Sophocles, power-fully came to occupy the breast of Shakespeare:

> O Thou whose Spirit most possest
> The sacred seat of *Shakespeare's* Breast!
> By all that from thy Prophet broke,
> In thy Divine Emotions spoke:
> Hither again thy Fury deal,
> Teach me but once like Him to feel:
> His *Cypress Wreath* my Meed decree,
> And I, O *Fear*, will dwell with *Thee!* (Collins 1747: 9)

Following Collins's example, several poets from the mid-eighteenth century onwards composed poems specifically addressed to Horror, a figure often personified in these Odes as a Muse, Prophet, Deity or abstract literary and psychological sensibility. By the early nine-teenth century, in fact, the Ode to Horror had become something of a poetic commonplace. Thomas Warton, for instance, the grave-yard poet and future Poet Laureate, published his 'Ode to Horror' in *The Student; or, The Oxford, and Cambridge Monthly Miscellany* in 1751, addressing his personified subject as the 'Goddess of the gloomy scene, / Of shadowy shapes thou black-brow'd queen' (Warton 1751: 313). What were, by the 1750s, already coming to be established as

the distinctive conventions of horror feature prominently throughout the poem, including a 'mouldering abbey' and 'charnels damp
and dim', a 'sheeted spectre grim', the 'terrors of a tomb', an Egyptian
'mummy' in a winding sheet and a 'grave-like grot[to]' (Warton 1751:
313–14). Sketching out Horror's literary genealogy, Warton renders it
as a distinctively English cultural phenomenon, one that begins with
Edmund Spenser's *The Faerie Queene* (1590–6) and continues in John
Milton's *Paradise Lost* (1667; 1674). Like Collins, Warton figures himself in the poem as Horror's 'pensive votary', ending his verse on the
powerful wish that he, too, may 'look madly wild like thee' (Warton
1751: 315).

Though it was probably written as early as 1791, Romantic poet and
future Poet Laureate Robert Southey published his poem 'To Horror'
in his *Poems* in 1797, beginning his verse with an invocation that recalls
the distinctive spatial location of horror employed in Addison, Blair and
Collins:

> DARK HORROR, hear my call!
> Stern Genius hear from thy retreat
> On some old sepulchre's moss-cankered seat,
> Beneath the Abbey's ivied wall
> That trembles o'er its shade. (Southey 1797: 140)

As in the earlier poems, Horror for Southey is associated with the forces
of the 'midnight gloom', the 'perturbed sprite' and the 'heavy gales of
night' (Southey 1797: 140). Wreaking havoc with the natural world, as
it did in Collins's 'Ode to Fear', Horror resides in 'dark-wing'd tempests'
that prove the scourge of mariners at sea: 'the black billows to the thunder rave / When by the lightnings [*sic*] light / Thou seest the tall ship
sink beneath the wave' (141–2). In an interesting political turn, Southey
employs as a particularly arresting manifestation of horror the image of a
mother clasping her dead child to her breast – one based, by all accounts,
on a description that he had read of the British retreat to Deventer,
Holland, during the French Revolutionary Wars of 1794 and 1795: 'The
Mother to her frozen breast, / On the heap'd snows reclining clasps her
child / And with him sleeps, chill'd to eternal rest!' (Southey 1797: 143).
Indeed, throughout Southey's poem, the 'Black HORROR' that speeds

towards the 'bed of Death' is highly political in nature, a ghastly force that, for a radical, humanitarian eye such as Southey's, manifests itself in its most gruesome form in the heinous practice of slavery: 'HORROR! I call thee yet once more! / Bear me to that accursed shore / Where round the stake the impaled Negro writhes' (144). 'Arouse the race of Afric!', he implores the 'holy Power' of Horror in the poem's closing lines, and 'Lead them to vengeance! And in that dread hour / When Ruin rages wide / I will behold and smile by MERCY'S side' (144). If Horror is slavery's by-product, it is also, for Southey, its ultimate source of vanquishing. Appropriating the nocturnal settings of horror from earlier graveyard verse, Southey inflects notions of 'blackness' and 'darkness' in the poem with racial concerns.

Other radical writers in the 1790s and early 1800s did much the same, for if there is one place in which the term 'horror' features prominently in literature of the Romantic period, it is in the titles of Abolitionist and anti-slavery tracts written and published on both sides of the Atlantic. *The Horrors of Slavery* (1824) by Robert Wedderburn, the son of a Jamaican house-slave and plantation owner, is probably the best-known example. In the work of radical writers in the 1790s, the accreting conventions of horror fiction were put to urgent political use, decrying in a fiction such as William Godwin's *Things as They Are; or, The Adventures of Caleb Williams* (1794) the horrific perpetuation of an unfair legal and punitive system, and in Mary Wollstonecraft's *The Wrongs of Woman; or, Maria* (1798) the persistence of an antediluvian system of patriarchal oppression.

Theorising Horror's Pleasures

The poems by Warton and Southey were by no means the only poetic invocations of the powers and pleasures of horror in the eighteenth century. Other examples include Anna Matilda's 'Invocation to Horror', a poem that was published in *The British Album* in 1790; Nathaniel Howard's 'To HORROR', published in his *Brickleigh Vale, With Other Poems* in 1804; and the Scottish poet Robert Fergusson's 'Ode to Horror' from *The Works of Robert Fergusson* of 1807. A host of anonymous odes, tributes and poetic invocations were also published in the newspapers and periodicals of the day. This sheer proliferation of material begs the question of what it was that writers of the period saw in the literary expression of horror. The answer, in this context, lies in the strange forms of pleasure and enjoyment that horror was thought to offer, a conviction that pertains as much to the appreciation of horror fiction and film today as it did in the eighteenth century. That the dark and bloody excesses of horror could, indeed, be a source of pleasure was something that perplexed many of the major aestheticians and essayists of the period. In his *A Philosophical Enquiry into the Origin of our Ideas of the Sublime and Beautiful* (1757), Edmund Burke argued that sublimity, that painful yet pleasurable feeling of awe and astonishment experienced in the face of grandeur, irregularity and obscurity, was in certain ways analogous to the emotion of terror:

> Whatever is fitted in any sort to excite the ideas of pain, and danger, that is to say, whatever is in any sort terrible, or is conversant with terrible objects, or operates in a manner analogous to terror, is a source of the sublime; that is, it is productive of the strongest emotion which the mind is capable of feeling. (Burke 1757: 13)

Although Burke in the *Enquiry* is thus more concerned with describing the danger and pain that underpin sublime terror than the workings of horror *per se*, the *Enquiry* went a long way towards constructing the experience of uncomfortable emotion – shock, disgust, fear – as a source of aesthetic pleasure. Indeed, 'horror' is a term that Burke habitually conflates with 'terror' throughout his work on the sublime, a fact that points to the same historical lack of distinction between the two that we see in Walpole's Gothic fiction and drama of the 1760s. With no clear distinction between them, horror and terror, though both indistinguishably steeped in the negative emotions of pain and danger, are both rendered as the source of aesthetic enjoyment in Burke's influential treatise.

It was precisely Burke's 'delightful horror' (Burke 1757: 129), that paradoxical coupling of pleasure and pain in his discourses on the sublime, that prompted Anna Laetitia Aikin's 'On the Pleasure Derived from Objects of Terror', an essay published in *Miscellaneous Pieces, in*

Prose, the collection of literary and cultural reflections that she published with her brother John Aikin in 1773. Like Burke and Walpole before her, Aikin's essay makes no attempt to differentiate between the experience of horror and terror. Rather, in the piece she attempts to explore 'the apparent delight with which we dwell upon objects of pure terror', or account for the strange enjoyment that we derive from such scenes of 'horror' as 'tales of ghosts and goblins, or murders, earthquakes, fires, shipwrecks, and all the most terrible disasters attending on human life' (Aikin and Aikin 1773: 126, 121). While this 'paradox of the heart' (Aikin and Aikin 1773: 120) may partly be accounted for by a sense of curiosity – it is our eagerness to satisfy our curiosity, she argues, that makes us endure horror and terror's torments – this does not adequately account for situations in which human beings willingly expose themselves to such objects when matters of curiosity are no longer at stake. 'Here', Aikin argues, 'though we know beforehand what to expect, we enter into them with eagerness, in quest of a pleasure already experienced' (125). The answer, then, lies in the expansive sense of marvel and wonder that tales of horror and terror, stories of ghosts, spectres and other 'invisible beings', evoke in the child listener or adult reader. However, as Aikin's metaphor of torture suggests, such experiences of the marvellous are not without their pains:

> This is the pleasure constantly attached to the excitement of surprise from new and wonderful objects. A strange and unexpected event awakens the mind, and keeps it on the stretch; and where the agency of invisible beings is introduced, of "forms unseen, and mightier than we," [a paraphrase of lines from Alexander Pope's *Essay on Man* (1734)], our imagination, darting forth, explores with rapture the new world which is laid open to its view, and rejoices in the expansion of its powers. Passion and fancy co-operating elevate the soul to its highest pitch; and the pain of terror is lost in amazement. (125)

It thus follows that 'the more wild, fanciful, and extraordinary are the circumstances of a scene of horror, the more pleasure we receive from it' (126). For Aikin, then, it is the imaginative expansiveness of wonder that anaesthetises the pain of horror and terror when reading a fiction such as *The Castle of Otranto*, a narrative, she observes, that successfully adapted and applied these emotions 'to the model of Gothic romance' (126).

It was in the Scottish poet and philosopher James Beattie's *Dissertations Moral and Critical* of 1783 that the complex, oxymoronic pleasures of horror first came to be theorised on their own terms. Although conceived very much in the tradition of Burke and Aikin, Beattie's 'Illustrations on Sublimity' sought to harness notions of horror, a concept no longer coterminous here with terror, to the 'pleasurable astonishment' or 'agreeable astonishment' (Beattie 1783: 610, 613) that was his conceptualisation of the sublime. 'There is a kind of horror', Beattie argues,

> which may be infused into the mind both by natural appearances, and by verbal description; and which, though it make the blood seem to run cold, and produce a momentary fear, is not unpleasing, but may be even agreeable: and therefore, the objects that produce it are justly denominated sublime. (Beattie 1783: 615)

As in *Hamlet*, and then later in Horace Walpole, horror for Beattie is distinguished by its corporeal effects, its ability to 'make the blood' of the spectator 'seem to run cold'. Evoked in natural scenes such as 'vast caverns, deep and dark woods, overhanging precipices' and 'the agitation of the sea in a storm' (615), sublime and pleasurable horror for Beattie might also be conjured up by literary description, particularly in tales of ghostly superstition. In turning to address the same question that perplexed Anna Laetitia Aikin - that is, what is the source of horror's inexorable attraction and pull? - Beattie concludes by figuring the mature taste for horror as a childhood pleasure that we never quite outgrow, an innate delight in that which rouses the soul, even on the pain of horror, anxiety and sorrow.

The care that Beattie had taken to theorise the sublime pleasures particular to the experience of horror in his *Dissertations Moral and Critical* was complemented first by Nathan Drake in his *Literary Hours; or, Sketches Critical and Narrative* of 1798 and then by Ann Radcliffe, the most popular and successful writer of Gothic romance in 1790s Britain. Drake's account of 'Gothic superstition' in *Literary Hours* turned upon a distinction between terror, on the one hand, and 'horror and disgust' on the other (Drake 1798: 246) – a conceptual differentiation that

Radcliffe would elaborate upon in an essay published posthumously
in *The New Monthly Magazine* in 1826. Responding to Burke, Aikin,
Beattie and Drake before her, Radcliffe in 'On the Supernatural in
Poetry' articulated a clear distinction between horror and terror, in
the process providing a conceptual framework through which, albeit
with frequent modification, horror in literature has been perceived ever
since. It is during a discussion of the relative merits of Shakespeare's
Hamlet and *Macbeth* that two gentlemen travellers, Mr S[impson] and
Mr W[illoughton], that Mr Willoughton, a fictional stand-in for Radcliffe herself, is led to make the following remark:

> Terror and horror are so far opposite, that the first expands the soul, and
> awakens the faculties to a higher degree of life; the other contracts, freezes,
> and nearly annihilates them. I apprehend, that neither Shakspeare [*sic*]
> nor Milton by their fictions, nor Mr. Burke by his reasoning, anywhere
> looked to positive horror as a source of the sublime, though they all agree
> that terror is a very high one; and where lies the great difference between
> horror and terror, but in the uncertainty and obscurity, that accompany
> the first, respecting the dreaded evil? (Radcliffe 1826: 149–50)

In the context of Mr Simpson's discussion, the blood-drenched *Macbeth*
epitomises horror, while the ghostly *Hamlet* exemplifies the sentiment
of terror; Mr Willoughton's privileging of sublime terror over horror
is repeated in the preference that he expresses for the Danish over the
Scottish play. His distinction between horror and terror is worth paus-
ing over. Terror, he claims, expands and enlarges the soul, while horror
constricts the observer's faculties almost to the point of death. Terror
is sublime, while 'positive horror' lacks sublimity insofar as it dispenses
altogether with the principle of obscurity, one of the Burkean sublime's
most necessary properties. If terror is generated by vagueness, mystery,
uncertainty and a prevailing lack of clarity, horror resides in immediacy
and the positive 'presence' of the 'dreaded evil'. Implicit in this is Radcliffe's close reading of Burke's *Enquiry*, in which matters of immediacy
and proximity are invariably described as compromising and frustrating
the workings of sublime terror. 'When danger or pain press too nearby,'
Burke had opined, 'they are incapable of giving any delight'; 'terror is
a passion,' he later continues, 'which always produces a delight when

it does not press too close' (Burke 1757: 13–14, 24). Radcliffe adopts a similar aesthetic position. Rather than using horror and terror interchangeably, however, she specifically defines 'terror' in the essay as that pleasurable effect that is generated when the sublime object is placed at an appropriate distance from the spectator, and horror as its ghastly, all-too-immediate opposite. For Radcliffe, the distinction between horror and terror is fundamentally one of proximity.

It is true that Radcliffe's 'On the Supernatural in Poetry' was not intended as a stand-alone critical dissertation on the differences between these two aesthetic modes; it was in fact extracted, seemingly without her knowledge, from the manuscript of the Introduction to *Gaston de Blondeville*, the writer's final Gothic romance that was posthumously published in the same year. Nor does it provide much insight into Radcliffe's own Gothic fictions, in which the terms 'horror' and 'terror' are often used interchangeably. Nonetheless the distinctions that Radcliffe put forward in 1826 have proved to be useful to the critical appreciation of Romantic-era Gothic writing that arose in the early twentieth century with such studies as Dorothy Scarborough's *The Supernatural in Modern English Fiction* (1917) and Montague Summers's *The Gothic Quest* (1938). Although they possess more critical and retrospective than historical purchase – Gothic romancers in the period 1764–1820 would not have considered themselves, primarily, as writers of either 'horror' or 'terror', to the exclusion of the other term – the distinctions nonetheless provide a convenient and generally defensible means of ordering the vast number of Gothic fictions that were published in the late eighteenth and early nineteenth centuries. With the rise of Anglo-American literary-critical feminism in the 1970s, horror and terror were reconfigured in gendered terms, with horror being superimposed upon a 'masculine' tradition of Gothic writing, and terror becoming synonymous with the feminine or female. While horror is the writing of immediacy, shock and confrontation, terror relies upon obscurity, deferral and suspense; if horror is the fiction of the fully-realised supernatural, terror merely gestures towards the possible but ultimately improbable existence of ghosts. Terror is the writing of sublimity, horror the literature of sensation, the former the writing of the fraught and haunted consciousness, the latter always firmly rooted in the body. While horror is visually graphic to the point of being lurid, terror as a mode often frustrates the visual sense by occluding sites of disturbance with veils, curtains, tapestries and palls. Like any taxonomic distinction, though, none of these categories is absolute or without its exceptions: mixtures of horror and terror may be identified in several Gothic fictions of the period, while a male author such as T. J. Horsley Curties could pen a highly 'feminised' version of terror in *Ethelwina; or, The House of Fitz-Auburne* (1799) and Charlotte Dacre a strongly 'masculinised' fiction of Gothic horror in her *Zofloya; or, The Moor* of 1806. Even so, they provide a convenient means through which to approach one of the most outrageous Gothic fictions of the late eighteenth century, Matthew Lewis's *The Monk; A Romance* of 1796 – a text that scandalously marked its difference from the fictions of Radcliffe and others that went before it and, in so doing, unwittingly brought the literature of horror into its own.

Horror and Disgust in Matthew Lewis's *The Monk*

Though it is filled with several interpolated narratives, the primary plot of Lewis's novel concerns the story of Father Ambrosio, the seemingly pious Abbot of the Church of the Capuchins in Madrid. Behind this outwardly respectable facade, however, lurks a cesspool of unfilled carnal desire that, having been somewhat blasphemously stirred by an erotic image of the Virgin Mary, is realised to extreme proportions throughout the rest of the narrative with the aid of Matilda, a cross-dressing Satanic temptress. Filled with scenes of ghostly conjuration and magical congress with the world of the dead, *The Monk*, unlike the earlier fictions of Radcliffe, refuses to dispense with the supernatural through a last-minute recourse to rational explanation. Its narrative, though, is as grounded in the desires of the corrupted and corrupting flesh as it is in the immateriality of the spirit world, and Father Ambrosio's libidinous path eventually comes to include, albeit unconsciously, the rape of his sister, Antonia, and the murder of his mother, Elvira. Brought to justice for the crimes of rape, murder and necromancy by the office of the Inquisition in the novel's final chapters, Ambrosio makes a Faustian pact with Satan, who then reneges on the deal and plunges the monk from a great height to his bloody, gruesome and lingering death on the rocks below.

The Monk, Mathew Gregory Lewis, 1796. Frontispiece from edition published by W. Mason, 1818.

The first moment of recognisable horror in the novel occurs in the second volume, when an extended inset narrative turns to tell the tragic tale of two lovers, Agnes and Raymond, the relationship between whom is prohibited by the fact that Agnes has, since birth, been destined to a celibate life in a convent. Seeking to end Agnes's virtual imprisonment in the Castle of Lindenberg in Germany, the lovers hatch an elaborate plan of escape and elopement that involves Agnes disguising herself as the ghost of the Bleeding Nun, a phantom that apparently returns every five years to haunt the Castle on 5 May. The scheme goes disastrously awry, however, when, at the critical moment of rendezvous, Raymond realises that he clasps in his arms not the disguised body of his beloved but the ghost of the legendary Bleeding Nun herself:

> God Almighty! it was the bleeding nun! It was my lost companion! Her face was still veiled, but she no longer held her lamp and dagger. She lifted up her veil slowly. What a sight presented itself to my startled eyes! I beheld before me an animated corse. Her countenance was long and haggard; her cheeks and lips were bloodless; the paleness of death was spread over her features; and her eye-balls, fixed stedfastly [sic] upon me, were lustreless and hollow. (Lewis 2004: 155)

Anticipations of love are replaced by a glimpse of absolute horror. Raymond's responses at this moment clearly display horror's corporeal effects: remaining as 'inanimate as a statue' with his nerves 'bound up in impotence', his blood is 'frozen' in his veins (Lewis 2004: 156). His shock, however, is coupled with a morbid sense of fascination, as Raymond comes to experience the manifold ambivalences, the simultaneous attractions and repulsions of horror such as those theorised by Burke, Aikin, Beattie, Drake and Radcliffe: '[m]y eyes were fascinated, and I had not the power of withdrawing them from the spectre's' (Lewis 2004: 156). Returning on subsequent nights to haunt Raymond, the ghost of the Bleeding Nun sings a ghastly refrain, ' "Raymond! Raymond! Thou art mine! / Raymond, Raymond! I am thine!" ' (157), and at one particularly nauseating moment attempts to caress him with her 'rotting fingers' (158) and kiss him with her lifeless lips.

Although, through the exorcism performed by the Wandering Jew and effects of a proper burial, the ghost of the Bleeding Nun, really one Beatrice las Cisternas, is eventually laid to rest in *The Monk*, her departure from the narrative by no means brings a cessation of horror. Indeed, the prevailing mood is only amplified in the events that lead up to Ambrosio's suffocation of Elvira, one whom he will only later discover is his biological mother. Gazing upon her lifeless body, the monk recoils in disgust at the sight:

> Her face was covered with a frightful blackness: her limbs moved no more: the blood was chilled in her veins: her heart had forgotten to beat; and her hands were stiff and frozen. Ambrosio beheld before him that the once noble and majestic form, now become a corse, cold, senseless, and disgusting. (264)

Indeed, the forces of horror and disgust become inextricably linked from this moment onwards in the narrative. Upon waking, Antonia, daughter to Elvira and Ambrosio's own sister, sees her mother's livid corpse before her and draws 'the inanimate form to her bosom', but 'with a movement of disgust, of which she was not the mistress' (Lewis 2004: 267) she throws it hastily from her. Horror invokes in the spectator uncontrolled revulsion and involuntary shuddering. A similar coupling of horror and disgust occurs when, her crimes having been exposed, the cruel Prioress of the Convent of St Clare is brutally torn limb from limb by an enraged crowd in the streets of Madrid. Dissatisfied with her death, they proceed to punish her body until it is reduced to an unrecognisable, bloody mass: '[t]hey beat it, trod upon it, and ill-used it, till it became no more than a mass of flesh, unsightly, shapeless, and disgusting' (302). While horror may thus seem graphically to reduce the body to its material, ahistorical basis, it is important to remember that the way in which it does so is always historically defined and culturally specific: perceived as a threat to the process of national, Protestant identity-formation in the eighteenth century, Catholics in early Gothic fiction become the objects, sources and causes of horror *par excellence*.

Another historically specific source of horror in the eighteenth century was that of live burial, a danger that was rendered more likely, perhaps, by the relative underdevelopment of contemporary medical practices. Lewis drew strongly upon this cultural fear in *The Monk*, particularly in his account of Lorenzo's discovery of Agnes, the pregnant nun who has been consigned by the Prioress to a form of live burial in the cavernous vaults beneath the Convent of St Clare. The sight of Agnes, clutching the maggot-infested body of her dead son to her bosom, occasions in her brother all of horror's corporeal and psychological effects: 'petrified with horror', he gazes upon the 'miserable object' with 'disgust and pity' (311). As the rescued Agnes herself later describes these travails, she has been exposed in the vaults to such objects of repulsion and horror as a rotting human head, reptiles that crawl and leave slimy tracks on her body and worms that have bred 'in the corrupted flesh of my infant' (343). Her ambivalent responses to her baby's rotting corpse, in particular, illustrate horror's contrary impulses particularly well: '[i]t soon became a mass of putridity', she notes, 'and to every eye was a loathsome and disgusting object, to every eye but a mother's.

In vain did human feelings bid me recoil from this emblem of mortality with repugnance' (342). An equally horrific scene of live burial occurs when Ambrosio, intent upon rape, drags the drugged Antonia into the vaults of St Clare. Surrounded by 'rotting bones and disgusting figures' (318), not even the monk and his Satanic accomplice are immune to horror's powers. *The Monk* as a whole, in turn, inspired anger, outrage and disgust in literary circles of the late 1790s and, seemingly driven to counteract its lurid and horrific excesses through her own distinctive style of terror, Ann Radcliffe penned what, in several crucial moments, reads as a corrective and disciplinary response to the text in her *The Italian: or, The Confessional of the Black Penitents* in 1797.

Horrors of the German School

As Lewis's 'Advertisement' to *The Monk* declares, the story of the Bleeding Nun derived ultimately from German sources, in particular the gruesome ballad of 'Lenore' (or 'Lenora' or 'Ellenore') by Gottfried August Bürger of 1773/4. The story concerns Lenore, the mournful lover of the ballad's title, who yearns for the return of her absent lover, William, who has gone abroad to participate in the Crusades against the infidel. When news arrives to say that William has died in battle, Lenore's grief takes her to the limits of reason. Inexplicably, though, his figure returns and takes her off on his galloping steed. At the moment when the two lovers joyfully anticipate their union in marriage, however, Lenore is revealed as the victim of a cruel supernatural joke: although he looks just like her beloved, the William that returns is nothing more than a ghost, intent upon dragging Lenore back with him into the land of the dead. Reconciled in the end to nothing more than a death's head and a skeleton, the heroine, like Raymond in *The Monk*, is left suitably wide-eyed and horrified as William's spectral vision vanishes before her eyes. It is difficult to over-estimate the importance of Bürger's tale to depictions of ultimate horror lurking in the place of love in Gothic fictions of the late eighteenth century. Translated into English and reworked by William Taylor, it was eventually published as 'Lenora' in the *Monthly Magazine* in 1796, the year of *The Monk*'s publication, although it had circulated in oral and manuscript versions in England long before this. Known to writers such as John and Anna Laetitia Aikin, Samuel Taylor Coleridge and Walter

Lenore, Gottfried August Bürger, 1773/4. Plate depicting the world of the dead. Illustrations by D. Maclise. Edition published in 1847.

Scott, Bürger's ballad continued to influence literary representations of horror well into the nineteenth century, resurfacing in such later poems and fictions as Coleridge's 'Christabel' (1816), Percy Bysshe Shelley's *St Irvyne; or, The Rosicrucian* (1811) and Charles Maturin's *Melmoth the*

Wanderer (1820). In *The Monk* a version of the story reappears in 'Alonzo the Brave and Fair Imogine', a poetic tale that Ambrosio's sister Antonia at one point in the narrative turns to read.

Influential though it was, Bürger's ballad was only one instance of a larger process of horrific transmission between Germany and Britain in the late eighteenth century. This steady import of translated horror fiction from the Continent led critics of popular romance in the period to inveigh against the Gothic as a foreign, 'German' literary phenomenon. In the 1800 Preface to *Lyrical Ballads*, for instance, William Wordsworth would describe his and Coleridge's 'revolutionary' collection of poems as, in part, an attempt to combat the 'frantic novels, sickly and stupid German Tragedies, and deluges of idle and extravagant stories in verse' (Gamer and Porter 2008: 183) that was contemporary Gothic fiction and drama. Similarly, a review of Francis Lathom's Gothic romance *Astonish-ment!!!: A Romance of a Century Ago* (1802) that was published in *Flowers of Literature; for 1803* emotively exclaimed that '[w]e should wish to see banished from our literature those *hobgobliana*, which the German school first suggested, and which Mrs Ratcliff [*sic*], by her superior talents, rendered popular' (Anon. 1804: 442). To a certain extent, these concerns seem justified: in addition to 'Lenore', other German fictions, dramas and writers that exerted a profound influence upon Romantic-era British popular literature include Schiller's play *Die Räuber* (translated into English as *The Robbers* in 1792) and novella *Der Geisterseher* (partly translated into English as *The Ghost-seer; or, Apparitionist* in 1795), as well as a host of German *Schauerromane* (or 'shudder novels') that were rapidly translated into English. Of the seven 'horrid' novels that Isabella Thorpe recommends to the heroine Catherine Morland in Jane Austen's *Northanger Abbey* (written in the late 1790s, published in 1817 but dated 1818), at least six of them claimed in either title, title page or setting to have been derived from German sources: *The Castle of Wolfenbach* (1793) and *The Mysterious Warning; A German Tale* (1796) by Eliza Parsons; *The Necromancer; or, The Tale of the Black Forest* (1794) by Carl Friedrich Kahlert; Francis Lathom's *The Midnight Bell* (1798); Eleanor Sleath's *The Orphan of the Rhine* (1798); and *Horrid Mysteries* (1796) by the Marquis de Grosse. That only the fictions of Kahlert and Grosse are, indeed, of German-language origin attests to the broader appeal that the tradition of German horror held for readers and writers of Gothic in late eighteenth-century

Britain – a taste exploited by such low-end publishers of horrid novels as William Lane's Minerva Press in London. When Coleridge, in a review of Charles Maturin's Gothic drama *Bertram* (1816), conceded in embarrassment that this mode of entertainment was ultimately English rather than German in origin, he returned the mode of Gothic horror to a British tradition that, he claimed, originated in the graveyard verse of Edward Young and James Hervey.

The Monstrous Horrors of Mary Shelley's *Frankenstein*

Despite the outrage that *The Monk* occasioned, it is clear to see that, as the titles of several bluebooks indicate, horror was fast becoming a marketable fictional commodity at the turn of the nineteenth century. Bluebooks, named for their flimsy blue-paper covers, were shorter,

The Black Forest or The Cavern of Horrors! A Gothic Romance, 1802. Frontispiece from edition published by J. Bonsor, 1802.

often illustrated redactions of longer Gothic novels. A popular, cheaply available and even disposable form of street literature, they were aimed primarily at a literate, working-class audience. These successors to the cheap, disposable broadsides and chapbooks of the earlier eighteenth century would eventually be replaced by the horror-mongering 'penny bloods' (later 'penny dreadfuls') of the Victorian publishing scene. Even if these short, highly sensational and plot-driven narratives did not always detail scenes of horror within their pages, titles such as the anonymous *The Black Forest; or, The Cavern of Horrors! A Gothic Romance* (1802), *The Night of the Broom Flower; or, Horrors of the Priory. A Romance* (1804), *The Bloody Hand; or, The Fatal Cup. A Tale of Horror* (c.1810), *Midnight Horrors; or, The Bandit's Daughter. An Original Romance* (c.1810) and *The Cavern of Horrors; or, Miseries of Miranda, a Neopolitan Tale* (c.1813) nonetheless demonstrate the extent to which publishers such as Thomas Tegg and Ann Lemoine saw in urban, working-class readers a lucrative market for the consumption of horror. With the exception of a text such as Mrs Carver's *The Horrors of Oakendale Abbey* (1797), horror was infrequently used as a titular, generic and marketing device in longer Gothic fictions of the period. Instead, as I argued at the outset of this chapter, such texts were more likely to be grouped together under such nebulous and ill-defined generic categories as the 'horrid' novels satirised by Jane Austen or the 'horrible romances' described in the *Encyclopædia Londinensis*. Thus when Mary Shelley began writing *Frankenstein; or, The Modern Prometheus* in 1816 – a fiction that, in time, would become enshrined as one of the most influential texts in the history of horror literature – she was not seeking to align herself with any tightly defined set of generic conventions so much as to innovate upon the diffuse British literary tradition of 'horrible' fiction that I have outlined in this chapter. As Percy Bysshe Shelley put it in his Preface to the first edition of *Frankenstein* in 1818, though the proceeding work was not to be conceptualised as 'merely' a tale of 'supernatural terrors' that had been woven together by the work of fancy, it derived from the same sources as those outlined above, among them Shakespeare's *The Tempest* and *A Midsummer Night's Dream* and 'most especially Milton, in *Paradise Lost*' (Shelley 1996: 5). Stirred by the presence of Shelley, Lord Byron, Polidori and Claire Clairmont and inspired by the reading of *Fantasmagoriana* (1812), 'some [French translations of] German stories of ghosts, which

Frankenstein, or the Modern Prometheus, Mary Wollstonecraft Shelley, 1818. Frontispiece, by Theodore von Holst, from edition published by Henry Colburn and Richard Bentley, 1831.

happened to fall into our hands' (Shelley 1996: 6), Mary Shelley's imagination in *Frankenstein* is as hybrid a Gothic construction as its resident monster.

Unmitigated horror is certainly the result, as Mary Shelley fashions in *Frankenstein* a tale that describes the construction and awful travails of an innocent creature-turned-murderous-monster, part-human and part-animal in form. His body parts drawn together from dissecting rooms, charnel houses and slaughterhouses by the hands of Victor Frankenstein, a deranged, megalomaniacal scientist, the creature is animated and brought to life by the forces of galvanism, electricity and other principles of modern science. His coming into being marks the advent of horror in the text, one that is suitably sunk in the responses of repulsion and disgust similar to those detailed in *The Monk*: 'now that I had finished', Frankenstein subsequently narrates, 'the beauty of the dream vanished, and breathless horror and disgust filled my heart' (Shelley 1996: 34). In its account of the anticipation of beauty that is replaced by sentiments of loathing and disgust, Shelley's fiction recalls the dynamics of horror previously explored in Bürger's 'Lenore': just as Lenore's anticipation of a return to the arms of her lover ends in shock and horror, so Victor's anticipation of a beautiful creature results in untold disgust. Echoes of Bürger recur almost immediately thereafter in the narrative, when an exhausted Victor falls into bed to dream about his beloved Elizabeth. As he turns in his dream to embrace and kiss her, the vision horrifically mutates into the worm-eaten corpse of his dead mother:

> I thought I saw Elizabeth, in the bloom of health, walking in the streets of Ingolstadt. Delighted and surprised, I embraced her; but as I imprinted the first kiss on her lips, they became livid with the hue of death; her features appeared to change, and I thought that I held the corpse of my dead mother in my arms; a shroud enveloped her form, and I saw the grave-worms crawling in the folds of the flannel. (34)

As in earlier fiction, horror in *Frankenstein* resides in the exposure of the mortality that lurks always just below the surface of an apparently more pleasing reality. Victor's responses recall those hypothetically outlined to Hamlet by the ghost of his father: 'I started from my sleep with horror; a cold dew covered my forehead, my teeth chattered, and every limb became convulsed' (34–5). Throughout the remainder of the text, horrors upon horror's head accumulate – culminating, perhaps, in the scene in which the creature, now self-consciously monstrous, chillingly threatens to 'be with' Frankenstein on his wedding night. In Burkean terms, horror in the text most certainly presides in that which presses 'too close'; throwing off the ineffability of earlier horrid fictions, narrators, including the monster himself, are distinguished by their remarkable eloquence. But if Shelley's narrative, in this light, reads as only a reiteration of the discourse of literary horror that had taken formation in British culture at least since the early modern period, it is important to acknowledge the primary innovation in the field that it achieves. Like the vampire that takes shape in another product of that notoriously bad summer of ghost-story-telling, John Polidori's *The Vampyre* of 1819, *Frankenstein* bequeaths to the horror tradition a preoccupation with the monstrous body, the manifold shudders, repulsions and revulsions provoked by an ugly, misshapen, deformed physical and psychological entity that will lunge heavily through the literature of horror from the nineteenth century through to the present day.

References

Addison, Joseph, 'No. 111. Friday, July 6, 1711', *The Spectator*, vol. II (1711; Boston: Hastings, Etheredge, and Bliss, 1809), pp. 229–34.

Aikin, John, and Anna Laetitia Aikin, *Miscellaneous Pieces, in Prose* (London: Printed for J. Johnson, 1773).

Anonymous, 'On the Titles of Modern Novels', *Monthly Magazine and British Register, for 1797. From July to December, Inclusive*, vol. IV (1797), 347–9.

——, 'Review of Francis *Lathom's Astonishment!!! A Romance of a Century Ago*', *Flowers of Literature; for 1803* (London: Printed by J. Swan for B. Crosby and Co., 1804), p. 422.

——, *Encyclopædia Londinensis; or, An Universal Dictionary of Arts, Sciences, and Literature*, vol. XXII (London: Printed for G. Jones, 1827).

Beattie, James, *Dissertations Moral and Critical* (London: Printed for W. Strahan and T. Cadell; Edinburgh: W. Creech, 1783).

Blair, Robert, *The Grave: A Poem* (London: Printed for M. Cooper, 1743).

Burke, Edmund, *A Philosophical Enquiry into the Origin of our Ideas of the Sublime and Beautiful* (London: Printed for R. and J. Dodsley, 1757).

Coleridge, Samuel Taylor, *Biographia Literaria: or, Biographical Sketches of My Literary Life and Opinions* (London: R. Fenner, 1817).

Collins, William, *Odes on Several Descriptive and Allegoric Subjects* (London: Printed for A. Millar, 1747).

Drake, Nathan, *Literary Hours; or, Sketches Critical and Narrative* (London: Printed by J. Burkitt and sold by T. Cadell, Junior, and W. Davies, 1798).

Gamer, Michael, and Dahlia Porter, 'Preface', in Samuel Taylor Coleridge and William Wordsworth, *Lyrical Ballads 1798 and 1800*, ed. by Michael Gamer and Dahlia Porter (Peterborough, ON: Broadview Press, 2008), pp. 171–87.

Gray, Thomas, *Odes by Mr Gray* (London: Printed at Strawberry-Hill for R. and J. Dodsley, 1757).

Lewis, Matthew Gregory, *The Monk; A Romance* (Peterborough, ON: Broadview Press, 2004).

Radcliffe, Ann, 'On the Supernatural in Poetry. By the Late Mrs. Radcliffe', *The New Monthly Magazine and Literary Journal, Part I* (London: Henry Colburn, 1826), pp. 145–52.

Reeve, Clara, *The Champion of Virtue: A Gothic Story* (Colchester: Printed by W. Keymer, 1777).

Shakespeare, William, *The Norton Shakespeare*, ed. by Stephen Greenblatt, Walter Cohen, Jean E. Howard and Katharine Eisaman Maus, 2nd edn (London and New York: W. W. Norton & Co., 2000).

Shelley, Mary, *Frankenstein; or, The Modern Prometheus* (New York: W. W. Norton and Co., 1996).

Southey, Robert, *Poems* (Bristol: Printed by N. Biggs, for Joseph Cottle; London: G.G. and J. Robinson, 1797).

Walpole, Horace, *The Castle of Otranto* (Oxford: Oxford University Press, 2014).

——, 'The Mysterious Mother; A Tragedy' (1768), in *Five Romantic Plays*, ed. by Paul Baines and Edward Burnes (Oxford: Oxford University Press, 2000), pp. 1–70.

Warton, Thomas, 'Ode to Horror', *The Student; or, The Oxford, and Cambridge Monthly Miscellany* (London: Printed for J. Newbery, 1751), pp. 313–5.

What to Read Next

Charlotte Dacre, *Zofloya; or, The Moor* (1806; Oxford: Oxford University Press, 2008).

Matthew Gregory Lewis, *The Monk; a Romance* (1796; Peterborough, Ontario: Broadview Press, 2004).

Charles Robert Maturin, *Melmoth the Wanderer* (1820; Oxford: Oxford University Press, 2008).

Mary Shelley, *Frankenstein; or, The Modern Prometheus* (1818; New York: W. W. Norton and Co., 2012).

Horace Walpole, *The Castle of Otranto* (1764/5; Oxford: Oxford University Press, 2014).

A

N A R R A T I V E

OF THE

CAPTIVITY, SUFFERINGS AND REMOVES

O F

Mrs. *Mary Rowlandson,*

Who was taken Prifoner by the INDIANS with feveral others, and treated in the moft barbarous and cruel Manner by thofe vile Savages : With many other remarkable Events during her TRAVELS.

Written by her own Hand, for her private Ufe, and now made public at the earneft Defire of fome Friends, and for the Benefit of the afflicted.

B O S T O N

Printed and Sold at JOHN BOYLE's Printing-Office, next Door to the *Three Doves* in Marlborough-Street. 1773.

A Narrative of the Captivity, Sufferings and Removes of Mrs Mary Rowlandson, Mary Rowlandson, 1682. Titlepage, showing Mary being taken prisoner, from edition published by John Boyle, 1773.

Chapter 2

American Horror: Origins and Early Trends

Agnieszka Soltysik Monnet

GOTHIC HORROR ARRIVED IN AMERICA in the latter half of the eighteenth century as one of many imports – literary and cultural – from England during this period of intense transatlantic circulation. As an experimental and often transgressive genre, the Gothic novel found a congenial home in the fiercely independent new nation. By the 1790s the American Gothic was well on its way to establishing a set of themes and concerns that would become uniquely its own. These included the frontier and its native inhabitants, Puritanism and its tendency towards religious excess and the individual in relation to the larger body politic. Aesthetically the Gothic novel embraced several different modes; of these, horror was the most significant and the most deeply rooted in American rhetorical and literary traditions. Present already in the uniquely American form of writing known as the captivity narrative, horror writing emerged in full force in the late eighteenth century as a modern reaction-formation to shifts in the political and religious landscape. As historian Karen Halttunen (2000) has shown, modern American horror was born at the moment when religious narratives had lost their purchase on explaining crime and, especially, murder. While Protestant religious narratives about evil had regarded it as a natural and inevitable fact of fallen existence on earth, the new, secular paradigms of the Romantic movement and the Enlightenment could only consider violent crimes as mysterious aberrations. The result of this epistemological gap was a fascination with the details of bodily mutilation and the life history of killers that has persisted until today.

The moment of horror's arrival in the fledgling United States also corresponded with a time of intense social transition as the new nation struggled to define itself and decide upon the precise character of its political institutions. For example, there was the public debate about federalism against republicanism, with its choice between centralised authority as opposed to greater states' rights. The country had committed itself to a democratic government, but many practical and philosophical questions about what this meant and how to implement it remained. Novelists took up the challenge of thinking through some of the dilemmas raised by the curious phenomenon of a disparate set of colonies banding together to cast off the trappings of empire and now facing the task of inventing themselves as a coherent political unity. Inherently engaged with questions of ethics and moral judgement, the horror mode lent itself to such experiments in political thought, as did the specific historical circumstances and background of the young republic. These included the popular genre of captivity narratives (first-person accounts of violence and kidnapping by 'Indians') and the tradition of Puritan sermons, both of which provided a wealth of imaginative material for early American horror's anxious examination of the individual in the New World.

Captive Narratives and Puritan Beginnings

The first indigenous form of the horror mode was the captivity narrative. These were usually written by women who had been abducted by Native Americans, often during a violent attack resulting in the death of the woman's husband and/or children and other relatives. The most famous captivity story, *A Narrative of the Captivity, Sufferings and Removes of Mrs. Mary Rowlandson,* written by Mary Rowlandson herself, was published in 1682, but the greatest number of captivity narratives appeared in the last decades of the eighteenth century – at exactly the moment when the Gothic novel and its horror aesthetics were becoming popular. There are many structural and thematic similarities between the two forms, including gory descriptions of violence, sequestration and the threat of rape, and the focus on an intrepid female survivor. In this respect the captivity narrative inaugurated a core dimension of the Gothic genre: the heroine who faces and overcomes male violence. The captivity narrative can also be seen as a way of thinking about various models of government in the way it stages scenarios in which different kinds of people (such as Native American tribes and European settlers) either possess enough common ground to co-exist or do not, depending on the political inclinations of the writer.

Another specifically American Gothic literary background is the Puritan tradition. Puritanism was originally a reform movement within the Church of England in the 1560s, but it soon parted ways from the mainstream of English society, its followers believing that the reforms had not gone far enough. The name 'Puritan' derives from the idea that these reformers sought to restore the 'purity' of the church. Although not necessarily separatists at the start, Puritans neverthe-less began to leave England because of persecution; several thousand eventually sailed to the American colonies in the early seventeenth century. Many believed that they had a pact with God to create a new kind of holy community. Such a conviction would remain a running thread throughout American history and self-definition, developing insidiously over the centuries into what twentieth-century scholars would call 'the myth of American exceptionalism' – that is, the belief that the United States of America is qualitatively different from any other country in the world and chosen by God for a special destiny. Puritans have been represented quite negatively in the contempo-rary media, portrayed as a dour and humourless people. Although this image is mostly exaggerated, it is undeniable that the Puritans held a number of beliefs that were quite dark and deterministic, including the existence of hell and the devil, original sin and innate (or total) depravity. Looking at their surroundings through the prism of their religious beliefs, the Puritans saw a wilderness peopled by devils, in which they had to wage daily and endless war against both Satan and their own inherent sinfulness. Ironically, later generations of Puritan settlers often became even more severe in their application of Puritan doctrine than their forefathers had been, due in large part to their cultural and geographical isolation.

Joseph E. Baker, *The Witch No. 1*, lithograph. Published by Geo. H. Walker & Co., Boston, *c.* 1892. Library of Congress, Prints and Photographs Division.

Few incidents in American history have left such an indelible mark on the history of horror – and its literary legacy – in the New World as the Salem witch trials of the 1690s. These were a series of hearings and prosecutions that resulted in 20 executions, almost entirely of women. Nineteen of these were by hanging, and one man was pressed to death with heavy stones laid on a plank over his body for three days in an effort to force a guilty plea. Seven more people died in prison, including a child. Although the Salem witch hysteria was over within a year, its impact on the American imagination has been enduring. One immediate effect was a permanent loss of power of Puritan authorities, as the ease with which respected officials were carried away by the frenzy and its murderous results led colonists to view religious fervour with a new wariness. This mistrust has never worn off, just as the Puritans have never shaken off their association with religious intolerance and murderous irrationalism. Narratives about the witch trials proliferated in the nineteenth century, including several stories by Nathaniel Hawthorne (discussed below). These have served as a basis for horror-inflected novels, plays and films throughout the twentieth century, such as Esther Forbes' *Mirror for Witches* (1928), Arthur Miller's *The Crucible* (1953) and the recent *The Lords of Salem* (Rob Zombie, 2012).

Charles Brockden Brown, America's First Horror Writer

The first acknowledged American novelist, Charles Brockden Brown, was a writer of horror fiction. The subject of his most famous and important novel, *Wieland; or, The Transformation* (1798), is religious fanaticism, and therefore indirectly interrogates America's Puritan legacy. *Wieland* is also a product of the Age of Enlightenment, as is Gothic horror in general, and therefore a novel that confronts rationalism with religious enthusiasm and discovers that the seemingly disenchanted modern world is full of mysteries. Like the British Gothic novels of Ann Radcliffe, the narrator of *Wieland* is a young woman, Clara Wieland. She begins the novel by telling readers that she is about to recount a narrative that ends with a mangled victim and a rage that 'exterminated' every 'remnant of good' (Brown 1998: 5) in her world. She then narrates the circumstances of her father's strange death by spontaneous combustion and her childhood as an orphan alone with her brother. The novel contains many strange and sometimes seemingly tangential details and plots, including the story of the villain's life, which was later developed by Brown and published as a separate novella, *Memoirs of Carwin the Biloquist* (1803–5). I say 'villain', but Brown's narrative makes it quite hard to determine who is the villain and who the victim. A spectacular and harrowing scene of violence occurs mid-way, the murder by Clara's brother of his wife and children, one so brutal that the victims are scarcely recognisable. A young woman living in the household like an adopted daughter had been beaten so savagely that '*not a lineament remained*' (Brown 1998: 147; emphasis in original) of her face. Equally chilling is Wieland's written testimony that he had merely acted upon the promptings of a voice he took to be that of God. The first complication here is the whole matter of the legal status of such claims. In a modern court of law the brother's testimony would be taken as the ravings of a madman. Yet claims of direct communication with

God are not entirely foreign to the Protestant tradition, and some religions, such as Mormonism, allow for such phenomena. Moreover, the rage and brutality accompanying the slayings also add a layer of horror to the situation that Wieland's testimony does little to assuage or explain.

Further complicating matters in the novel is the fact that Clara's family is being spied upon by a con man of sorts who uses his powers of ventriloquism to manipulate them for his own amusement. One of his ventriloquist tricks is to pretend to be the voice of God. Yet, confronted with Wieland's testimony, Carwin denies having instructed Wieland to murder anyone. The resulting mysteries are thus entirely secular and naturalistic, but no less irresolvable and mystifying. Is Wieland mad? Is Carwin lying? Did Carwin's ventriloquist games set off Wieland's religious madness?

Moreover, such uncertainties call into question the whole issue of how anyone can know what they know with any certainty and make judgements, moral or otherwise, based on that imperfect knowledge. The fact that Brown sent his novel to Thomas Jefferson suggests that he believed it contained useful insights about political philosophy, but scholars have disagreed about what these might be. One way to understand the violence that brings the narrative to a climax is that religion is a form of madness and therefore dangerous in a liberal republic. One could also read the relative freedom enjoyed by the protagonists as a tacit argument that a strong central government could keep such excesses in check. This reading would ascribe a deeply conservative slant to the book. Alternatively, more progressively, we could suppose from the fallibility of *all* the characters that a strong central government would be equally vulnerable to errors of judgement, and that therefore a full democracy is the least of all political evils.

In raising these issues, Brown participates in a longstanding tradition in horror fiction of implicitly exploring the connections between psychology and political theory. Inspired by the English radical writer William Godwin (1756-1836), Brown wrote a series of novels focusing on young protagonists navigating the volatile social space of the young nation and confronting situations that strained both their abilities, and that of the reader, easily to judge people and actions. Psychological and physical violence, deadly illness, crime, mental disorders and mysteries abound in the novels. For instance, in *Arthur Mervyn, or Memoirs of the Year 1793* (1799), the protagonist recounts his experiences during an epidemic of yellow fever in Philadelphia. Like today's contagion films, such as *28 Days Later* (Danny Boyle, 2002), the novel is full of horrific descriptions of the physical symptoms of the disease, often plunging into abject details of bodies become monstrous, as well as disturbing descriptions of the breakdown of civil society under the pressure of the epidemic. We hear of family members abandoned by their loved ones, of the dying heaped with the dead and of the cowardice of persons trusted to care for the infected. Once more Brown complicates this already richly horrific plot by making his first-person narrator ambiguous and possibly unreliable. Readers are left wondering if Mervyn is not himself a con man, or at least an opportunist. Questions of motive and character are constantly raised and rendered uncertain, as people themselves scarcely know the reasons for their actions.

Although Charles Brockden Brown is little known today outside of universities, he had a huge influence on the subsequent tradition of American horror. All the great American Gothicists of the nineteenth century – including Poe and Hawthorne – were influenced by his work. Brown made horror a genre of the social and political thought experiment, freeing himself of novel conventions that required consistent characters and unified plots. Instead, in seeking a higher realism, Brown permitted himself complex and ambivalent characters and allowed contingency and the messy complexities of life to seep into his plots. He also made each of his character's subjective experience of his or her world as true and valid as any other – recreating in this respect the individualistic dynamics of American democracy. Such a scenario was both exciting and potentially frightening to Brown and other people of his time, and horror fiction permitted him to explore the more extreme peripheries of individual behaviour and psychology. By placing complex characters in violent or terrifying circumstances, Brown tried to discover certain universals of human nature, or at least to examine the range of its possible reactions. This acute awareness of the diversity and complexity of human motives and behaviour emerged naturally in a nation composed of states which had previously had less contact with each other than with the mother country (and even that had been quite attenuated by distance). American states had been quite autonomous up until the Revolution, each with unique local cultures and values. Moreover, each state was composed of even more subcultures, ethnic enclaves, races, religions and other communities with markedly different moral and political frameworks. Now these radically different entities had to create a single political organism. Brown's horror fiction offered him and his readers a safe space in which to think through some of the meanings and implications of that diversity.

Subtle Horror in the Short Stories of Washington Irving

A more familiar name is Washington Irving, whose story 'The Legend of Sleepy Hollow' (1820) has been the basis of several films, most notably the 1999 Tim Burton adaptation, and a recent television series in the United States (2013-present). Irving also wrote a companion piece called 'Rip Van Winkle' (1820), about a man who falls asleep and wakes up 20 years later. Both stories are examples of fairly gentle horror fiction, though admittedly 'Sleepy Hollow' is remembered mainly for its headless Hessian horseman. Both stories develop Brown's interest in the question of competing value systems and cultures. In 'Rip Van Winkle', the protagonist wakes up in a dramatically different world from the one in which he fell asleep because the American Revolution has happened in the meantime. His utter dislocation, and the horror of finding all familiar faces and cultural landmarks gone, is part of the darkness of the tale. Similarly 'The Legend of Sleepy Hollow' is about a confrontation of two different worlds – that of the inhabitants of Tarry Town, a remote Dutch village in Pennsylvania, and that of Ichabod Crane, the itinerant teacher who represents the grasping, materialistic values of the new business culture taking hold of American society in the 1820s. Although he seems to represent modernity and progress, Crane's goal is less to teach the town's children than it is to marry the town's richest heiress and acquire her wealth. Despite his education, Ichabod Crane is also terribly superstitious and this is what allows the local admirer of the same young woman to chase him away. Brom, as the local suitor is called, takes advantage of a story-telling session to revive a legend about a headless horseman from the Revolutionary War who roams the woods outside town. Later that evening, as Crane is riding home, he is accosted by a horseman who resembles the Hessian mercenary of the story:

> There was something in the stranger's moody silence that was appalling. It was soon fearfully accounted for. On mounting a rising ground, which brought the figure of his fellow traveler in relief against the sky, gigantic in height, and muffled in a cloak, Ichabod was horrorstruck on perceiving that he was headless! But his horror was still more increased on observing that the stranger's head was carried before him on the pommel of the saddle. (Irving 1983: 1083)

The mysterious figure chases him through the woods and throws what appears to be his head at him (1085). The story of Crane's terrifying chase by the horseman has been part of American popular culture for nearly two centuries, often represented visually with a 'real' headless ghost. In the story, however, the reader is subtly but unmistakably invited to read between the lines and understand that the supposed headless horseman is none other than Brom himself. The young man takes advantage of Crane's cowardice and superstition to drive him from the town by pretending to be the horseman and throwing a pumpkin at him. In short, the story is basically a satire of the Gothic, but one so subtle and effective that many superficial readers miss the parody or ignore it. However, the story is representative of the way in which humour and self-irony have been essential features of the horror mode since its inception.

Edgar Allan Poe, The Master of the Early American Horror Story

Probably the best known writer of American horror fiction is Edgar Allan Poe. Not particularly appreciated at home, especially after a scurrilous obituary damaged his reputation by wildly exaggerating his eccentricities, Poe became a sensation in Europe in the second half of the nineteenth century; his fame started in France with Charles Baudelaire's translations and eulogies and then spread across the globe. Poe's work is a perfect example of how horror and humour often go

Portrait of Edgar Allan Poe, *Illustrations to Edgar Allan Poe. From drawings by Aubrey Beardsley*, limited edition. Published by Aubrey Beardsley Club, 1926.

together. One of the greatest challenges – and pleasures – for readers of Poe is how to take the often ironic tone of his stories, especially the most horrific ones. This tonal ambivalence, as we could call it, has been responsible for many Anglo-American critics dismissing Poe as a charlatan or boys' writer. Yet it is precisely this complexity that caused French readers to admire him, and that made Poe something of a star in deconstructionist circles in the late twentieth century (Soltysik 2007: 137–8). For instance, both Jacques Lacan and Jacques Derrida wrote extensively about him (see Johnson 1977).

Poe's biography has been the subject of much exaggeration and distortion, yet remains one of the most fascinating in American letters. He was indeed spared few horrors in his own life. Orphaned as a toddler, he was raised by a wealthy merchant in Virginia and Scotland, only to lose his beloved stepmother to tuberculosis and to be disowned by his stepfather as a young man. Accustomed to a certain comfort as a child, Poe struggled with poverty his entire adult life. He was the first American writer to support himself entirely by writing, in a literary marketplace where copyright laws were weak and writers earned very little. Poe clung to what little biological family he had, marrying a young cousin, largely in order to become her legal guardian and to be able to care for her and her mother. When his young wife also fell ill with tuberculosis and began to slowly waste away, Poe was disconsolate. Much of this grief and horror found its way into his writing, especially into works such as 'Morella' (1835), 'Ligeia' (1838) and the long poem 'The Raven' (1845).

At the same time, Poe was a writer of tremendous wit and satirical genius. His experience of living abroad as a child and of being a perpetual outsider, even in his own family, gave him a privileged insight into the strangeness and absurdity of many cultural conventions. This critical distance, which included a fascination with the arbitrariness of standards of good taste and good judgement, would be translated into an acute sense of irony, and even self-irony, in his writing. A good example of this tonal ambivalence can be found in 'Ligeia'. The story is told by an unnamed male narrator, who describes his marriage to a beautiful, mysterious and extremely erudite woman with whom he spends days in recondite studies, and who tells him that death can be overcome by willpower (Poe 1984: 269). Ligeia contracts tuberculosis, even as did Poe's beloved stepmother and later his wife, and dies, leaving the narrator despondent, bitter and addicted to opium. He remarries a fair-haired woman he does not love and neglects her cruelly until she too dies. The main part of the story consists of a scene in which the shroud-wrapped body of the dead second wife seems slowly to re-animate as the black-haired Ligeia – a horrific process of seeming perception and denial complicated by the narrator's opium-induced intoxication. As if these ambiguities were not enough, the entire story is riddled with pretentious foreign references and over-the-top pseudo-scientific riffs that have led many readers to suspect the whole piece is a parody of the Gothic genre, something Poe did more overtly in several other stories of the same period. The result is a radically unstable narrative that succeeds as a tale of horror for many readers while simultaneously working as a subtle piece of mock-horror or self-reflexive metafiction for others.

Poe's skilful manipulation of writing conventions occasionally led to genuine uncertainty about the status of certain tales. One of the more gruesome of Poe's short stories, 'The Facts in the Case of M. Valdemar'

(1845), for example, was taken by some readers to be an authentic scientific report. The story purports to be an account by a mesmerist of an experiment in hypnotising someone at the moment of death. The result is described as some form of suspended animation in which the test subject is technically dead but still manages to speak, uttering in a thoroughly uncanny way, 'I have been sleeping – and now – now – I am dead' (Poe 1984: 840). The reaction to such a violently unnatural utterance is pure horror and recoil:

> No person present even affected to deny, or attempted to repress, the unutterable, shuddering horror which these few words, thus uttered, were so well calculated to convey. Mr. L___l (the student) swooned. The nurses immediately left the chamber, and could not be induced to return. My own impressions I would not pretend to render intelligible to the reader. (840)

This passage bears all the elements of horror as a modern cultural phenemenon: the physical reactions of fear and flight as well as fainting, the seeming inability to describe one's feelings – in other words, an invocation of the unspeakable – and finally a curious self-consciousness about emotion as a calculated product of a certain kind of verbal production. Just as M. Valdemar's words seem 'calculated to convey' a 'shuddering horror' to his listeners, so are they – and the story itself – calculated to convey horror to Poe's readers. The tale ends with a line that is itself clearly meant to produce the purest horror in readers. When the narrator releases M. Valdemar from the hypnotic spell that had bound him after his death, the body instantly melts as seven months of suspended putrefaction rot it away: '[u]pon the bed, before that whole company, there lay a nearly liquid mass of loathsome – of detestable putridity' (842). The reduction of the human body to something that bears no resemblance to the human, to a thing, here a puddle of decay, is the very essence of horror.

Slavery was a real-life issue at a time in which humans were being systematically reduced to things, and horror became a favoured strategy among abolitionist writers trying to stir outrage against it. Although Poe is scarcely considered an abolitionist, generally avoiding the topic of race and slavery in his work, one of his last published short stories does address this topic, though displacing it to a fictional and fantastic world. 'Hop-Frog' (1849) explicitly dramatises the plight of a slave, a dwarf who

Edgar Allan Poe, 'Hop Frog; Or, The Eight Chained Ourangoutangs', short story in *The Flag of Our Union*, 17 March 1849. Illustration by Arthur Rackham for the same story, re-titled 'Hop-Frog', in *Tales of Mystery and Imagination*, published by G. G. Harrap & Co., 1935.

has been kidnapped from his native land to serve a cruel king as court jester, and a young girl slave, also a dwarf. Told by an unnamed courtier who fails to understand much of what he is witnessing, the story is a brilliant example of Poe's use of unreliable narration. (Unreliable in this context does not mean dishonest or deceptive, but merely stupid or slow, unable to correctly interpret what he or she sees.) Poe frequently used this device in order to allow readers to make connections and inferences that he wanted to leave unsaid, believing that they made a more powerful impression if suggested rather than stated. The story begins with a scene of cruelty, in which the king and his ministers abuse both Hop-Frog and the other slave, a tiny girl named Trippetta, by forcing them to drink, shoving them, throwing wine in their faces and laughing uproariously at their discomfort, all the while making cruel jokes, such as asking them to toast their absent friends (Poe 1984: 903). Subtly and with indirection, Poe allows the reader to see something that the narrator misses entirely: that the cruelty of the scene leads Hop-Frog to devise an equally cruel plan for revenge. In the rest of the story the reader discovers, with growing horror, the plan that Hop-Frog has devised, namely to cover the king and his ministers with tar, chain them together like orang-utans and set them on fire – a horrific allusion to some of the most brutal punishments meted out to Southern slaves and later free blacks under Jim Crow (namely tarring and feathering or burning alive).

The story ends with a scene of carnage almost unparalleled in American fiction, with the king and his ministers hanging from a chandelier – '[t]he eight corpses swung in their chains, a fetid, blackened, hideous, and indistinguishable mass' (Poe 1984: 908) – as the two dwarfs run away, never to be seen again. The story takes place in a fantasy kingdom and therefore does not appear on the surface to be a comment on the Southern institution of slavery, and moreover the grotesque and seemingly comic features of the main character can be seen as examples of racist caricature. Nevertheless, the tale is a devastating rebuke to the Southern defence of slavery on the grounds that slaves are childlike creatures needing the care and control they receive from masters, who were depicted in pro-slavery ideology almost in the role of parents or guardians to their slaves. This argument was predicated on a total denial of the repressive and cruel character of slavery as an institution – including a denial of the possibility that slaves resented their servitude and would take revenge if given the opportunity. That such a fact was likely was the unspeakable open secret of Southern existence, but the official discourse around slavery always represented it as a benevolent and civilising institution. In this light one can see to what extent Poe's story gives the lie to such fictions, by allowing the reader to perceive something the narrator does not: namely, that the slave hates his master and wishes to be free.

In this way, horror fiction was able subtly to expose social realities in a way that would have been immediately discredited had Poe written an editorial or non-fiction account. Abolitionists and pro-slavery defenders rarely read one another's work, and neither would have been swayed by the other's arguments. However, by weaving abolitionist horror into a fictional narrative Poe was able to undermine Southern propaganda about the benevolence of slavery and the seeming acquiescence of slaves to their captivity. In this way, he illustrated the craft and cunning with which writers of horror have been able to participate in larger conversations about social values and practices while appearing to be concerned with wholly imagined or fantastic worlds.

Witchcraft in Nathaniel Hawthorne's Short Stories

The other major writer of horror fiction from the pre-Civil War era in American history is Nathaniel Hawthorne, probably best known for his novel *The Scarlet Letter* (1850). Hawthorne was America's first great writer of historical horror, often setting his tales and novels in the past. No aspect of American history obsessed Hawthorne more than its Puritan origins and especially the witch trials that had taken place in his native town of Salem, Massachusetts. Hawthorne's interest in this dark moment of American history was personal as well as professional – he was descended from the only judge from that period who had not publicly repented for having sent people to their deaths.

As previously mentioned, it is fair to say that the Salem witch trials of 1692–3 have had a hold on the American horror imagination like few other events, though they lasted no more than a year. When the episode had passed and people realised that a kind of mass hysteria had gripped their communities, Puritan authorities found themselves with considerably less power and influence. One of the issues that has particularly bothered Americans about the trials is the harrowingly

Lady Eleanore's Mantle.

Twice-Told Tales, Nathanial Hawthorne, 1837 (vol 1), 1842 (vol 2). Frontispiece from The Complete Works of Nathanial Hawthorne, published by Houghton & Co., 1883.

irrational attitude towards evidence. It sufficed for a person to testify in court that someone's spirit or spectral shape appeared to him or her in a dream – this was called 'spectral evidence' – for the accused to be considered guilty. In practical terms, this meant that anyone could condemn anyone else of witchcraft and there was little the victim could say to defend herself or himself.

Nathaniel Hawthorne returns to this problem of spectral evidence again and again in his work. His most famous story dealing with the Puritans and their problematic relationship to signs is 'Young Goodman Brown' (1835). In this early tale Hawthorne tells of a young Salem man who leaves his pretty wife alone for a night while he travels through a wood for an unspecified 'evil purpose' (Hawthorne 1982: 276). Like many of Hawthorne's stories, the tale leans heavily toward allegory (the wife's name, for example, is 'Faith' and Brown must leave her behind to accomplish his dark journey) while still sounding quite individualised and realistic. The story quickly takes a dark turn as Brown encounters a character who is clearly a version of the devil, an association made more allegorically explicit as we are told his staff resembled a 'great black snake, so curiously wrought, that it might almost be seen to twist and wriggle itself like a living serpent' (277). This mysterious personage accompanies Brown through the dark forest, telling him that he was friends with many of his Puritan forefathers – including his grandfather, who lashed a Quaker woman in the streets, and Brown's father, who burned down an Indian village. Here Hawthorne evokes the violent excesses of the Puritans in their persecution of others, and suggests that the devil figuratively had a hand in them. As the pair penetrate further into the wood, Brown sees a series of people he knows from his life and town, and is astonished to discover how many of his townsmen have given themselves over to the devil. At one point, he refuses to walk any further, but ends up following the voices of two men who seem to be the minister and the deacon of the town. He then discovers almost the entire town cavorting. Hawthorne is careful to remind the reader that these apparitions may all be spectral illusions of some kind, and sometimes refers to them as merely voices or images of the people they resemble. Brown despairs when he sees what appears to be his wife Faith, and the language of the passage takes a dark turn as Brown loses his mind and metamorphoses into 'the chief horror of the scene', not shrinking 'from its other horrors' (284). Like a character from Charles Brockden Brown or Edgar Allan Poe, Young Goodman Brown is pushed into momentary insanity:

> In truth, all through the haunted forest there could be nothing more frightful than the figure of Goodman Brown. On he flew among the black pines, brandishing his staff with frenzied gestures, now giving vent to an inspiration of horrid blasphemy, and now shouting forth such laughter as set all the echoes of the forest laughing like demons around him. The fiend in his own shape is less hideous than when he rages in the breast of man. (284)

He participates in a dark mass, discovering that all the most revered figures of his life are sinners in thrall to the dark arts, and emerges from the forest the next day a changed man: 'stern, [...] sad, [...] darkly meditative' (288–9), living the rest of his life distrustful and distant from all the people around him, including his wife. With this story Hawthorne alludes to the problem of spectral evidence – after all, Brown's only proof is what he believes he has seen in the forest – leavening the religious allegory with conventions of the fantastic.

Also in 1836, Hawthorne wrote another story which developed his preoccupation with the witch trials even more pointedly. 'Alice Doane's Appeal' borrows from a popular non-fiction genre of the time, the sketch, and consists of a frame narrative and an embedded story. In the frame narrative a young man, a writer, accompanies two young women to Gallows Hill in Salem. He takes advantage of the opportunity to read them a horror story he has written about a brother and sister and an evil wizard, a story that ends with fratricide and also includes a scene of demonic spectres in the woods. For the sake of effect, the narrator tries to connect his story to the real world by ending with a claim that the wizard's bones are buried on Gallows Hill – a strain on his listeners' credulity that leads them both to laugh. Annoyed by their reaction, the young narrator now tells them of the real history of Salem, conjuring up the gloomy procession to Gallows Hill as the condemned witches are led to their death. Here the mock-horror of the embedded story is replaced by the real horror of history, and the narrator is gratified to see his listeners moved and terrified by the scene he evokes as he attempts 'to realize and faintly communicate, the deep, unutterable loathing and horror, the indignation, the affrighted wonder, that wrinkled every brow' (Hawthorne 1999: 112) as the accused approach the gallows. Hawthorne refers to the deluded townspeople as a mass, a 'universal heart' (112), while describing many of the condemned individually, stressing their suffering and anguish: 'one, a proud man once, was so broken down by the intolerable hatred heaped upon him, that he seemed to hasten his steps, eager to hide himself in the grave hastily dug, at the foot of the gallows' (112). In one of the few stories where Hawthorne designated moral polarity explicitly and without irony, the narrator describes these condemned witches as 'victims' and their accusers as 'a guilty and miserable band of villains, wretches and lunatics' (112). He compares the minister Cotton Mather to 'the fiend himself' and describes him as 'blood-thirsty' and 'sternly triumphant' (112) as he leads the small procession to the gallows. In this way, the story exemplifies the complexity of expected victim and villain roles that often characterises American horror writing.

Women of Horror

No portrait of nineteenth-century American horror is complete without exploring the work of women writers. The three most important are Harriet Beecher Stowe, Louisa May Alcott and Charlotte Perkins Gilman. The first two names may be surprising because they are best known for popular sentimental works – *Uncle Tom's Cabin* (1852) in the case of Stowe and *Little Women* (1868) for Alcott. However, like Brown, Poe and Hawthorne, all three writers addressed historical and cultural issues with devices borrowed from the horror genre. In Stowe's case, horror elements are mixed into her *magnum opus*, *Uncle Tom's Cabin* (1852), a novel that has been credited with turning the tide of American public opinion against slavery.

Louisa May Alcott, aged 26.
Unknown photographer, 1858.

In Alcott's case her horror writing had been totally eclipsed by her sentimental novels, but has been rediscovered and appreciated in recent decades. This work includes the now widely anthologised 'Behind a Mask, or, A Woman's Power' (1866), as well as numerous short stories she called 'blood and thunder tales' and a suspense thriller about obsession and stalking titled *A Long Fatal Love Chase* (written 1866, published 1995). Finally Charlotte Perkins Gilman is remembered as one of America's most important feminist activists from the First Wave – a journalist, social theorist and author of the ground-breaking *Women and Economics: A Study of the Economic Relation Between Men and Women as a Factor in Social Evolution* (1898). She is also the author of the extraordinary horror story *The Yellow Wallpaper*, first published in 1892. It was republished in 1973 by the Feminist Press, whereupon it became a bestseller and is now recognised as the most important horror story written by a woman in the nineteenth century. Together these three authors comprise a formidable triptych of American horror writing.

Harriet Beecher Stowe created some of the most popular and beloved American characters of her era: Uncle Tom, Little Eva and the little black girl Topsy. She also created one of the most terrifying villains, the slave master Simon Legree, and situated him on a Southern plantation that was meant to represent an earthly hell. Decayed and unkempt, Legree's plantation is a demonic concentration camp where two brutal black overseers terrorise an exhausted workforce, pushed to the limits of its endurance and humanity by a policy of exploiting slaves until they die. Violence, despair and fear reign supreme. Legree is depicted as cruel and sadistic, his only weaknesses alcohol and superstition. His slave mistress, Cassy, is able to escape with the adolescent girl that Legree has bought to replace her by playing upon Legree's irrational fear of ghosts – itself a symptom of his lifetime of cruelty and heartlessness, since it is his repressed conscience that feeds his fear of the supernatural. The two women pretend to escape through the swamps, but in fact remain in the attic of the plantation house until the hunt with bloodhounds has been called off. When they do finally escape, they are dressed in white like two ghosts, a sight arousing little notice in a place as haunted and troubled as Legree's plantation. Stowe plays the two kinds of horror – the real historical horror of slavery and the Gothic stratagem of impersonating ghosts – off against each other to evoke a multi-layered network of fear and terror that permeated the institution of slavery and corrupted everyone involved with it.

Known around the world as the author of sentimental novels for young adults, Louisa May Alcott was also a secret writer of horror fiction. The story that has been the most widely read and anthologised from this hidden trove of dark treasures is a novella titled 'Behind a Mask: or, A Woman's Power'. A tale of psychological perversity and deceit, it reads like the mirror opposite of the guileless sentimentality of *Little Women*. The protagonist, a divorced actress, is a hardened woman of 30, who pretends to be an innocent young girl hired as a governess by a wealthy family. Using her theatrical skills and cynical insight into human nature, she seduces every male member of the family into falling in love with her, playing cruelly with some in order to punish them for perceived slights or character flaws. Finally she marries the elderly *pater familias*, partly for his title and partly for his genuine kindness. The horror of the tale lies less in any overt violence than in the cynical machinations of the main character, whose insight into other people is as uncannily penetrating as her unscrupulous manipulation of them is sociopathic. At the beginning of the narrative Alcott also depicts her villainess like a witch: a 'haggard, worn, and moody woman' (Alcott 2013: 12) who transforms herself into an 18-year-old girl with the help of make-up, false teeth, a wig and consummate acting skills. When the family acquires the letters she has written to a female friend during her stay with them, they are horrified to discover how cunningly each has been appraised and punished. Like Stowe's work, the tale is also an intervention into the social situation of the time: the protagonist's plight is symptomatic of the dearth of economic opportunities for women of a certain class and age in nineteenth-century America. Though conniving and sometimes cruel, the protagonist also inspires pathos, and at the end is described as genuinely grateful for the security she has found with her elderly husband. The larger social issue at stake is the economic vulnerability of women in a society where there are few respectable jobs for them. Such a situation makes marriage an economic imperative and invaluable safety net for women who could easily face a wide range of real-world horrors if alone and poor.

The social and economic constraints on women also preoccupied Charlotte Perkins Gilman. Her most important contribution to American horror fiction consists of the brilliantly effective 'The Yellow Wallpaper', a first-person narrative of a young woman descending into madness because of her confinement at home. The story is loosely based on Gilman's own experience of post-partum depression and treatment by the famous physician Weir Mitchell, whose 'rest cure' forbade female patients from activity of any kind (male patients were treated very differently), including reading or writing. Forced to lie passively in bed, Gilman reported later that she felt her own sanity in danger. Her nameless protagonist, whose husband is a doctor and an acquaintance of Mitchell's, does not confine her to bed, but does discourage any intellectual activity or stimulation. By insisting on what he calls 'rest', the husband drives her deeper and deeper into madness, as she begins to believe there is a woman trapped behind the wallpaper and finally convinces herself that she is that very woman. Gilman's story also includes unsettling details suggesting a history of madness, imprisonment and horror in the house: the windows in the room with the wallpaper have bars on them; the bedframe has teeth marks; the walls have rings as if to attach chains. The remarkable story blends a Poe-esque first-person narrative mode with a feminist critique of nineteenth-century gender ideology, and even anticipates the rise of asylum horror in the twentieth century.

With its origins rooted in religious enthusiasm and tales of captivity, American horror fiction has often expertly woven psychological and political concerns into its tales of cruelty and violence. Subjective distortions of perception and interpretation are foregrounded, while the subtexts frequently involve political philosophy and theory. Women have played an important role in American horror writing, as have African Americans and Native Americans (especially later in the twentieth century). Horror often looks forward, even as it appears to look back. In the case of Charlotte Perkins Gilman's classic feminist horror story, for example, we have the first intimations of the subgenre of medical or asylum horror, which has assumed significant contemporary proportions. A major genre of American literature in the nineteenth and twentieth centuries, horror shows no signs of abating in the twenty-first.

References

Alcott, Louisa May, *Behind a Mask: A Woman's Power* (London: CreateSpace, 2013).

Halttunen, Karen, *Murder Most Foul: The Killer and the American Gothic Imagination* (Cambridge, MA: Harvard, 2000).

Hawthorne, Nathaniel, 'Young Goodman Brown' (1835), in *Nathaniel Hawthorne's Tales*, ed. by James McIntosh (New York: W. W. Norton, 1982).

——, 'Alice Doane's Appeal' (1835), in *American Gothic: An Anthology 1787–1916*, ed. by Charles L. Crow (Malden, MA: Blackwell, 1999).

Irving, Washington, *History, Tales and Sketches: The Sketch Book, a History of New York, Salgamundi, Letters of Jonathan Oldstyle, Gent.* (New York: Library of America, 1983).

Johnson, Barbara, 'The Frame of Reference: Poe, Lacan, Derrida', *Yale French Studies*, 55/6 (1977), 457–505.

Poe, Edgar Allan, *Poetry and Tales* (New York: Library of America, 1984).

Soltysik, Agnieszka, 'Poe's Aesthetics', *American Aesthetics,* ed. by Deborah L. Madsen (Tübingen, Germany: Gunter Narr Verlag, 2007).

What to Read Next

Louisa May Alcott, *Behind a Mask: The Unknown Thrillers of Louisa May Alcott,* ed. by Madeleine Stern (New York: William Morrow, 1997).

Charles Brockden Brown, *Three Gothic Novels*, ed. by Sidney J. Krause (New York: Library of America, 1998).

Nathaniel Hawthorne, *Young Goodman Brown and Other Tales*, ed. by Brian Harding (Oxford: Oxford University Press, 2008).

Washington Irving, *The Legend of Sleepy Hollow and Other Stories*, ed. by Elizabeth L. Bradley (London: Penguin, 2014).

Charlotte Perkins Gilman, *The Yellow Wallpaper* (1892; London: Penguin, 2015).

Edgar Allan Poe, *The Fall of the House of Usher and Other Writings*, ed. by David Galloway (London: Penguin, 2003).

The Mysteries of London, George W. M. Reynolds, 1844–5. Plate from chapter 25, 'The Enchantress'. Vol I, edition published by John Dicks, no date.

Chapter 3

Horror in the Nineteenth Century: Dreadful Sensations, 1820–80

Royce Mahawatte

The Horrors of Modern Times

In 1832–3 *The Lancet* published a stern criticism of the Anatomy Act, which had been passed earlier that year. After lengthy debate in Parliament, the act sought to replace the illegal trade in cadavers, for the study of human anatomy, with the controlled distribution of the bodies of anyone who died destitute. The act came about after the West Port murders (1828–9) in Edinburgh and the copycat 'London Burkers' cases of 1831. Here vulnerable members of the public (minors, prostitutes, the mentally ill) had been murdered and sold to surgeons for their dissection classes. While being taught, some students had actually identified some of the cadavers as locals familiar to them. The author of the article felt that the Anatomy Act did nothing to protect the public across the country: their 'dead human bodies', as he put it, were left to the 'suffocating grasps of the Bishops and Burkes' (Anon. 1832–3: 245) – John Bishop and William Burke were the notorious body snatchers of the London and West Port murders. The article concluded that it was: 'disgusting to talk of anatomy as a science, whilst it is cultivated by means of practices which would disgrace a nation of cannibals' (245).

After reading a piece like this, with its images of death, asphyxiation and cannibalism – and even considering that details from these cases found their way into the most popular fiction serial of the era, George W. M. Reynolds's *The Mysteries of London* (1844–5) – it may come as a surprise to find that there is no 'horror-literature' of the nineteenth century. Horror is not a nineteenth-century literary concept. It did not classify or warn us against certain kinds of narratives. 'Horror' was certainly not identified as a genre of popular writing. Any discussion of the literature of the nineteenth century, in terms of horror, can only be retroactive and very much influenced by twentieth-century uses of the word that tried to bring together a vast array of work 'located in both the real and the nightmarish imaginary' (Wisker 2005: 2). The category is an anachronism for a chapter on the nineteenth century, but, as the piece in *The Lancet* indicates, horror was certainly present and used as a word in this period. As early as 1814, in Jane Austen's *Mansfield Park*, 'William and Fanny were horror-struck at the idea' (Austen 2005: 430) of Mrs Norris joining them on their carriage journey to Portsmouth. Social horrors of Regency England take on greater meaning when perhaps viewed in terms of scientific discourse. Our journey into nineteenth-century horror, therefore, should begin with medical terminology.

In 1822 John Mason Good's use of the word in his *The Study of Medicine* describes a tropical fever: '[t]he first attack generally commenced with a horror; but the subsequent paroxysms, though often beginning with a sense of cold, were chiefly without horror' (Good 1822: 95). Good, a learned physician and prolific medical writer, used the word clinically, as a noun to indicate the physical symptom of fever. This gloss perhaps makes Austen's understatement about a socially awkward moment all the more telling. At Madame Tussaud's, in 1835, the word approached our contemporary usage. Here the 'Separate Room', showing criminals and crime tableaux, was renamed the 'Chamber of Horrors'. The attraction became such a part of the contemporary imagination that in William Makepeace Thackeray's *Pendennis* (1848) it was jokingly compared with a drinking club in Saint James that was frequented by 'old fogies' (Thackeray 1994: 460). The terrifying thing here, clearly, was to be thought of as unfashionable.

Although they did not use the word to classify entertainment, as the period continued, the Victorians came to have a 'horror' all of their own, and it was encompassing and intricate. In fact 'Victorian horror', if we are to use such a term, can be used to describe the emerging culture that depicted fear and the afflicted body. One of the most enduring elements of horror is the presence of the unstable body – a body that is somehow confusing, disturbing or at least medically inscrutable. The rise of medical and pseudo-scientific epistemologies contributed to the institutionalisation of the body as a source of horror. It is a body dismantled, in pain, dead, or even undead. It is a body that at times wants to cannibalise, or one that is itself snatched and cannibalised by forces around it. The eating of human flesh is an extensive metaphor in this period, in use even before the popular awareness of evolutionary theories and the accompanying fear of atavism. Cannibalism represents an interface between self and society that is lawless, degenerate and literally inhumane. The chaos and brutality Thomas Carlyle depicted in *The French Revolution* (1837) emphasised the degradation of the social and body politic. It came down to the 'lowest, least blessed fact' of 'Cannibalism: That *I* can devour *Thee*' (Carlyle 1902, I: 65). Could the savagery of revolutionary France be contagious?

The period was a dehumanising era, but it was also one of voting reform; it saw the abolition of slavery in the colonies and the expansion of the middle classes on home soil. What kind of society was the prevailing economic and social system creating? Two years after the Anatomy Act was passed the Poor Law Amendment Act of 1834 came into effect, placing social welfare under the domain of the harsh workhouses. The poor were criminalised in life and objectified in death, and these themes can be seen in the literary culture of the period. The rising popularity of crime reporting meant that horror was both monitored and mythologised as being a part of urban life. In the late 1830s the accounts in the *Morning Chronicle* of 'Spring-heeled Jack', a protean figure who terrorised the inhabitants of south London, became an urban legend. The group of publications known as the *Newgate Calendar*, which ran from the late eighteenth to the mid-nineteenth century, reported on, and harshly judged, criminals brought to their lowest. The case of the 'London Burkers', with its detailed confessions of how the snatched victims were drugged and drowned in a well, was published with fascination here for an eager readership: '[t]he boy struggled a little with his arms and legs in the water, and the water bubbled a minute. We waited till these symptoms were passed [...] and afterwards I think we went out and walked down Shoreditch to occupy the time' (Anon. 1831). Here the mixture of brutality and banality highlights the everyday nature of Victorian horror. One did not need to be a cannibal to be inhuman.

So in order to see horror in the nineteenth century we need to strip away the word, and also the literary hierarchies, to focus instead on the literary effects, the disturbing bodies and the ideas that lie beneath them. The nineteenth century was the period in which the Gothic novel of the eighteenth century proliferated into a network of tropes, subgenres and plot threads. These were deployed by major and minor writers alike, in both fiction and non-fiction. Regency horror from the early eighteenth century had been shaped by social changes and literary innovations that created new forms for a new type of reader. Yet horror was also created by the literary or bourgeois authors of the period, writers more associated with its dominant narrative mode: Realism. Though scholars tend not to emphasise it too much, Victorian writers such as George Eliot, Charles Dickens and Elizabeth Gaskell all deployed horror at various points in their careers. The names of Wilkie Collins, Mary Elizabeth Braddon, James Hogg and Edward Bulwer-Lytton sit more comfortably, perhaps, with the effects of horror, though their work was labelled with different and quite telling terminology.

Victorian horror did not discriminate – it was distributed by gentleman and trade publisher alike. Consequently horror sometimes cost a shilling, if in magazines, which was relatively expensive. More likely it cost no more than a penny, and sometimes less, in those cheaply produced serials, often from the pen of George W. M. Reynolds and James Rymer who, if we were to look at sales alone, were probably the most widely read writers of the nineteenth century. Horror presents a problem for critics. By reason of its popularity it is easy to see why it was often dogged by panics in the mainstream press about its poor quality and the ease by which it could be accessed by the impressionable minds of working-class boys and women. Despite the cheap serial really reaching its height in the 1840s, before becoming a youth-orientated format, its legacy in subsequent decades cannot be underestimated.

From this perspective Gothic writing became such a part of the general literary scene that it ceased to have a name to identify it. In a sense, horror entered the Victorian frame of mind unannounced. Nineteenth-century bodies are repeatedly associated with horror, and readers were believed to experience their own embodied responses, in the form of formidable physical sensations, as they consumed, and were consumed by, this broad literary culture.

Early Developments and Strange Cases

The defeat of the French Army in 1815 heralded a new, and relatively more stable, European order. The ideological horrors of the eighteenth century had, to a degree, had their day; across Europe the middle classes were slowly gaining dominance, as they reaped the rewards of technological change in the colonies, in the country and in the city and town. In case we might overlook it, through developments in science, pseudo-science and medicine, they also found new ways of understanding the workings of their bodies and minds. These people monitored themselves: they noticed life around themselves, and they looked to the future. And from this observation a new kind of horror began to emerge.

An emerging middle class wanted to read fiction about their own changing society, presented in a way that reflected their own position as consumers of culture. Changes occurred in the making of paper and in magazine production, and these, combined with the relaxation of stamp duty on paper, meant that there was a growing market for bourgeois magazines that offered a rich variety of content, of which original fiction was part. The *New Monthly* and *Blackwood's* magazines were established in 1814 and 1817 respectively. By the 1820s there was something of a Gothic revival, with the publication of works such as Mary Shelley's *Frankenstein*, Charles Maturin's *Melmoth the Wanderer* (1820) and James Hogg's *Confessions of a Justified Sinner* (1824). *The New Monthly* published Polidori's 'The Vampyre' in 1819 and established the magazine format as a competitive, and thrilling, alternative to the triple-decker novel, which, in a certain light, was beginning to look rather traditional. *Blackwood's* would soon follow suit with its own, more conceptual handling of horror. So the writing of fear and revulsion found a new literary idiom. The aspirational middle class created the very conditions that in turn produced the foundation of Victorian horror.

An innovative serial that ran in *Blackwood's* early period was Samuel Warren's *Passages from a Diary of a Late Physician* (1830–7). This work, an international hit in its day, is an example of the medical casebook genre, which is vital to understanding the beginnings of horror writing in the nineteenth century. Warren, who started medical training, but eventually practised as a lawyer, presented the memoirs of an erudite gentleman doctor. We are taken through the early career of the narrator, through his financial and personal struggles. The work proceeds into a series of medical cases, where the social context is clearly explained; symptoms and afflictions are vividly described, and final, and often fatal, outcomes are discussed with an evangelical Christian implicitness. 'A Man about Town', for example, first published in 1830, told of the hard-drinking and socially ambitious Mr Effingstone: 'an abandoned profligate, a systematic debauchee, an irreclaimable reprobate' (Warren 1834, I: 210). The doctor receives a letter from him, asking for assistance from 'the tortures of the damned, both in mind and body' (228) and rushes to give what aid he can. What follows is a deathbed sequence, in which Effington rants and raves in his death throes and questions his past behaviour, 'his flesh creeping from head to foot' (233). After failing to provide a remedy, the doctor grimly realises that 'it was beyond human power to dislodge the harpy that had fixed its cruel fangs deeply, inextricably in his vitals' (232).

In another case, 'Spectre Smitten', Warren deals with Mr M, a patient with paranoid schizophrenia. The doctor's report states that the man started out as a law student and member of London society until he began to tire of the frivolity of his social life. On returning home one evening, where he lives alone, M spies a figure sitting in an armchair: '[t]he appalling spectre, while M's eyes were riveted upon it, though glazing fast with fright, slowly rose from its seat, stretched out both its arms, and seemed approaching him, when he fell down senseless on the floor, as if smitten with apoplexy' (Warren 1834, II: 5). From this point

Mr M, 'spectre smitten' as he puts it, descends into a violent mental illness, which the doctor diagnoses as 'a very severe congestion of vessels
of the brain' (9). M, with a pulse 'beating at about 115 a minute' (10),
grinds his teeth, froths at the mouth, brandishes a razor and threatens to
kill those around him.

There are no supernatural events in *Passages*. Warren's work is acutely
empirical, and it is down to the imagery and literary allusions in the
prose to create a terrifying parallel world clearly aimed at readers familiar with Gothic literature. The doctor, for example, looks at Effingstone
'with feelings of concern, alarm, and wonder, akin to those with which
one might contemplate the frightful creature brought into being by
Frankenstein' (Warren, 1834 I: 213). This technique creates a very peculiar and contemporary form of horror. Mister M's unfortunate condition
is imagined, through his speech, as a demonic possession. The narrator, however, is far more measured. He presents literary comparisons
with Milton's Lucifer and Charles Maturin's Melmoth to the reader,
and leaves it at that. The work is an intriguing combination of Gothic
intertextuality and observation of the human subject. Warren presents
both the bourgeoisie and modern social practices as being debilitating to
the body and mind. The cases in *Passages* are vivid and violent, and they
rarely have positive outcomes. The patients in this narrative fall ill, and
hence out of society, largely due to its dangerous and detrimental effects.
Warren was following the contemporary trend by choosing to write
about society and fashionable life. His particular approach was to warn
against social frivolity by manifesting evangelical Christian retribution as
medicalised bodily horror. His depiction of the well-meaning but often
ineffectual physician contrasted with the more problematic figure of the
surgeon, notorious after the 'Burking' crimes and the debates around the
Anatomy Act that took place during the serial's run.

Warren's influence can be seen throughout the nineteenth century
as doctors started publishing their casebooks and memoirs for a popular readership, reporting particularly on the horrors of sexual ill-health.
We can also arguably see Warren's influence in Dickens's 'A Madman's
Manuscript' in *The Pickwick Papers* (1837) and in the numerous retribu-
tive deathbed scenes of the period, for example Anne Brontë's rendering
of the death of Arthur Huntington in *The Tenant of Wildfell Hall* (1848)

and the death of Robert Dempster in George Eliot's 'Janet's Repentance' (1857). The mode of storytelling, which capitalised on unreliable narration, can be seen in Sheridan Le Fanu's editorial strategy for *In a Glass Darkly* (1872) and, of course, in Robert Louis Stevenson's *Strange Case of Doctor Jekyll and Mister Hyde* (1886).

Medical casebook literature presented a modern brand of horror to a post-Napoleonic society who wanted both their aspirations and their anxieties reflected back to them. The distinctive synergy between imagination, empiricism and social critique in *Passages* brought the Gothic into line with what would be the dominant literary mode of the nineteenth century, Realism – one that we do not directly associate with horror at all.

Horror and Victorian Realism

Henry James, in the 1909 preface to *The Tragic Muse*, described the novels of the nineteenth century (works by Thackeray, Fyodor Dostoyevsky, Leo Tolstoy) as 'large, loose, baggy monsters' (James 2004: 477) mainly because of their complicated structure, size and range, and the fact that these authors had to tame the immense creatures to which they had given life. The description is telling. Victorian Realism is not the literary scene where we first locate horror in the era. Horror effects, however, were deployed by writers as they attempted to represent a vast and modernising Britain, where people had to do battle with monsters of the less literal kind. Following on from Samuel Warren's medical cases, if the higher ranks of society contained their own kind of intangible hell, one that was observable as shocking illness, then what did the lower parts of social life hold?

The 'Condition of England' novel often depicted horrifying or degraded bodies when exploring social problems and inequality. The polemical description of the experiences of the working and lower-middle classes was a feature of Realism, and authors used familiar Gothic techniques to elicit powerful reactions. For example, the Dotheboys Hall chapters from Charles Dickens's *Nicholas Nickleby* (1839) were a scathing and affecting critique of the Yorkshire schools abuse scandals of the 1820s and 1830s. A year before publication, Dickens and Hablot Browne, his illustrator, had visited Bowes Academy in Yorkshire. Subsequently the author chose to expose the maltreatment of boys. Their bodies are abject and distorted: '[p]ale and haggard faces, lank and bony figures, children with the countenances of old men, deformities with irons upon their limbs, boys with stunted growth, and others whose long meagre legs would hardly bear their stooping bodies' (Dickens 1998: 88). With their youth and vitality robbed from them, these are bodies in pain. The pathos is increased by the lack of sympathy they are afforded at the hands of Wackford Squeers, whose name already indicates violence and greed. '[T]here were the bleared eyes, the hare-lip, the crooked foot, and every ugliness of distortion' (88): this catalogue of horror is also a list of the grotesque and unwanted. Dickens was writing horror with a purpose. The passage continues:

> [w]ith every kindly sympathy and affection blasted in its birth, with every young and healthy feeling flogged and starved down, with every revengeful passion that can fester in swollen hearts eating its evil way to their core in silence, what an incipient Hell was breeding here! (88)

This is fundamentally a horror of the body with an ethical slant: the long visceral sentences, the exclamation, the comparison with 'Hell' itself. Of course, the real horror was not in the physicality, but actually the outrage at the social system which allowed Squeers and William Shaw, the headmaster of Bowes Academy in Yorkshire, to trade in unwanted children. This writing deploys a campaign of horror effects in order to engender sympathy as a way to social change – and it did achieve some success. Bowes Academy and a number of Yorkshire schools were closed down after the novel's publication.

Similarly in Elizabeth Gaskell's *Mary Barton* (1848) Margaret Jennings's fears for her failing sight are Gothicised, but without the grotesquery. The needlework she has to take in, in order to support her family, has a debilitating effect on her eyes: '"There now, Mary", continued she, shutting one eye, "now you only look like a great black shadow, with the edges dancing and sparkling. [. . .] I suppose I'm going dark as fast as may be"' (Gaskell 2006: 47). This supernatural image, conveyed via only a few words, is a product of illness, but the poignancy of Margaret's economic situation is increased by the fact that the sewing is black mourning wear. The condition of the working classes is a frightening one. Karl Marx opened *The Communist Manifesto* (1848) with the line: '[t]here is a spectre haunting Europe – the spectre of communism' (Marx and Engels 2008: 2). This ghost he writes about is the remnant of a communism dismantled and outlawed by the bourgeoisie. One interpretation is that this vestige finds its way back into bourgeois culture as horror images in Realist fiction.

If not directly concerned with social problems, mid-Victorian writers, particularly female ones, deployed images of horror as a way of depicting their characters' psychological make-up. Most striking is Emily Brontë's *Wuthering Heights* (1847), where Lockwood cutting open Catherine's ghostly wrist and Heathcliff's gaping dead face are heightened moments in an already brutal world where characters are haunted by their pasts and tormented by their desires. Charlotte Brontë, whose work is provocatively poised between Victorian Gothic and Realist forms, used moments of horror when depicting psychological states. In *Villette* (1853) Lucy Snowe's loneliness and isolation during the school vacation contributes to her 'hypochondriasis' or low spirits, 'wherein the worst evils are apprehended upon the slightest grounds', to quote from Thomas John Graham's *Modern Domestic Medicine* (1827: 382), of which the Brontës possessed a copy. This state is shown through a Gothic reverie, where 'the ghostly white beds were turning into spectres – the coronal of each became a death's head, huge and snow-bleached' (Brontë 2004: 177). Although informed by the eighteenth-century Gothic that the Brontë sisters devoured as young girls, this moment of haunting is located within Lucy's frustrated mind.

In *Jane Eyre* (1847) Charlotte Brontë had expressed in her letters that with Bertha Mason, the attic-bound first Mrs Rochester, she had wanted to explore 'a phase of insanity which may be called moral madness, in which all that is good or even human seems to disappear from the mind and a fiend-nature replaces it' (Wise and Symington 1980, II: 173). The description of Bertha reads: 'whether beast or human being, one could not, at first sight, tell: it grovelled, seemingly, on all fours, it snatched and growled like some strange wild animal' (Brontë 1996: 327). Bertha is truly non-human, a terrorising presence in the novel. She is not even gendered ('*it* grovelled'; emphasis added). In a novel that guides the reader to the understanding of unconventional female

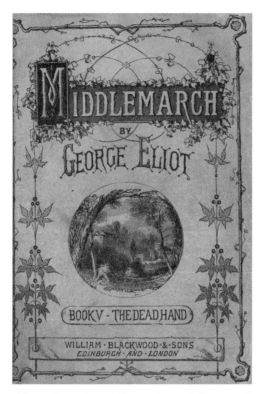

Middlemarch. Book V – The Dead Hand, George Eliot,
1871–2. Front cover of Book V (eight books in total),
published by William Blackwood & Sons, 1871–2.

aspiration, she is a problematic and censuring horror character. She
is Jane's unwholesome alter ego, yet also an unsettling indictment of
Edward Rochester's ties to the slave economy of Jamaica.

The thoughtful realism of George Eliot is also disturbing at times.
The author took the reader to moments of horror with her characters'
minds as a way of disclosing their psychological states or dark personal
circumstances. She used *ekphrasis*, the writing of visual arts, in *Romola*
(1862–3) to show the terror in Tito Melema's conscience, which is only
captured when he sits for Piero di Cosimo. Despite the reputation of
Middlemarch (1871–2) as being the highest development of the English Realist novel, there are moments of understated horror that slowly
work on the reader. Dorothea Brooke's ill-advised marriage to the
elderly scholar Casaubon is described as 'a noose' (Eliot 1986: 41) and

the 'most horrible of virgin sacrifices' (351), violent images which fore-
shadow the arguably unconsummated state of the marriage. In chapter
28 Dorothea's post-honeymoon depression is conveyed via a sense of
haunted incarceration in her boudoir at Lowick: 'the ghostly stag in
a pale fantastic world that seemed to be vanishing from the daylight'
(268). Casaubon himself is presented as 'a shadow of a man' (67) and
'death's head skinned over for the occasion' (87). After his sudden death,
Dorothea finds out that his will forbids her from marrying his nephew,
Will Ladislaw, whom she secretly loves, without losing her inheritance.
The title of the part-published segment of the book that contains this
sequence was called 'The Dead Hand', giving an embodied and chilling perspective on the situation. In all of these examples we find that
the language of horror finds its way into the mainstream of Victorian
fiction, and is quite detached from any Gothic origins it might have
had. Ironically, of course, this method depended on readers' familiarity
with the very conventions that the Realist novel, at least on the surface,
rejected.

Mid-Century Sensations, or Preaching to the Nerves

Domestic and psychological realism began to encroach on what
remained of Gothic conventions in the mid-nineteenth century. This
literary absorption produced some remarkable results that further
extend our understanding of horror in the period. The first instalment of the bestselling novel of 1860, Wilkie Collins's *The Woman
in White*, ends with the protagonist Walter Hartwright walking at
night up the Hampstead Road, back towards London. Suddenly, he
narrates: '[i]n one moment, every drop of blood in my body was
brought to a stop by the touch of a hand laid lightly and suddenly on
my shoulder from behind me' (Collins 1975: 15). The unchaperoned
and quite spectral woman, 'dressed from head to foot in white gar-
ments' (15), whom he meets on the roadside is hard for him to place:

> There was nothing wild, nothing immodest in her manner: it was quiet
> and self-controlled, a little melancholy and a little touched by suspicion;
> not exactly the manner of a lady, and, at the same time, not the manner
> of a woman in the humblest rank of life. (15)

THE WOMAN IN WHITE.

"I TURNED ON THE INSTANT, WITH MY FINGERS TIGHTENING ROUND THE HANDLE OF MY STICK."

The Woman in White, Wilkie Collins, 1860. Illustration showing the climax of the first installment where Walter Hartwright meets a mysterious woman dressed in white on the Hampstead Road. Edition published by Harper & Bros, 1860.

Her appearance indicates a degree of social mobility. This is worrying. Her air of suspicion, however, and her lack of immodesty rule out that Hartwright has been approached by a prostitute, something which would be far scarier than him meeting a ghost, it would seem. After they part, Walter overhears two men in a carriage telling a policeman they are searching for a woman: '[s]he has escaped from my Asylum. Don't forget; a woman in white. Drive on' (22). The instalment ends with this revelation.

As I have proposed, 'horror' did not technically occur in the nineteenth century, but it seems that the Victorians did have their own similar word for it, 'sensation'. This term had been previously used sarcastically in relation to stage melodramas and was influenced by popular physiology and medicine. At the same time, and much like the medical use of the word 'horror', it described the physical experience of being thrilled, distressed and disturbed. *The Woman in White* became the classic exponent of the 'novel of sensation' and was closely followed by the work of Mary Elizabeth Braddon, Mrs Henry (Ellen) Wood and Charles Reade. Novels of sensation could expose the horrors of modern life: domestic crime, infidelity and fraud, the most prevalent forms of which were impersonation, identity theft and bigamy. Such a trend can be understood as the popularisation of the Realist novel, which, as we have seen, was already using literary techniques to mobilise readers' concern. Although exploitative in its handling, sensation fiction showed the failures of institutions, legal and medical in particular, that could not, in most cases, protect the vulnerable, especially women and the working classes. The stories were set in ostensibly everyday or unremarkable settings. As the narrator of Mary Braddon's *Lady Audley's Secret* (1862) points out: '[n]o crime has ever been committed in the worst rookeries about Seven Dials that has not been also done in the face of that sweet rustic calm which still, in spite of all, we look on with a tender [. . .] yearning, and associate with – peace' (Braddon 1998: 54).

The narratives themselves often came from true crimes. In *The Woman in White*, for example, the drugging of the heiress Lady Laura Glyde and her incarceration in a lunatic asylum were shaped by the famous Madame de Douhault case of the previous century. Nor was it just the subject matter that came from real crimes. According to John Sutherland, the trial of William Palmer, the Rugeley poisoner, in 1856, 'was England's mania that year', and the reporting of the case influenced the 'high impact' (Sutherland 1991: 248–9), suspenseful style of narration that Collins later deployed in his novel. Sensation novels were distinguished by their use of personal statements and written confessions, cliff-hanging endings, revelations and coincidences. In eager readers, they elicited physical manifestations of excited fear, which commentators wanted to understand.

Henry Mansel in the *Quarterly Review* in 1863 saw sensation fiction as 'preaching to the nerves instead of the judgement' (Mansel 1863: 482). A reviewer in an article in *The Living Age* of 1863 tried to clarify: '[t]he one indispensable point in the sensation novel is, that it should contain something abnormal and unnatural: something that induces,

in the simple idea, a sort of thrill. [. . .] There is appeal to the imagination, through the active agency of the nerves, excited by the unnatural
or supernatural' (Anon. 1863: 353). This literature had a clear physiological effect on the body. Mansel gave a catalogue of them: there were
novels 'which carry the whole nervous system by steam', while others
'aspire to set his [sic] hair on end or his teeth on edge'; still others 'are
strongly provocative of that sensation in the palate and throat which is
a premonitory symptom of nausea' (Mansel 1863: 485). It was not simply the content of sensation fiction that was objectionable to him, but
rather the terrible things these stories *did* to the reader. Such a physical,
embodied response to literature was highly suggestive.

It follows, then, that the fiction itself often concentrated on the instability of meaning when it came to understanding the human body. In
Braddon's fiction, the double plot was used to exploit anxieties around
differing types of social mobility, presented as a kind of fraud, as in
Lady Audley's Secret or *Henry Dunbar* (1864), where revenge is a motive.
Braddon's third-person narrators are often entertainingly arch and
never let on who has been replaced by whom. The result is that people are repeatedly misread, and those unfortunate enough to discover
an imposter's true identity become mentally afflicted or worse. This
produces a horror effect. In *Lady Audley's Secret*, only a portrait by a
Pre-Raphelite can hint at the dark secret of the bigamist Lady Audley,
when he gives 'a lurid lightness to the blonde complexion' and 'the hard
and almost wicked look [. . .] of a beautiful fiend' (Braddon 1998: 70).
The sensational appealed to all senses, hence the use of visual art. It was
fundamentally erotic. The body and the senses of the readers were in the
thrall of the writing, as were the characters to the changing whims of
the heroine-villainess. These horrors were far, far worse than supernatural hauntings. They sprang from status anxiety and the fear of social and
sexual impropriety. Sensationalism had worrying implications.

Twists and Innovations in Supernatural
Tales and Ghost Stories

The rise of magazine culture supported short form fiction, and horror
found a fitting medium there. Victorian sensationalism was very much

a cultural condition: sensation fiction and tales of the supernatural were often classed together in contemporary reviews by reason of the chilling effects they sought to elicit in the reader. Sheridan Le Fanu moved seamlessly between both formats and innovatively connected his short stories via the medical casebook format when he published them as a collection in *In a Glass Darkly* (1872). Short tales often signalled new literary trends or, more commonly, exploited public interest in current sensational events. James Hogg's 'Some Terrible Letters from Scotland' (1832), published in the *Metropolitan Magazine*, was in essence three accounts of the cholera epidemic in rural Scotland, each one ending in a supernatural twist. The first is told through the point of view of a man who, after being struck down by the illness, mysteriously remains alive as 'a sensitive corpse' (Hogg 2008: 101). The story described the experience of being wrongfully pronounced dead, of being 'burked' and nearly buried alive.

Despite the ephemeral conditions of their publication, there were enduring concerns in these short form works. The tensions between human values and monetary value had always been a part of the Gothic tradition – ghosts appear to signal the wrongful appropriation of title, land or property. Victorian ghost stories often developed these themes into anxieties about the ghostly or fleeting nature of money itself. The 'promissory notes', the money in circulation, were a representation of gold and had a virtual value. As Andrew Smith suggests, '[p]aper money was perceived as spectral money (not "real" money), which like the ghost had a liminal presence' (2010: 5). The popular appeal of Dickens's *A Christmas Carol* (1843) lies less in its status as horror, although there are many ghosts in it, and more in its deployment of these ghosts to critique Ebenezer Scrooge's narrow-minded miserliness. In a society that was slowly secularising on the one hand and yet becoming more denominational and sectarian on the other, ghost narratives explored themes of Christian charity in the broadest sense.

Major and minor writers clearly worked with the form from one time to another. George Eliot, Elizabeth Gaskell, Mary Braddon, Catherine Gore, Sheridan Le Fanu and Edward Bulwer-Lytton all had their own ways of building up suspense, fear and aversion into a horrific climax or twist. In George Eliot's tale 'The Lifted Veil', published by *Blackwood's* in

1859, the dead maid who is reanimated by a blood transfusion delivers a secret that the clairvoyant protagonist could not otherwise divine. Elizabeth Gaskell's 'The Old Nurse's Story' was published in 1852 in a festive special edition of *Household Words*. In this story a spirit child haunts the nurse's young charge and reveals, via a spectral projection, a fatal domestic conflict of betrayal and jealousy between sisters. A year before Gaskell had published 'Disappearances' in the same publication, which linked the true disappearance of a medical student to Burke and Hare (in fact, the young man had died of cholera in the colonies).

What is noticeable about these tales is that the endings often problematise the kind of closure usually found in sensation fiction and in the Gothic writing of the earlier period. In them, a sense of malevolence usually lingers after the final page. This was a challenge to the satisfying conclusions of the Victorian Realist project, where virtue was rewarded and society's ills hopefully corrected. In August 1859 Bulwer-Lytton, then very much a major writer, published 'The Haunted and the Haunters, or, the House and the Brain' in *Blackwood's* and drew much from Catherine Crowe writing on ghost seeing. Crowe wrote novels and the short story collections *The Night Side of Nature* (1848) and *Ghosts and Family Legends* (1859), both first-hand accounts of supernatural events which were told to the author and presented to the reader as documented fact. Bulwer-Lytton wrote a narrative with a baffling twist at the end, investing it with all the elements of a haunted house story that twenty-first-century readers would recognise. An unnamed protagonist decides to spend a night in a haunted house to investigate the mysterious occurrences that have been scaring previous tenants. In this house he witnesses paranormal and inexplicable phenomena: disembodied footprints, secret rooms and a floating hand. During the course of a terrifying vision the protagonist draws on his knowledge of the occult sciences. He comes to the conclusion that the house must be under the influence of a 'Brain', a mesmerist practised in the magic arts, who is using the secret room as a kind of conduit. The room is eventually demolished. The tale reaches its climax in a coda where the protagonist discovers the mesmerist in a London club and is suddenly put under a spell by him.

Bulwer-Lytton was a playful writer, who sought to beguile both his friends and his readers. In supernatural tales the startling endings often beckoned an exploration of contemporary pseudo-science within a medical and psychological context. Because of their tendency towards implicitness, they were experiments in literary form and narrative method. They had a wide appeal in the nineteenth-century literary scene and, although condemned by critics like E. S. Dallas, were endorsed by major publishers. The same could not be said for the penny serials that ran alongside them and to which they clearly owed a debt.

Panic and the Penny Dreadful

If medical epistemologies revived horror in the nineteenth century, the cheap literature of the 1840s made it virulent. It consolidated not only the trajectories of the liminal cityscape, the vampire and the werewolf, but also the theatrical style in which horror was presented. More broadly, the critical reception to this form of sensational writing gave horror an enduring allure. Though loosely termed 'penny dreadful', this term actually only applies to the post-1860 serials, which were melodramatic adventures aimed at boys. A good example is Colin Henry Hazlewood's *Spring-Heeled Jack, The Terror of London* (1867), which removed the inhuman elements of the 1830s newspaper reports and told of a creature (a bull, a clawed monster, a ghost) rampaging in the night. Here Jack was recast as a masked and heroic vigilante. In fact, before the 1880s, urban adventure tales of vigilantism were the dominant subject matter of most cheap literature. The first penny 'blood', a highway robbery narrative, was published in 1836, and together with those of the 1840s were called 'penny bloods', 'blood books' or 'blood and thunder books'. These were published in the innocuously titled *Lloyd's Penny Atlas* and *The People's Periodical and Family Library*.

Soon the depiction of murders, 'burking' and subsequent hangings aligned with the proliferating Gothic tradition. A series of 'penny blood' horror classics emerged, most notably *Varney the Vampyre, or, the Feast of Blood* (1845–6) and *The String of Pearls* (1846–7), which evolved into *Sweeney Todd, the Demon Barber of Fleet Street* – the story of the bloodthirsty barber who murdered his clients and baked them in pies for an unsuspecting public. Both

"THERE IS BLOOD ON THE NOTES!"

'The Black Band, or The Mysteries of Midnight', Lady Caroline Lascelles
(Mary Braddon), *The Halfpenny Journal*, 22 July 1861. Illustration to chapter
10, depicting one of the text's many sensational moments.

of these texts are now attributed to James Malcolm Rymer. *Wagner
the Wehr-wolf* (1846–7) and *The Mysteries of London* (1844–8) were
authored by George W. M. Reynolds. Set in a London heavily influenced by Dickens's depictions of the city, the latter work contained
the cadaverous-looking Anthony Tidkins, the 'Resurrection Man'
who made his living from the acquisition and selling-on of corpses.
At its height, the serial sold nearly 40,000 weekly copies.

Rather interestingly Mary Braddon wrote, as 'Lady Caroline Lascelles',
'The Black Band, or, The Mysteries of Midnight', for *The Halfpenny
Journal* in 1861. Though not supernatural, the events in this work, over
240,000 words in length and generally written in the present tense, present a world in which bigamy, plotting, poisonings and disguise are rife.
The horror lies in the violent fragility of social structures and personal
ties as working-class, self-made men suffer the machinations of those of
a higher rank. The cunning Lady Edith Vandeleur, after her wedding to
a hard-working millionaire, is described in the language of horror: '[i]f

her lover could have read the depths of her soul, he would have shrunk with a shudder from the false and perjured creature' ([Braddon] Lascelles 1861: 10).

Cheap literature, of course, had its literal monsters. Rymer's Lord Francis Varney was *the* Victorian vampire, not Polidori's Lord Ruthven nor Bram Stoker's *Dracula*. In a work of over 600,000 words,

" HE DASHED THROUGH THE FUNERAL TRAIN." (See p. 23.)

Wagner the Wehr-wolf, George W. M. Reynolds, 1844–5. Illustration showing Fernand Wagner the wehr-wolf disturbing a funeral procession. Facsimile of an 1848 edition (*Reynolds' Miscellany*), published by Dover, 1975.

in 220 chapters, the story is truly episodic and the horror theatrical. The first chapter contains what is now the familiar trope of the vampire stalking the maiden from outside her bedroom window: '[t]he figure is there, still feeling for an entrance, and clattering against the glass with its long nails, that appear as if the growth of many years had been untouched' (Rymer 1845: 3). What ultimately qualifies this writing as horror is the description of fear as a physical, embodied experience: the 'weighed down' limbs of the fear-stricken heroine, the 'choking sensation' and the *inability* to scream out: 'she can but in a hoarse faint whisper cry, —"Help – help – help – help!"...' (3). This inability to express fear was a popularised representation of the Romantic idea that intense feeling was somehow beyond expression. Characters, and sometimes even the narrator, are rendered speechless. This kind of theatrical writing relished the telling of the events: '–a gush of blood, and a hideous sucking noise follows', 'the vampyre is at his hideous repast!' (4).

Taken up by writers such as Catherine Crowe, the wolf-man and she wolf were very popular in both magazine and penny serial fiction. George W. M. Reynolds' *Wagner the Wehr-wolf* has fewer man-to-wolf transformation scenes than we might expect; the serial is more of a romance and mystery. The transformation scene from chapter 12, however, will be very familiar. In it, 'a man – young, handsome, and splendidly attired – has thrown himself upon the ground, where he writhes like a stricken serpent, in horrible convulsions' (Reynolds 1975: 23). As with the vampire, the horror here is about a moment of contact where: '[h]is handsome countenance elongates into one of savage and brute-like shape. [...] His body loses its human contours, his arms and limbs take another form; and, with a frantic howl of misery [...] the wretch starts wildly away, no longer a man, but a monstrous wolf!' (23). The human meets the non-human, and is subsequently and violently consumed. The action, again described in the present tense, offered a theatrical sensibility to readers who might not experience drama or melodrama on the contemporary stage.

These serials' status as horror was confirmed by the critical reception they increasingly encountered. As with the debates on sensation fiction, there was an ongoing posturing about the effects that cheap literature had on readers, ostensibly working-class and newly literate boys. In 1865 the sociologist and campaigner Harriet Martineau wrote in the *Edinburgh Review* that the youth in the 'garrets of large cities' were, through this writing, exposed to 'animal passion and defiant lawlessness' (Martineau 1865: 347). By the end of the nineteenth century the concern had moved almost entirely towards young readers. Francis Hitchman, the literary critic, wrote in the *Quarterly Review* of 1890: '[w]hen it is remembered that this foul and filthy trash circulates [. . .] amongst lads who are at the most impressionable period of their lives, it is not surprising that the authorities have to lament the prevalence of juvenile crime' (152). Penny serials, 'dreadful' literature, hardly needed a moral panic to increase their sales, but this is certainly what happened. Reading such works marked a resistance to dominant modes of literary taste.

Horror Classifies the Classifier

Although not a distinct genre, Victorian horror anticipated the violation of both the body and the body politic. It was a medically inspired criticism of everyday life, in which bodies were snatched and cannibalised both figuratively and literally. The Victorian era was the period when the Gothic became everyday and the everyday became horrific. Horror literature, however, cannot be horror without a social movement to control, or at least to advise against, its consumption. To adapt the words of sociologist Pierre Bourdieu, horror classifies. Victorian horror was a discourse that marked both hostile critics and subject matter. It is a position of taste that was neither secure in its categories nor confined to prose fiction alone.

Whether labelled as 'horror' or not, the writing of the non-human and the language of fear was a way of looking at social change and also the changing self. Victorian writers blurred the boundary between the Gothic in fiction and the horrific in life; this is their enduring legacy to contemporary horror. If they were not explicitly conscious of it, then they were certainly attuned to it. In 1860 Joseph Randall

Tussaud, Madame Tussaud's grandson, attempted to change the name of the popular 'Chamber of Horrors' to the 'Chamber of Comparative Physiognomy', where onlookers could view the waxworks of criminals to see if their facial and bodily proportions revealed their criminality according to the tenets of the pseudo-science. Randall did not have good instincts. The name did not stick (it appears the public did not want scientific theory to mix with their thrills) and 'The Chamber of Horrors' title remains to this day. The Victorians might not have identified a horror tradition themselves, but they could certainly seek it out with relish.

References

Anonymous, 'John Bishop and Thomas Williams, Notorious Body-Snatchers, Who Murdered People and Sold Their Bodies to Hospitals, and Were Executed at Newgate, 5th of December, 1831', *Newgate Calendar*, vol. V (1831). <http://www.exclassics.com/newgate/ng609.htm> [accessed 1 July 2015].

——, 'Our Female Sensation Novelists', *The Living Age*, 78 (1863), 352–4.

——, 'The Anatomy Bill', *The Lancet*, vol. I (1832–3), 243–5.

Austen, Jane, *Mansfield Park* (Cambridge: Cambridge University Press, 2005).

Braddon, Mary Elizabeth, *Lady Audley's Secret* (Oxford: Oxford University Press, 1998).

Brontë, Charlotte, *Villette* (London: Penguin, 2004).

——, *Jane Eyre* (Harmondsworth: Penguin, 1996).

Carlyle, Thomas, *The French Revolution, A History*, 3 vols (London: George Bell and Sons, 1902).

Collins, Wilkie, *The Woman in White* (Oxford: Oxford University Press, 1975).

Dickens, Charles, *Nicholas Nickleby* (Harmondsworth: Penguin, 1998).

Eliot, George, *Middlemarch* (Oxford: Clarendon Press, 1986).

Gaskell, Elizabeth, *Mary Barton* (Oxford: Oxford University Press, 2006).

Good, John Mason, *The Study of Medicine*, 4 vols (London: Baldwin, Cradock and Joy, 1822).

Graham, Thomas John, *Modern Domestic Medicine* (London: Simpkin and Marshall et al., 1827).

[Hitchman, Francis], 'Penny Fiction' *Quarterly Review*, 171 (1890), 152.

Hogg, James, 'Some Terrible Letters from Scotland', in John Polidori, *The Vampyre and other Tales of the Macabre* (Oxford: Oxford University Press, 2008), pp. 99–112.

James, Henry, *The Portable Henry James* (London: Penguin, 2004).

Lascelles, Lady Caroline [Mary Braddon], 'The Black Band; or The Mysteries of Midnight', in *The Halfpenny Journal,* No. 2, 8 July 1861, pp. 9–11.

Mansel, Henry L., 'Sensation Novels', *Quarterly Review*, 113 (April 1863), 481–514.

[Martineau, Harriet], 'Life of Criminal Classes', *Edinburgh Review*, 122 (1865), 347.

Marx, Karl, and Friedrich Engels, *The Communist Manifesto* (Oxford: Oxford University Press, 2008).

Reynolds, George W. M., *Wagner the Wehr-wolf* (London and New York: Dover, 1975).

[Rymer, James Malcolm], *Varney the Vampire, or the Feast of Blood* (London: E. Lloyd, 1845).

Smith, Andrew, *The Ghost Story, 1840–1920* (Manchester and New York: Palgrave, 2010).

Sutherland, John, 'Wilkie Collins and the Origins of the Sensation Novel', *Dickens Studies Annual: Essays in Victorian Fiction*, 20 (1991), 243–57.

Thackeray, William Makepeace, *Pendennis* (Oxford: Oxford University Press, 1994).

Warren, Samuel, *Passages from the Diary of a Late Physician*, 2 vols (Edinburgh: William Blackwood; London: T. Cadell, 1834).

Wise, Thomas James, and John Alexander Symington (eds), *The Brontës: Their Lives, Friendships and Correspondence*, 4 vols (Oxford: Basil Blackwell, 1980).

Wisker, Gina, *Horror Fiction: An Introduction* (New York and London: Continuum, 2005).

What to Read Next

Mary Elizabeth Braddon, *The Face in the Glass and Other Gothic Tales* (London: British Library Publishing, 2015).

Wilkie Collins, *The Woman in White* (1860; Oxford: Oxford University Press, 2008).

Charles Dickens, *Bleak House* (1853; Oxford: Oxford University Press, 2008).

George Eliot, *The Lifted Veil* and *Brother Jacob* (Oxford: Oxford University Press, 2008).

Elizabeth Gaskell, *Gothic Tales* (London: Penguin, 2000).

James Malcolm Rymer, *Varney, the Vampyre* (1847; Hertfordshire: Wordsworth Editions, 2010).

The Three Impostors, Arthur Machen, 1895. Front cover of first edition, published by John Lane/The Bodley Head.

Chapter 4

Transitions: From Victorian Gothic to Modern Horror, 1880–1932

Roger Luckhurst

THE PERIOD COVERED IN THIS chapter begins with the late Victorian Gothic revival in Britain and ends with the consolidation of the elements of modern horror in America in both fiction and film. What feverish conditions produced this intensely creative period, where enduring icons such as Dr Jekyll and Mr Hyde, Dorian Gray, Count Dracula, Doctor Moreau, Cthulhu and the Dunwich Horror were all spawned in such close proximity? To begin to explain this avalanche of major horror classics, I want to use the long career of the definitive 'minor' writer Arthur Machen as a lens to focus what might otherwise be a rather diffuse discussion.

Arthur Machen's *The Three Impostors* appeared in 1895 in the famous 'Keynotes' series, then synonymous with the British Decadent movement. The book is a chain of teasing, interlinked stories, and stories within stories, about strange and horrifying events told to a couple of investigators: Dyson, a man about town, and Phillipps, ostensibly a man of empirical science. Both, however, seem willing to believe anything they are told. The book was constructed in the manner of Robert Louis Stevenson's *New Arabian Nights* (1882), tall tales inside a shared frame, and rather similar to that odd collection of after-dinner gossip, letters and strange confessions that makes up the text of Stevenson's shilling shocker *Strange Case of Dr Jekyll and Mr Hyde* (1885). Stevenson died in 1894, and a year later something had curdled in Machen's Decadent imagination. This was the year in which Oscar Wilde had been arrested, prosecuted and convicted for his sexual transgressions; in which rumours of scandal swirled around the British Prime Minister, Lord Rosebery; and in which a bestselling screed by Max Nordau called *Degeneration* predicted the rapid decline and fall of Western civilisation.

The wild goose chase in *The Three Impostors,* the hunt for the man with spectacles, ends the book with this memorably gruesome dénouement:

> A naked man was lying on the floor, his arms and legs stretched wide apart, and bound to pegs that had been hammered into the boards. The body was torn and mutilated in the most hideous fashion, scarred with the marks of red-hot irons, a shameful ruin of a human shape. But upon the middle of the body a fire of coals was smouldering; the flesh had been burnt through. The man was dead, but the smoke of his torment mounted still, a black vapour.
> 'The young man with spectacles,' said Mr Dyson. (Machen 1995: 154)

While Machen's book remains obscure, two of the interpolated stories from it are frequently anthologised as quintessential examples of late Victorian horror. 'The Novel of the Black Seal' is about the researches of Professor Gregg in the West Country; he discovers a degenerate survival of the 'little people' who occupied the land before our human ancestors and possess grotesque, shape-changing powers, still possible to conjure through a magical language inscribed on a seal discovered during an archaeological excavation. This curious survival, a boy native to the region, seems to be a biological reversion, capable of exuding tentacular pseudo-pods from his body that leave trails of primordial ooze. 'Never will I write the phrases which tell me how man can be reduced to the slime from which he came, and be forced to put on the flesh of the reptile and the snake' (Machen 1995: 82), Gregg's confession states. The other justly notorious tale is 'The Novel of the White

Powder', about a dissolute student whose sister watches in horror as his non-specific moral corruption in the fleshpots of London turns into a full-scale physical degeneracy. He retreats to his locked room in shame, just as Dr Jekyll does. Through the door, Miss Leicester glimpses first 'not a hand [...] but a black stump [...], a beast's paw' and 'two eyes of burning flame' (119–20). At the culmination of the tale, heavy with anticipatory dread, she discovers 'a pool of horrible liquor' dripping through her ceiling onto the white sheets of her bed. Her brother's door is smashed open and:

> There upon the floor was a dark and putrid mass, seething with corruption and hideous rottenness, neither liquid nor solid, but melting and changing before our eyes, and bubbling with unctuous oily bubbles like boiling pitch. And out of the midst of it shone two burning points like eyes, and I saw a writhing and stirring as of limbs, and something moved and lifted up that might have been an arm. (122)

The critics soon wearied of Machen's piling up of these deliberate outrages on good taste. The book was called 'gruesome and unmanly' by the *Ladies' Pictorial*, while the *Bookman* wished Machen 'had some restraining qualities that would keep him from writing such horrors as those in his last chapter' (Machen 1995: 156, 158). Somehow, it was the cleverness of the construction that made this worse, revealing considerable aesthetic talents squandered on mere provocation. The book felt brash and cynical. Even the title was a joke, a reference to the ultimate blasphemous book that named Moses, Jesus and Mohammad as the 'three impostors', but which had only ever existed in the feverish imagination of church authorities. The reader struggled through 'The Novel of the White Powder' only for the earnest narrator, Miss Leicester, to go off 'into a shriek of laughter' (Machen 1995: 128), pulling out the rug from under the reader's suspended disbelief, cruelly exposing the artifice.

Machen had received even more of a mauling for his previous Keynotes book that comprised two nasty novellas, *The Great God Pan* and *The Inmost Light* (1894). The first hints at the horrors associated with Helen Vaughan, the result of a horrific experiment on a young girl that opens the pathways of her brain to other dimensions. The rather strong implication is that the woman has had sexual congress with Pan, the priapic pagan spirit whose death is traditionally meant to herald the beginning of the Christian era. The story pulsed with erotic allure, the promise of the unspeakable horrors and delights always just on the verge of being spoken, but breaking off or lapsing into obscure Latin to hide the awful truth. In late Victorian London, a wave of suicides after a night in Helen's company in a nefarious street somewhere north of Oxford Street suggests unimaginable extremities of experience.

The Inmost Light, a tall tale again told to the credulous Mr Dyson, featured another instance of unnameable scientific experiment and sexual transgression. This seemed all the worse for happening behind the dull facade of an anonymous London suburb: it is horror in Harlesden. *Pan* was memorably described as 'an incoherent nightmare of sex and the supposed horrible mysteries behind it, such as might conceivably possess a man who was given to a morbid brooding over these matters' (review cited in Machen 1993: 26) by the *Westminster Gazette* – and this was one of the politer comments. The reviews in general were so hyperbolically awful that Machen later delightedly published a collection of them under the title *Precious Balms* (1924).

After Wilde's arrest in March 1895, the windows of his publisher John Lane in Vigo Street were broken by a stone-throwing mob. This was the home of the Keynotes series, too, and there was considerable risk for other authors of guilt by association. Decadence as a form of London's public culture was severely curtailed, and Machen was caught in the backlash. He largely abandoned publishing fiction for a number of years before becoming established as the emblematic 'minor writer', struggling in relative obscurity on the margins of 'Grub Street', the capital's epicentre of hack writing, for decades. He became briefly famous again in the First World War when his story 'The Bowmen' was published in the *Evening News* in 1914. The story describes a supernatural vision of English bowmen from the Battle of Agincourt appearing in the sky to protect the retreating soldiers from slaughter after the failure of the first action of the British Expeditionary Force at Mons in August 1914. Machen was astounded to discover this fiction had become a 'true' myth among the troops themselves, who took great umbrage at Machen's claims to be the origin of the enduring myth of the 'Angel of Mons'.

He continued to write stories about fleeting access to other planes of existence – sometimes in the horrific mode, but also in a kind of religious ecstasy, for example in the visions of the Holy Grail that break through the dusty squares of London in books such as *The Secret Glory* (1922). There was another revival of interest in his fiction a decade later, when the American writer H. P. Lovecraft declared Machen to be one of the four English masters of 'weird fiction' in his long survey essay, *Supernatural Horror in Literature* (1927). Machen's works remained rare, however, his ornamental, Decadent prose finding favour only among connoisseurs of the perverse. Penguin issued a slender paperback collection of selected tales, sips of a heady and fortified wine, called *Holy Terrors* in 1946, the year before Machen's death.

For all these signals of Machen's marginality, his fiction has been resolutely championed by writers of weird fiction, from Lovecraft to the contemporary British author M. John Harrison, and he has been claimed as the archetypal 'lost' London writer by the poetic documentarist of the city, Iain Sinclair. I want to propose that Machen's fiction can be taken as representative of a crucial transition from eighteenth-century Gothic to twentieth-century horror. We can use Machen as a portal into the other fiction being produced at the time to make this case. I am going to pursue three avenues: the question of the new forms that writing took in the late Victorian era; the waning of religious terrors and rise of more secular sources of horror; and specifically the continual revolution in biological understanding in this era that definitively pinpoints the body as the locus of modern horror.

The Form of Horror

Print culture expanded massively in the 1880s. A mass literate population was the market for a host of new dailies, weeklies and monthlies. These were price- and class-sensitive publications, and those that found a niche in the mass market sold hundreds of thousands. In America a language of 'slick' versus 'pulp' emerged, naming the journals from the relative quality of the paper on which they were printed. The model for

Dr. Jekyll and Mr. Hyde, colour lithograph (theatrical poster). Published by
National Prtg. & Engr. Co., Chicago, 1880s. Library of Congress, Prints
and Photographs Division.

all subsequent pulp fiction journals was Frank Munsey's first all-fiction
Argosy, published in 1896. By the 1930s these sold in the tens of millions,
and the subset of horror collections were known as the 'shudder pulps'.

These conditions created a boom in short stories, novels and serial fiction and made celebrities of those accomplished in the new forms, such
as Rudyard Kipling and Arthur Conan Doyle. The linked tale helped to
create continuity and reader loyalty: this was the form that gave Sherlock
Holmes his fame in the *Strand* magazine in monthly short stories (from
1891), where the earlier stand-alone novel, *A Study in Scarlet* (1887), had
not. Commercial considerations consolidated emergent genres, such as
detective fiction or the scientific romance. The late Victorian Gothic
revival, with so many rushing to imitate the global success of Stevenson's
short novella *Jekyll and Hyde,* was part of this boom, but also provided
a locus of anxiety. Some complained that the new mass literature was
merely debased distraction for a population that the writer George Gissing in *New Grub Street* (1891) described as the 'quarter educated' (1993:
460). The graphic horrors depicted in contemporary fiction were crude

sensation for jaded, over-stimulated nerves, a tactic that inevitably had steadily to broaden and coarsen its effects to maintain the same effect. This concern was exacerbated by a distinct sense that the moral censorship and control of public discourse once imposed by respectable Victorian publishers and circulating libraries such as Mudie's and W. H. Smith's was coming to an end. The upstart presses were selling crude sensation to the mass public directly, with no filters for taste or morality.

In this era there emerges a distinct formation of 'high' and 'low' literature – although confusingly this was a line that often cut across the middle of an author's output. Henry James was the defender of the 'art of the novel' as the highest aesthetic form, but he also desired commercial success and symptomatically returned to writing ghost stories in the 1890s. Stevenson was congratulated by the literati for the genius of what he called his 'Gothic gnome', *Jekyll and Hyde,* but was also repeatedly told by friends that he should apply himself to completing an enduring work of art to preserve his name. Even within the Gothic revival, we can identify a division of high and low. The canonical fictions are those of psychological subtlety and ambiguity: the ghost stories of Vernon Lee's *Hauntings* (1890), for instance, or Henry James's *The Turn of the Screw* (1898). The 'golden age' of the ghost story reaches its apogee in M. R. James, who pushed material horrors to the very edges of the page and preferred a donnish treatment of a largely undemonstrative supernatural realm. In a late essay, 'Ghosts – Treat Them Gently!' (1931), James disowned those ghost tales that simply hoped 'to make their readers' flesh creep'. 'These are shameless in their attempts,' he said, '[t]hey are unbelievably crude and sudden, and they wallow in corruption. And if there is a theme that ought to be kept out of the ghost story, it is that of the charnel house' (James 1987: 351). James defined his cerebral terrors against the lowly forms crammed into the popular journals with their breathless plots, shattering screams and shuddering dread, an intensive focus on extreme emotional states or bodily dissolution. Horror was decidedly for the pulps.

For students of the Gothic, this divide strongly echoes that put forward by Ann Radcliffe in her essay 'On the Supernatural in Poetry' (1826), discussed by Dale Townshend in chapter 1. Terror leads in steps towards the sublime, as used in the works of Shakespeare and Milton. Horror is the broken arc of this ambition, dragging the reader back into the abysmal

Vernon Lee, at Sestri, Italy. Unknown photographer, 1914.

mud and the coils of the body. This lowly realm of horror was the locale of writers such as Bram Stoker and H. Rider Haggard in the late Victorian period. The men sought to revive the romance form in a movement against what they perceived as the enervation of filthy French Naturalists and the 'analytic' Realist novel, both of which they believed to be too focused on the social and psychological depths. Haggard found astonishing success with his colonial romances *King Solomon's Mines* (1885) and *She* (1886) – fantasies of lost civilisations in the African interior built on his experience as a colonial administrator in the Transvaal in the 1870s. These books are considered to be conservative reinforcements of imperial ideology by current critics, but at the time they were received by some with deep dismay for their brash, informal and near-illiterate style and for the crude horrors that peppered their narratives. In the culminating battle scene in *King Solomon's Mines,* the usurper king Twala is beheaded in gruesome detail: '[f]or a second the corpse stood upright, the blood spouting in fountains from the severed arteries; then with a dull crash it fell to the earth' (Haggard 2008: 147). Haggard's signature scenes of the weird and uncanny feature royal corpses transformed into stalactites in *King Solomon's Mines* or preserved with unnerving perfection in catacombs beneath the city in *She*.

As both Sigmund Freud and Carl Jung acknowledged, Haggard seemed to have a direct route into the mythopoeic realm of the unconscious. More typically, however, the *Church Quarterly Review* declared Haggard to be the figurehead of a new 'Culture of the Horrible' (Anon. 1887–8: 389) emerging in public discourse, delivering gaudy romances marked by 'naked intellectual indolence', 'pernicious stimulus' and the 'neglect of self-restraint' (390). They transgressed every Christian virtue in presenting 'all the minutiae of the charnel-house' (396). 'Why should the imagination be educated to revel in the bestial?' (403) the outraged reviewer demanded. Always stung by slights on his gentlemanly status, Haggard toned down his bloodthirsty epithets in subsequent editions. Yet he knew that however many millions of copies he sold, he was regarded as entirely outside literature. We do not regard Haggard as a horror writer now, but he was to his contemporaries.

Ten years later there was little moral outrage about Bram Stoker's *Dracula* (1897), although this too focused relentlessly on sexual and bodily corruption, and also hinged on gruesome matters of the grave. Like Haggard, Stoker had a fixation with the uncannily preserved corpse, staging gatherings of men around dead female bodies in *Dracula,* his mummy horror *Jewel of the Seven Stars* (1903) and again in *The Lady of the Shroud* (1909). One fixes the shape-shifting, perambulating vampire properly back in the body at the point of a stake hammered pitilessly into the heart. Sever the head and turn it to the earth for good measure. This punitive act, performed in *Dracula* on the corrupted and licentious Lucy Westenra in a cemetery crypt in North London by her promised husband and his band of blood brothers, is emblematic of the bodily fixation of horror fiction. Stoker, who penned these shockers in his spare time while working as the business manager of the Lyceum Theatre in London, was also considered outside literature for many years. His obituary in *The Times* ignored *Dracula* and considered him most likely to be remembered, if at all, as the biographer of his boss, the actor Sir Henry Irving.

Dracula, Bram Stoker, 1897. Front cover of first paperback edition, published by Archibald Constable & Co., 1901.

Stoker's ephemeral fiction was typical of genre writing fostered by the commercial conditions of publishing at the turn of the century. Horrors, Gothic romances and ghost stories sold, as the mildly disgusted author Grant Allen discovered early on in his career. Allen hoped to be a serious man of science; his first book, a self-financed tome called *Physiological Aesthetics* (1877), was dedicated to his hero, the social evolutionary theorist Herbert Spencer. When academic posts proved elusive, Allen struggled to earn a living as a journalist. He wrote light science pieces for the general public before discovering that he could earn considerably more by selling ghost stories to the new periodicals. Allen's *Strange Stories*

(1884) were full of conflicted tales that at once indulged and lambasted the supernatural. He was good at tales of unnerving psychological and physiological unravelling. In 'The Pallinghurst Barrow' (1892), a feverish man enters a liminal, dreamy state in which he either imagines or actually encounters ancestral survivals in a Neolithic burial site. In 'The Beckoning Hand' (1887) it is racial regression that creates the horrors (the hidden taint of black blood in a young Englishman's wife calling her back to the savage rites of voodoo in the Caribbean). This was a signature theme in Allen's fiction, underpinned by his allegedly scientific grounding in biology and ethnography. Allen proved extremely adaptable to the market in the 1880s and 1890s, writing the controversial marriage-debate novel *The Woman Who Did* (1894). H. G. Wells subsequently acknowledged Allen as a crucial influence in his understanding of the emergent genre of the 'scientific romance' when he published *The Time Machine* (1895).

Allen's brief, tortured career (he died in 1899) exposed the tensions of this new fiction market. Others had less difficulty in writing horror to order. Some of these writers have only been rescued from oblivion by another publishing revolution a century later, with the low costs of digital reprinting allowing small presses to reissue new editions of long-lost books. Guy Boothby, M. P. Shiel and Bertram Mitford produced streams of exotic shockers, all of them using personal experience of the colonies to their advantage. Richard Marsh was another writer who produced a memorable cluster of horrors at the turn of the century amidst a hack career of over 80 novels. *The Beetle* (1897) briefly eclipsed Stoker's *Dracula* when it first appeared. The novel was written in an ingenious narrative construction reminiscent of Wilkie Collins. A series of overlapping documents record the pestilential presence in London of an uncategorisable ancient-modern, animal-human, female-male Thing – essentially an Egyptian monster seeking revenge on its colonial masters. *The Beetle* is obsessed with psychological and physical torture, and with the violent conjuncture of bodies. Marsh achieved the same memorable strangeness with his delirious, exotic oddity *The Joss: A Reversion* (1901), although he rarely invested in specific genres for long before moving on. And the times were moving too. In the new century the market for short horror tales helped to consolidate the early careers of John Buchan, William Hope Hodgson and Algernon Blackwood.

The Beetle, Richard Marsh, 1897.
Front cover of edition published by
Skeffington & Son, 1897.

Amidst this vibrant new market, Machen's fiction straddled the
divide between the Gothic sublime and grotesque horrors, the high and
the low. His style remained recognisably Decadent – a mode defined
by the poet Arthur Symons in 1893 as marked by 'an intense self-consciousness, a restless curiosity in research, an over-subtilizing refinement
upon refinement, a spiritual and moral perversity' (Symons 2000: 105).
This was the style of life and art that brought Wilde into disgrace, and
Symons largely abandoned it after Wilde's imprisonment, although
Machen retained allegiance throughout his career, long after it fell from
fashion and long after the disappearance of Decadent icons such as the
Yellow Book and the *Savoy*.

Such an enduring fascination is of a piece with Machen's love of
obscurity, occult lore and secret knowledge (he was a member, briefly,
of the magical society, the Hermetic Order of the Golden Dawn). At

the same time that he valued rarefaction, Machen struggled to write material for the market, fluttering in and out of the ranks of Fleet Street hacks. This produced strange contradictions, among them the idea that Machen fashioned the oblique Decadent horror story 'The White People' (1904), another menacing tale constructed from a set of Chinese box narratives, for *Horlick's Magazine* – the commercial publication of the malted drink manufacturers, presumably meant as a gentle accompaniment to the soporific bedtime drink. For all his Decadent sensibility, in his culminating moments of physical horror Machen is happy to exploit the most systematically condemned mode in the Gothic romance, invoking the horror that 'freezes the soul'. These were the market paradoxes that make Machen's fragile fictions oddly representative of the time.

Horror: A Secular Gothic?

The second avenue for thinking through the distinction of Gothic and horror is to entertain the conventional premise that the Victorian period was an era of progressive secularisation, a time that saw the shifting of authority from the Church to new institutions and discourses, particularly the sciences. After the British government reforms of the 1870s, which ensured state funding and formal schooling in science for the first time, the late Victorian period was marked by the rise of the scientific savant and the engineer/inventor as cultural heroes. The pace of change visibly accelerated and the world was transformed by an avalanche of new technologies and scientific discoveries that often directly challenged a Christian theological understanding of the world.

In the first wave of the Gothic romance, fear is associated with blasphemy, mortal sin and moral transgression. Vice has its moment in the sun, but writers such as Ann Radcliffe ensure that the Protestant Virtues are always ultimately victorious, however fearfully pressed. Those who threaten the moral order – the Marquis de Montalt in *Romance of the Forest* (1791) or Signor Montoni in *The Mysteries of Udolpho* (1794) – are pitilessly dispatched. Even those who acquired scandalous reputations for their Gothic texts – William Beckford for *The History of the Caliph Vathek* (1782) or Matthew Lewis for *The Monk* (1796), for example – stage their subversions through acts of religious sacrilege. In both texts the libidinous villains end by being literally dragged away to hell.

The late Victorian Gothic revival does not simply abandon this paradigm: there is some authentic Christian dread left in *Dracula,* for instance, and Jonathan Harker is entirely in the tradition of the modern Protestant menaced by priestcraft, superstition and evil on the edges of Catholic Europe as he suffers in Transylvania. However, horror initially seems to derive from a more secular framework, picking up on the radical materialism and atheism that underpins some of the ideas swirling in Mary Shelley's 1818 text of *Frankenstein,* a crucial progenitor in this regard. H. G. Wells's protagonists – the Time Traveller, Doctor Moreau or Griffin in his violent and disordered novella, *The Invisible Man* – have no religious frame of reference, and barely any notion of social morality supported by a Protestant state. The priest is openly mocked in *The War of the Worlds* (1898) and Christian values rapidly collapse. Haggard similarly eschews religion for a gentlemanly code of soldiering, white fraternity and empire in his fiction (something that also upset the *Church Quarterly Review* about the 'Culture of the Horrible'). By the end of the century, vengeful mummies are cross about the politics of colonial occupation rather than the presumptions of Christendom. Even the modern ghost, as the critic Andrew Lang opined, came less with a moral intention and a sense of holy outrage and was often a mute, psychical intrusion, with no moral purpose. Henry James's ghosts had nothing to do with religion, and even the historian of the medieval Church M. R. James rarely ascribed his malevolent presences to religious causes.

In the 1920s the American pulps introduced the aimless, shuffling zombie from Haiti, an emblematic modern monster that has little of the unholy transgressive glee of the un-Christian vampire. This trend reaches its logical conclusion in the radical atheism of H. P. Lovecraft, who espoused a philosophy of 'cosmic indifferentism': 'all my tales,' he said in a letter about his most famous story, 'The Call of Cthulhu', 'are based on the fundamental premise that common human laws and interests have no validity or significance in the vast cosmos-at-large' (Lovecraft 1968: 150). His monsters emerge entirely outside a Christian or even a humanist framework, beyond 'organic life, good and evil, love and hate' (Lovecraft 1968: 150). Is it that modern horror is what remains after Christian dread has drained from the Gothic body?

Any neat, linear narrative of secularisation in the nineteenth century should always be regarded with suspicion. Darwin's ideas were often rendered entirely compatible with religious beliefs about human perfectibility (and often by Darwin's fellow biologists), while leading men of science, for example the physicist William Thomson, Lord Kelvin, offered a workable synthesis of energy physics and Protestantism. The number of priests actually increased in England over the course of the century and religious organisations were thoroughly woven into public life, with new evangelical movements such as the Salvation Army or the Catholic Modernists prominent at the end of the century.

The specificity of the Victorian crisis around the competing authority of science and religion can be read in the weird compromise formations that emerged in belief systems and mass movements such as Spiritualism. This spread rapidly across the world from its cradle in the millennialist theologies of New England in 1848. Although it took many forms, Spiritualism often claimed to use the empirical experimental method of science to 'prove' the existence of the spirit's survival of bodily death. In the face of chronic doubt over biblical truths, here was proof one could touch. Trance mediums, attuned to receive messages through the ether, were treated indistinguishably from subjects of Mesmeric and hypnotic experiments on the fringes of orthodox medicine. Both seemed to have heightened perceptual powers that shaded into supernatural hyperacuity that could be tested and demonstrated in the 'laboratory' of the séance. In 1882, an eminent group of philosophers, physicists, psychologists and gentleman researchers formed the Society for Psychical Research (SPR) with the express aim of putting disorderly and chaotic Spiritualist investigations onto a proper, systematic scientific footing. These men and women of the establishment recognised the authority of science but feared that purely materialist explanations rendered social and moral purpose meaningless. In the scientised language of psychical research, weird extra-sensory communications in trance and dream became 'telepathy', ghosts became psychical projections called 'phantasms of the living' and haunted houses were 'phantasmogenetic centres'.

Another compromise formation from around the same time was a notable magical and occult revival. It included the Theosophical Society and various mystical groups who promised to unlock the forgotten secrets of the Hermetic tradition. These similarly fused various theological traditions with the latest language of physics and biology. In fact, the findings of energy physics in the 1890s – the discoveries of new kinds of invisible waves of 'dark matter', of radiation, X-rays and wireless telegraphy – all contributed to a sense that science and magic were merging. The new science and the new religion were identical to the influential newspaper editor W. T. Stead, who entertained notions from science, technology, the evangelical church, psychical researchers, astrologers, occultists and 'borderland' Gothic writers without any discrimination. The sociologist Max Weber famously talked about the advance of science as a progressive 'disenchantment of the world' (Weber 1948: 155) and the rolling back of childish magical thinking. However, cultural historians such as Alex Owen (2004) have since argued that phases of extraordinary science, in which sublime phenomena shown by the sciences astound the world, are moments of *re-enchantment* which get appropriated back into magical and religious thinking.

The late Victorian Gothic revival can be read as another version of these compromise formations. The fiction is full of men of science – physicists, medical doctors, experts in uncanny and weird phenomena – whose experiments blur the boundaries of the natural and the supernatural. They stretch from Doctor Hesselius in Sheridan Le Fanu's collection *In a Glass Darkly* (1872), via Professor Van Helsing in *Dracula*, to the various hapless professors of Miskatonic University in Lovecraft's fiction of the 1920s and 1930s. Sometimes their transgressions can be articulated both inside and outside Christian formulations. Stevenson's Dr Jekyll is a chemist whose chemical experiments on himself appear to accelerate a horrifying process of biological reversion, yet the split of Jekyll and Hyde also derived from the Calvinist notions of predetermined good and evil that dominated Stevenson's Edinburgh childhood. Jekyll and Hyde almost immediately became a short-hand term for dynamic psychologists investigating the rare puzzle of 'alternating personality', in which two streams of memory seemed to co-exist in the same consciousness, but it was simultaneously also the subject of many traditional sermons on the Christian virtue of self-restraint. The antisocial materialism of Wells's Doctor Moreau or Griffin, along with a whole host of mad doctors and evil geniuses of the era, are always hemmed in by questions of social morality.

The biggest impact on literature of the tension between traditional and scientific authority was felt in the ghost story, which became ambivalently 'psychical' at the end of the century. The ghost story occupied the liminal territory between the new psychology, occultism, magical and psychical researches. Grant Allen ridiculed the SPR from the view of science in his early stories, while Vernon Lee's *Hauntings* objected in far more aesthetic terms to the dogged literalisation of the ghostly metaphor. Yet this ambiguous state of the ghost was perfect for an author such as Henry James when he returned to Gothic trappings in the 1890s. Henry's brother William was an eminent psychologist at Harvard University and president of the SPR, who researched extensively in the area with an attitude of sceptical open-mindedness. His investigations clearly had an influence on Henry's tales. *The Turn of the Screw* notoriously leaves the status of the ghosts suspended between old-fashioned demonic presences, obtruding into the world to corrupt innocence, or the psychological projections of a governess who some readers confidently diagnose as a sexual hysteric. It has been claimed that the governess's 'case' has echoes not only of specific accounts of hauntings collected in the *Proceedings of the Society for Psychical Research*, but also to the case studies presented in Freud and Breuer's *Studies in Hysteria*. Nor is this a choice between the orthodox or unorthodox, by the way: Freud was a corresponding member of the SPR and believed in telepathy. The 'suspended' ambiguity of the ghost story in the late Victorian and Edwardian period was something new, a development from debates over the role of imagination and fancy in the eighteenth-century Gothic.

In terms of horror fiction, this set of compromise formations between knowledge and belief also exercised a strong influence. The genre of the 'psychic detective' was a tradition that stretched back to Le Fanu's Dr Hesselius and Edgar Allan Poe's Auguste Dupin, investigators with near-supernatural abilities called to investigate apparently inexplicable, uncanny crimes. This nascent genre was picked up in the new century by Algernon Blackwood in his *John Silence* collection (1908) and by William Hope Hodgson for the interlinked stories in *Carnacki, the Ghost Finder* (1913). Both construct recurrent protagonists who work in the space between the scientific, the occult and the psychical. Both men encounter disembodied super/natural forces that are implacably malignant and are attempting to obtrude their murderous presence into the human realm. This is what defines 'haunting' in these fictions. What is striking is the intense *physicality* of these encounters, the way they put the body under severe pressure. Blackwood's 'A Psychical Invasion' (1908) or Hodgson's 'The Thing Invisible' (1912) seem consciously to revert to the original derivation of horror from *horripilation,* defined by the *Oxford English Dictionary* as 'the erection of the hairs on the skin by contraction of the cutaneous muscles (caused by cold, fear, or other emotion, or nervous affection), producing the condition known as "goose-flesh"; "creeping of the flesh"'. As Carnacki waits for the ghost to appear in the chapel, he focuses intensely on physical reactions:

> A constant, queer prickling went up and down my spine, and a dull ache took me in the small of the back, as I fought with myself to conquer this sudden new feeling of terror and horror. I tell you, that no one who has not been through these kinds of experiences, has any idea of the sheer, *actual physical pain* attendant upon, and resulting from, the intense nerve-strain that ghostly-fright sets up in the human system. (Hodgson 1974: 25)

This first Carnacki story is in fact an instance of the 'explained supernatural' – it transpires that there is no ghost, only a 'mechanical dodge at the back of the whole queer business' (Hodgson 1974: 36). Elsewhere, however, the 'creep' that Carnacki waits to feel in his body, a prickling skin, a sickness to the stomach, indicates the presence of truly malignant forces from other dimensions – forces that he terms 'ab-human'. Carnacki responds to these intrusions with a bizarre set of strategies mixed together from psychical research and ritual magic, usually resorting to an Electric Pentacle and the flummery of technical invocations from the 'Saamaa Ritual' to protect himself from certain death. Blackwood also invoked formulae of ritual magic in his fiction, although more circumspectly (in his early years he had been a member of both the Theosophical Society and the Hermetic Order of the Golden Dawn, and took the discipline of magical and theological training very seriously). The absent presence of vast, invisible cosmic forces is brilliantly evoked in Blackwood's early classics such as 'The Willows' (1907) and 'The Wendigo' (1910). This is psychical horror, but focused almost entirely on lavish evocations of the physiological state of fear, a reiteration that horror always comes back down to the creeping flesh.

Once again we can return to Arthur Machen as representative of the ambiguities and contradictions that result from the imperfect process of secularisation that I have sketched out. His Gothic fiction acknowledges the growing authority of science, but Machen was more fascinated by the occult and Hermetic tradition, as the teasing references in his fiction to hidden lore attest. Doctor Raymond in *The Great God Pan* is an amoral vivisectionist, but, like Victor Frankenstein before him, he is less of a materialist than a dabbler in the alchemical and mystical fringes. Mr Phillipps, one of the antagonists of *The Three Impostors*, is also a scientist, but lambasted for it: 'he was in truth one of the most credulous of men, but he required a marvel to be neatly draped in the robes of Science before he would give it credit, and the wildest dreams took solid shape to him if only the nomenclature were severe and irreproachable' (Machen 1995: 37). Machen echoes the common complaint that it was actually naïve empirical scientists who were most likely to convert suddenly to Spiritualism because they claimed the authority of the evidence of their own eyes and could not conceive that they might be duped.

In contrast to brash modernity and the shallow authority of science, Machen eventually settled on the authority of the ancient Anglican Christian tradition. Although rumoured to have converted to Roman Catholicism, just like those other Decadents, Oscar Wilde and Aubrey Beardsley, Machen in fact clung to a set of beliefs older than the vulgar Protestant Reformation – those of the *original* 'Catholic' church buried in ancient Celtic and Anglo-Saxon traditions and left to linger in the ruins of dissolved abbeys and forest clearings (see Games and Machin 2014). No wonder his later fiction is punctured by visions of guardians of the Grail in England, vulgar modern horrors defeated by the authentic terror of glimpses of the divine.

Bio-Horror

The thread that truly binds together the physiological horrors of this period is biology. Charles Darwin tried to avoid addressing the question of man's development in *On the Origin of Species by Means of Natural Selection* (1859), although the implications of his proposals were clear. He finally spelt these out in *The Descent of Man, and Selection in Relation to Sex* (1871). Darwin offered just one of several rival theories of evolution circulating at the end of the century in the time before the mechanism of transmission – genes – had been identified or understood.

At mid-century, the implications of the theory of natural selection were traumatic. Darwin offered a monistic theory, explaining the origin of life solely as a material, biological process without reference to a spiritual sphere. There was no soul, no 'divine spark' of life that existed on another plane. Evolution required millions of years to work, placing humans within the vast extent of geological time, while the Christian convention from earnest calculations derived from biblical history was that the Earth was created by God in 4004 BC. Darwin also argued that the human biological form was tied both to an animal past and to an entirely *plastic* future, since morphology was not fixed but adaptive to external conditions. Far from being a 'separate creation' in a fixed divine image, the human being was embedded in universal biological processes and was actually one of the most malleable creatures. Human biology, Darwin declared in *The Descent of Man,* 'resembles those forms called by naturalists protean and polymorphic' (Darwin 1989: 205). This is the crucial underpinning for the view that horror in this period nearly always comes back to the body.

In late Victorian Gothic fiction, this unnerving malleability of human beings and the anxiety about the survival of an animalistic core explains the twin obsessions of the horror mode with degeneration and slime. Degeneration was a spurious off-shoot of biological theory, which argued that evolutionary 'progress' from simple to complex forms was not inevitable, and that it was just as possible to regress from the fragile height of civilisation into more savage and primitive forms (see Pick 1989). Whole races might do this, or descendants in a family – such as the Baskerville family in Conan Doyle's *Hound of the Baskervilles* (1902) or the Spanish family in Stevenson's story 'Olalla' (1885); the process could also occur in individuals who allowed themselves to unravel morally. This is why Dr Jekyll's transformation into Mr Hyde is figured in such animalistic terms, with hairy hands, simian features and ape-like gestures and violence. Moral degeneracy was much discussed among psychologists as an explanation for madness: such a regression is portrayed in the monstrous disfigurements that appear in Dorian's hidden painting in Oscar Wilde's *Picture of Dorian Gray* (1891).

More spectacularly, this regression happens to the whole working classes of London in H. G. Wells's *The Time Machine* (1895). Wells was trained in biology in the late 1880s by Darwin's 'bull-dog' T. H. Huxley and the prominent zoologist and degeneration theorist Edwin Ray Lankester. As a young journalist he wrote several provoking essays with titles such as 'The Rate of Change in the Species', 'On Extinction' and 'The Limits of Individual Plasticity', communicating the implications of the new biological theories to general audiences. In *The Time Machine* Wells sends his Time Traveller forward to the year 802,701, initially to what appears to be a utopia of leisure and ease (this is a satirical take on William Morris's 1890 text, *News from Nowhere*). The graceful Eloi, though, have mentally regressed; they are repeatedly compared to children or 'primitives', and their simplicity and stupidity upsets the Traveller's assumptions about continual evolutionary progress. He speculates that, without the continual 'struggle for existence', evolutionary advances simply cease and forms start to revert.

This analysis takes place before the Traveller encounters the creatures that live below the surface, the Morlocks. The descendants of the workers retain basic mechanical skills, but are also portrayed in degenerate forms, as bestial creatures such as apes or lemurs. They also carry the cultural marker of the most savage survivals: they are cannibals. The language that Wells uses around the Morlocks is striking: they continually evoke horror and physical revulsion in the Traveller, in part because he can trace his own past and future in their disgusting bodies. In this extrapolation of the condition of strife between Capital and Labour at the end of the century, Wells the socialist is also a biological pessimist: the future, he declares, is degeneration and race suicide. His vision, one of his early champions W. T. Stead said, 'dwells in my memory from

"I could not distinguish what he said."

The Island of Doctor Moreau, H. G. Wells, 1896. Frontispiece from the first edition, published by Heinemann, Stone & Kimball, 1896.

its horrible suggestiveness' (Stead 1898: 396) because it carried all the authority of the new biology. The horrors only multiply in *The Island of Doctor Moreau* (1896), where the mad doctor vivisects and splices together species in his House of Pain. The project starts as an optimistic attempt to accelerate the evolutionary progress in animals; it ends with an isolated Prendick watching these monstrous hybrids revert back to their animalistic past.

We have already encountered that other biological obsession with slime. In Machen's 'Novel of the Black Seal', the boy's reversion is signalled by trails of sticky matter and ooze. Phillipps listens to the tale, then wanders home musing on 'the outlines of a little work to be called *Protoplasmic Reversion*' (Machen 1995: 85). In *The Time Machine* the Traveller feels his face brushed at night by horrible 'palps' and dreams of tentacles: the *touch* of the Morlocks is always worse than seeing these 'bleached, obscene, nocturnal' (Wells 2008: 36, 38) things. Perhaps the English writer most consistently obsessed with slime was William Hope Hodgson. A large number of his seafaring tales involved encounters with disgusting lakes of ooze. In 'The Derelict' (1912), for example, the narrator's ship encounters an abandoned wreck entirely swallowed in some kind of suppurating jellied growth, 'carrying a queer, sickly, heavy odour with it, that somehow frightened me strangely' (Hodgson 2014: 448). It is only once the captain and his team have rowed into the ooze that they realise it is alive and hungry to absorb them as well:

> [T]he stuff heaped itself upon him, as if it were actually alive, with a dreadful savage life. It was simply infernal. The man had gone from sight. Where he had fallen was now a writhing, elongated mound, in constant and horrible increase, as the mould appeared to move towards it in strange ripples. (Hodgson 2014: 453)

This is typical of Hodgson's ocean tales in *The Boats of 'Glen Carrig'* (1907) and his linked Sargasso Sea tales, in which sailors are harried by weird hybridisations of human, seaweed and monstrous fungal growths.

This work had a clear influence on the American 'weird tale' – the very first story in the first number of the celebrated magazine *Weird Tales* in 1923 was indeed called 'Ooze'. It involves a backwoods experiment

Weird Tales, first issue, March 1923.

with protozoan matter that produces a giant amoeboid thing that goes on to devour the scientist's family. Lovecraft was similarly interested in triggering feelings of disgust and revulsion at slime; hybrid forms with rotting stenches either clamber out of the sea, as in 'The Shadow over Innsmouth' (1931), or land on Earth from the abyss of outer space and rot everything they touch from within in 'The Colour Out of Space' (1927). Lovecraft also wrote a sonnet sequence, 'Fungus from Yuggoth' (1930). In 'The Dunwich Horror' (1929), Lovecraft created a memorable hybrid monster, part human, part animal, 'with coarse black fur, and from the abdomen a score of long greenish-grey tentacles with red sucking mouths' (Lovecraft 2012: 98).

One might speculate that horror writers are touching on foundational human structures of taboo in these tales. The psychoanalyst Julia

Kristeva has written about 'abjection' (1982) as the powerful feeling of horror at fluids that ooze over fixed bodily boundaries – the mucus, pus, blood, semen and urine that all cultures police with elaborate social rituals to expel taboos. In this period, though, it is linked specifically to biological speculations on the origin of life. In 1868, T. H. Huxley believed that he had found the origin of all planetary life in ooze lifted from the seabed, primitive protozoan cells that he named *bathybius haeckelii*. Huxley asserted it was the missing link between organic and inorganic life. This theory was soon discredited, but similar speculations continued to drive biological theory – and thus horror fiction – long into the twentieth century. Horror fiction continues to have what Ben Woodard has termed a 'slime dynamics' (2012) because it harks on the ooze said to lie at the very origins of life.

The period at hand ends with the arrival of a new kind of medium termed 'horror'. The years 1931–2 mark the beginning of the horror film in Hollywood, with the innovative *Dr. Jekyll and Mr. Hyde* (Rouben Mamoulian, 1931) shortly followed by the Universal Studios cycle of films that included *Dracula* (Tod Browning, 1931), *The Mummy* (Karl Freund, 1932) and *Frankenstein* (James Whale, 1931). This was the period of the notorious adaptation of Wells's *Doctor Moreau, The Island of Lost Souls* (Erle C. Kenton, 1932), a film so queasily obsessed with miscegenation that it was banned for decades. The Halperin brothers independently produced *White Zombie* (1932) and launched the cinematic career of that distinctively modern monster. These were not yet called 'horror films' – as Alison Peirse records, they were variously called 'weird' or 'mysteries with a horror angle' (Peirse 2013: 7) – but in 1932 a new film classification emerged: 'H for Horrific'. After this, the interaction between fiction and film would become an essential part of the story of horror. Nearly a century later adaptations of stories from this critical period of the development of horror fiction continue to drive a now vast industry.

References

Anonymous, 'The Culture of the Horrible: Mr Haggard's Stories', *Church Quarterly Review,* vol. XXV (Oct 1887–Jan 1888), 389–411.

Darwin, Charles, *The Descent of Man, and Selection in Relation to Sex* (1871), *The Works of Charles Darwin,* ed. by Paul Barrett and R. B. Freeman, vols 21 and 22 (London: Pickering, 1989).

Games, Gwilym, and James Machin, 'Notes of Gawsworth's Account of Arthur Machen's Funeral', *Faunus,* 29 (2014), 9–16.

Gissing, George, *New Grub Street* (Oxford: Oxford University Press, 1993).

Haggard, H. Rider, *King Solomon's Mines* (Oxford: Oxford University Press, 2008).

Hodgson, William Hope, *Carnacki, The Ghost-Finder* (London: Sphere Books, 1974).

——, 'The Derelict' (1912), in *Horror Stories,* ed. by Darryl Jones (Oxford: Oxford University Press, 2014), pp. 439–62.

James, M. R., *Casting the Runes and Other Ghost Stories* (Oxford: Oxford University Press, 1987).

Kristeva, Julia, *Powers of Horror: An Essay on Abjection,* trans. by Leon S. Roudiez (New York: Columbia University Press, 1982).

Lovecraft, H. P., *Selected Letters, Volume II 1925–9,* ed. by August Derleth and Donald Wandrei (Sauk City, WI: Arkham House, 1968).

——, *Classic Horror Stories* (Oxford: Oxford University Press, 2012).

Machen, Arthur, *The Bowmen and Other Legends of War,* 2nd edn (London: Simpkin, 1915).

——, *Holy Terrors* (London: Penguin, 1946).

——, *The Great God Pan* (London: Creation, 1993).

——, *The Three Impostors* (London: Dent, 1995).

Owen, Alex, *The Place of Enchantment: British Occultism and the Culture of the Modern* (Chicago, IL: Chicago University Press, 2004).

Peirse, Alison, *After Dracula: The 1930s Horror Film* (London: I. B. Tauris, 2013).

Pick, Daniel, *Faces of Degeneration: A European Disorder, c.1848–c.1918* (Cambridge: Cambridge University Press, 1989).

Radcliffe, Ann, 'On the Supernatural in Poetry' (1826), in *Gothic Documents: A Sourcebook 1700–1820,* ed. by E. J. Clery and Robert Miles (Manchester: Manchester University Press, 2000), pp. 163–72.

Symons, Arthur, 'The Decadent Movement in Literature' (1893), in *The Fin de Siècle: A Reader in Cultural History c.1880–1900,* ed. by Sally

Legder and Roger Luckhurst (Oxford: Oxford University Press, 2000), pp. 104–11.

Weber, Max, 'Science as a Vocation' (1919), *Essays in Sociology,* trans. by H. Gerth and C. Wright Mills (London: RKP, 1948), pp. 129–56.

Wells, H. G., *The Time Machine* (New York: Norton, 2008).

Woodard, Ben, *Slime Dynamics* (Winchester: Zero Books, 2012).

What to Read Next

H. P. Lovecraft, *Classic Horror Stories* (Oxford: Oxford University Press, 2013).

Roger Luckhurst (ed.), *Late Victorian Gothic Tales* (Oxford: Oxford University Press, 2005).

Arthur Machen, *The White People and Other Weird Stories* (London: Penguin, 2012).

Robert Louis Stevenson, *Strange Case of Dr Jekyll and Mr Hyde and Other Stories* (1886; Oxford: Oxford University Press, 2006).

Ann and Jeff VanderMeer (eds), *The Weird: A Compendium of Dark and Strange Stories* (London: Corvus, 2011).

H. G. Wells, *The Island of Doctor Moreau* (1896; London: Penguin, 2005).

I Am Legend, Richard Matheson, 1954. Front cover of edition published by Bantam Books, 1964.

Chapter 5

Horror Fiction from the Decline of Universal Horror to the Rise of the Psycho Killer

Bernice M. Murphy

O<small>N THE</small> 26<small>TH OF</small> J<small>UNE</small> 1948 a housewife named Tessie Hutchinson was stoned to death in the pages of *The New Yorker*. The story was Shirley Jackson's instant classic 'The Lottery', and it was, despite the worrying assumptions of some of the magazine's more impressionable readers, entirely fictional. Published just before the release of Jackson's debut novel *The Road through the Wall* (1948), it instantly anointed her one of the nation's most promising young writers. It also attracted more hate mail than any piece of fiction previously printed in the magazine. Those who objected to the story may have done so in part because they recognised, even subconsciously, that it captured something about the true tenor of the times. Adding to the story's resonance was the fact that many contemporary critics felt it could be taking place in the aftermath of a nuclear attack.

The publication of 'The Lottery' was one of the many signs heralding the arrival of a new kind of horror fiction – one that would go some way towards capturing the complex, often contradictory spirit of the era after the Second World War. For many Americans – particularly those who were white, male and middle-class (or getting there) – this

was a time of unprecedented economic, social and technological progress. Although Britain had no choice but to embark upon an accelerated period of imperial decline and decolonisation after 1945, the
US was physically unscathed and, in fact, economically boosted by the
war. At the time that Jackson's story was published, the US was rapidly
consolidating its standing as both a consumerist paradise and the most
militarily powerful nation on Earth. And yet the self-satisfaction generated by these advances was from the very start intrinsically connected
to a genuine, and entirely appropriate, sense of dread.

In contrast to the most significant manifestation of American horror fiction prior to the war – the cosmic horror of H. P. Lovecraft's
Cthulhu mythos, whose 'terrors were not those of within, but those of
the unintelligible outside, of the individual cramped by alien encroach-
ment' (Punter 1996: 38) – it was horror that arose from the conditions
of everyday life that would take the lead in the 1950s and after. Many of
the genre's classic monsters and stereotypical settings were made over in
order to reflect this newfound appetite for psychological and situational
realism. As David J. Skal puts it, 'earlier, horror came from the irrational
and the ungodly encroaching from without – post-war stories increasingly show horror arising from aspects of life normally associated with
security and stability' (1993: 201).

Horror Fiction After the Second World War

By the late 1940s American horror cinema, dominated since the early
1930s by the larger-than-life Universal horror movies, was, albeit with a
few notable exceptions (such as the work of producer/director duo Val
Lewton and Jacques Tourneur), resolutely in the doldrums. While Tod
Browning's *Dracula* (1931), James Whale's *Frankenstein* (1931) and *Bride of
Frankenstein* (1935) had thrilled Depression-era audiences and spawned
the first cinematic horror boom, a succession of remakes, sequels and
comedic mash-ups meant that, by the late 1940s, horror had been sup-
planted by Noir as the most compelling manifestation of on-screen cultural anxiety. The years following the war were therefore characterised
by a 'sudden, and apparently complete, loss of interest in horror subjects
among filmmakers and audiences alike' (Rigby 2007: 294). It was hardly

surprising that the 'Old School' Gothic horrors of the Universal cycle had come to seem completely outdated to a world still trying to absorb the fact that mass murder on an industrial scale had just occurred in the 'civilised' heart of Europe. After all, 'a world forced to contend with the war's very real legions of the dead and the unalleviated apprehensions of the dawning nuclear age demanded horrors that were more believable, rather than more fantastic' (Dziemianowicz 1999: 200–1).

This move towards horror rooted in real-world anxiety was pioneered in the late 1940s and early 1950s by writers such as Ray Bradbury, Shirley Jackson and Richard Matheson. Although he was better known as a science-fiction writer, Bradbury's horror stories of the time were amongst his finest. Those collected in *Dark Carnival* (1947) and *The October Country* (1955) display a ghoulish streak that foreshadowed the work of many of his successors. For instance, Bradbury dramatised the unsettling underbelly of small town life in 'The Handler' (1947), a story about a seemingly mild-mannered local mortician who has been, for many years, secretly defiling the corpses of his friends and neighbours. This macabre conceit predated by a decade the infamous real-life case of noted amateur taxidermist Ed Gein, discussed in more detail later in this chapter. One of the most shocking of Bradbury's stories from this period was 'The October Game' (1948), in which the custody battle between a feuding professor and his wife culminates in a genuinely stomach-churning dénouement. As in many other notable horror stories of the time, the real horror lies close to home, in the form of a deranged husband and father who has decided to take the most terrible revenge of all upon his estranged wife.

During the 1940s and 1950s, the lines between horror, science fiction and fantasy, as we would now define them, were nowhere near as distinct as they would be once popular publishing categories had become more rigidly defined. Like Bradbury, most of the major genre writers of the time, including Charles Beaumont, Fritz Leiber, Jackson and Matheson, worked within several popular genres. They also often wrote stories that incorporated elements from several genres, with horror and science fiction in particular frequently being combined, as in Bradbury's twist-in-tale space exploration story 'Mars Is Heaven!' (1948). Another horror/science fiction hybrid text of the period is

Photograph of serial killer Ed Gein, Plainfield, Wisconsin, 18 November 1957. Courtesy Everett Collection/Alamy Stock Photo.

Jack Finney's hugely influential 1955 novel *The Body Snatchers*, which, among other things, epitomised the horror of creeping dehumanisation and political and cultural conformity that many contemporary thinkers saw as being a hallmark of the post-war US. Matheson, Beaumont and Bradbury also made major contributions to on-screen horror in the form of their screenplays for radio, film and, in particular, television, where both *The Twilight Zone* (1959–64) and *The Outer Limits* (1963–5) frequently dramatised their work.

Almost all of the major American horror writers of the 1940s and 1950s first established themselves as short story writers before turning to novel-length publications. Indeed, up until the early 1970s, when ever more lengthy novels began to dominate the industry, the short story remained one of horror fiction's main publication modes. For instance, although it ceased its initial run in 1954, *Weird Tales* served as an important publication venue for many of the post-war era's most important horror and science fiction writers. In Britain, two influential anthology series – *The Pan Book of Horror Stories* (1959–89) and *The Fontana Book of Great Horror Stories* (1966–84) – provided an invaluable showcase for the work of both established and emerging horror writers. In contrast to the genre's escalating cultural visibility in the US, horror fiction in Britain remained more of a niche than a mainstream publication category until the late 1970s and early 1980s, spurred into life by the arrival of a new wave of novels and stories by James Herbert, Ramsey Campbell, Clive Barker and others. There were, of course, some notable exceptions to this rule (such as Dennis Wheatley), but, by practical necessity, this chapter deals mainly with American authors – who did more than writers from any other nation to create modern horror fiction as we understand it today.

In addition to magazines, one of the period's most notable publication mediums for the genre was the horror comic. Many of the most prominent titles were published by the EC ('Entertaining Comics') group, led by William Gaines. During the 1950s the comics industry published a wide number of popular genres, releasing Western, romance, science fiction, crime and horror titles. It was the latter two categories in particular that aroused the ire of child psychiatrist Dr Fredric Wertham; his book *Seduction of the Innocent* (1954) condemned comics on the grounds that they featured material of a violent, immoral and over-sexualised nature, and were therefore harmful to the 'vulnerable' child reader. Wertham's charges helped to instigate a crusade against horror comics and, under tremendous political pressure, the industry voluntarily adopted a strict self-censorship code that helped bring their popularity and profitability to a screeching halt (even the use of 'horror' or 'terror' in titles was forbidden). However, the comics remained an immensely significant influence upon later horror writers (many of whom grew up reading them), not only because of their ghoulish, lurid charm, but also because they undercut the supposedly wholesome 'family values' of the decade so effectively. Though the horror comics were populated by abusive parents, battling couples, unrepentant adulterers, gangsters and murderers, evildoers almost always got their ironic just desserts in the end. As Skal (1993: 231) notes, what many of their critics overlooked was just how moral the comics actually were.

Certain themes and topics show up again and again in American
horror fiction during this period. These included paranoia, the subversion of traditional ideas of what 'normality' constitutes, a suspicion
(and even abhorrence) towards women and female sexuality (particularly in the work of Matheson, Bloch and Beaumont), the intrusion of
the irrational into the everyday and unstable identities. In addition, for
obvious reasons, the apocalypse was an important theme – although it
tended to be expressed much more overtly on screen, in the form of
the many apocalyptically inclined 'creature-features' of the period and
in science fiction novels such as Leigh Brackett's *The Long Tomorrow*
(1955), Bradbury's *Fahrenheit 451* (1953) and Walter Miller's *A Canticle
for Liebowitz* (1960). American horror fiction at this time tended to
focus upon individual, domestic and psychological terrors rather than
the overt spectacle of mass death, although one could argue that the
popularity of horror was itself an indication of the apocalyptic tenor
of the times. There was, however, one notable exception to this rule:
Richard Matheson's *I Am Legend* (1954), in which the main character's
psychological battle against loneliness and despair is just as compelling
as his physical struggle to survive.

Matheson is important first of all because, unlike Bradbury, who
often utilised an idealised 1930s small town setting, much of his work is
set in a recognisably contemporary, suburban milieu and features white-
collar husbands and fathers defined by their jobs and their role within
the family (Jancovich 1996: 131). Robert Neville, the protagonist of *I
Am Legend*, is certainly no different. As the novel begins, it is January
1976 and a devastating plague has swept the planet, killing off everyone except Neville and those whom the sickness has transformed into
bloodthirsty, pasty-faced ghouls. Neville characterises them throughout the novel as vampires, and even reads *Dracula* in a (fruitless) bit
of background research; but had he been familiar with the work of
George A. Romero (which in fact owed much to this novel), he would
surely have characterised them as zombies. The creatures that terrorise
Neville in his boarded-up suburban home every night, like Romero's
shambling 'Living Dead', are not alien 'others'; they are fellow citizens,
transformed, yet recognisable. In fact Ben Cortman, the leader of the
vampire mob, was formerly Neville's friend and next-door neighbour.

The novel also consistently upends conventional notions of what constitutes 'normality' and 'abnormality' – a characteristic of 1950s horror fiction in general and Matheson's work in particular. Even Neville himself realises that, on some level, he enjoys his stake-wielding, vampire-killing ways, and derives a particular frisson from 'experimenting' upon vampire women in a futile quest for a 'cure' that he is completely unqualified to create. This formerly upright family man, a blonde-haired, blue-eyed WASP who sees himself as the last defender of the world-that-was, is, to the human/vampire hybrids that we encounter in the final chapters of the novel, a fanatical killer who needs to be publicly executed so that the new world can rise from the ashes of the old. As Neville finally admits, 'I'm the abnormal one now. Normalcy was a majority concept, the standard of many and not just the standard of one man' (Matheson 1954: 160).

The dust storms that presage the outbreak of the plague in *I Am Legend* may also be an early indication of a then emerging form of apocalyptic anxiety that would gradually become even more terrifying than the prospect of nuclear annihilation. In fact, one of the most influential apocalyptic narratives of the period is actually a non-fiction text: biologist Rachel Carson's *Silent Spring* (1962). In her careful depiction of the environmental degradation and despoliation caused by the use of insecticides, and her lyrical evocation of a future in which 'no birds sang' (Carson 1962: 2), she helped bring to the surface the latent strain of eco-horror that has haunted the nation since the earliest days of European settlement. Little wonder, then, that although 'The Birds', Daphne Du Maurier's 1952 tale of avian apocalypse, was originally set in Cornwall, when it was adapted for film by Alfred Hitchock less than a year after the release of Carson's book the setting became a picture-perfect American town. By following *Psycho* (1960) with *The Birds* (1963), Hitchcock had unwittingly prefigured the turn towards psychological and environmental horror that would become ever more pronounced in the decades that followed.

Werewolves, Vampires, Witches and Little Devils

One of the most interesting developments in post-war horror was the way in which hackneyed old tropes, themes and settings were reconfigured in order to make them relevant for a post-atomic, post-psychoanalytical age. Between the late 1940s and the early 1970s American horror writers in particular revelled in updating familiar genre conventions in ways that teased out their latent, and not-so-latent, symbolic and psychological potential. For instance, in his 1953 novel *Conjure Wife* Fritz Leiber placed the horror genre's most resonant female icon – the witch – in a decidedly contemporary setting, which only highlighted the subversive potential that the witch held as both a symbol of female power and a source of considerable male unease. *Conjure Wife* was one of the first major 'witch-as-wife' narratives in American popular culture, with the most famous example being the immensely popular sitcom *Bewitched* (1964–72).

Leiber was also an important fantasy writer who helped to establish the 'sword and sorcery' subgenre. His horror fiction, like that of many of his contemporaries, consistently featured male protagonists whose otherwise ordinary existence is violently upended by the intrusion of terrifying supernatural forces. This tendency is exemplified in one of his most famous tales, the classic urban horror story 'Smoke Ghost' (1941) – a nightmarish evocation of the contemporary city as a grimy and terrifying metropolis haunted by modernity itself. Leiber would later return to many of the same themes in his 1977 masterpiece *Our Lady of Darkness*, in which ancient and immeasurably powerful supernatural forces are again located within a notably modern and in this case urban (San Francisco) setting. Meanwhile Shirley Jackson would later investigate the idea of the 'witch' as a more positive symbol of female empowerment in her final novel *We Have Always Lived in the Castle* (1962).

Although *I Am Legend* represents by far the most influential reimagining of the vampire mythos during this period and, as already noted, helped to create the modern zombie, there were other noteworthy attempts. These included Theodore Sturgeon's 1961 novel *Some of Your Blood*. Framed by a case study written by an army psychiatrist, who has asked one of his most troubled patients, a young private prone to extremely violent outbursts, to write out his life story, the novel is a poignant, gripping and complex portrait of an individual whose sense of himself has been irreparably warped by physical abuse and economic and emotional deprivation. In vague outline, it resembles the kind of premise one frequently finds in the work of Robert Bloch, whose stories and novels also often featured dangerously deluded young men. Here, however, Sturgeon's novel, like his science fiction novels of the same period, is characterised by a sense of psychological complexity and sensitivity that Bloch, for all of his liveliness, rarely achieved.

The werewolf tale was also tackled during this period in Jack Williamson's *Darker than You Think* (1948). The story features a premise that would in later years be replicated in countless urban fantasy novels: a secret and ancient race of werewolves exist alongside, and in intermittent battle with, humanity. Along with Guy Endore's 1933 *The Werewolf of Paris*, it remains one of the few major pre-2000s werewolf novels, although Anthony Boucher did make a tongue-in-cheek addition to the slender lycanthropic canon with his story 'The Compleat [*sic*] Werewolf' (1942). Perhaps one of the reasons why the werewolf tale never quite took off in the US during this period is that the themes of hidden identities and transformation into a bloodthirsty 'other' self inherent to the myth were, after the late 1940s, increasingly incorporated into more realistically inclined narratives of 'split personality'. As Stefan Dziemianowicz has noted, in *Psycho* Bloch took 'the basic premise of the werewolf story and transformed it into the foundation of the modern psychological thriller' (1999: 230).

The most archetypal horror setting of all, the haunted house, was also subjected to a makeover during the 1950s and after, most significantly in the work of Jackson and Matheson. In *A Stir of Echoes* (1958) Matheson's protagonist Tom Wallace is a contented corporation man, husband and father. After undergoing hypnosis at a neighbourhood party Wallace gains unwanted psychic abilities as a result; among other things he starts to see the ghostly figure of a murder victim. In addition to being horrified by the glimpses into the secret lives of his fellow suburbanites he experiences, Wallace asks himself, '[w]hy should a place like this be haunted? It's only a couple of years old' (Matheson 1958: 106). He has, of course, not yet realised that, as a myriad of haunted houses to come would remind us, people carry their own histories with them.

Having said that, the most influential haunted house story of the decade, and perhaps the century, does, in fact, feature such a setting – even if Hill House is not quite as old as one might think (only 80 years or so) and, to some of its more unfortunate guests, even seems quite cosy, welcoming and oddly *motherly*. Jackson's *The Haunting of Hill House* (1959) has influenced just about every major modern horror writer since. Part of the novel's lasting appeal lies in the fact that Jackson lays out her story in typically lucid, elegant prose, as in the famous opening paragraph:

> No live organism can continue for long to exist sanely under condi-tions of absolute reality; even larks and katydids are supposed, by some, to dream. Hill House, not sane, stood by itself against its hills, hold-ing darkness within; it had stood for eighty years and might stand for eighty more. Within, walls continued upright, bricks met neatly, floors were firm, and doors were sensibly shut; silence lay steadily against the wood and stone of Hill House, and whatever walked there, walked alone. (Jackson 1959: 3)

While we are left in no doubt from the outset that Hill House is most definitely what Stephen King would later characterise as a 'Bad Place' (King 2012: 296) – he would expand upon many of the ideas found in Jackson in *Salem's Lot* (1975) and *The Shining* (1977) – what is most compelling and heartbreaking about the novel is the way in which the house appears to manipulate its most vulnerable resident, Eleanor Vance. As a single woman in her early thirties, Eleanor is, by the standards of her time, an unwanted spinster, and her claustrophobic emotional neediness is vividly conveyed. She comes to Hill House as one of a small group of paranormal investigators trying to determine whether or not it is truly a haunted house. As the novel progresses, it becomes increasingly difficult both for the reader and her fellow investigators to determine whether the 'haunting' is caused by Eleanor or by the house, with which she has become increasingly and dangerously infatuated.

Richard Matheson would use the same basic premise as Jackson in his gleefully lurid 1971 novel *Hell House*, which also focuses upon a small group of investigators setting out to explore a notorious New England mansion. However, the tone, execution and conclusion of the two novels could not be more different. In contrast to Jackson's low key atmospherics, *Hell House*, though tremendously readable, features graphic depictions of murder and sexual violence. As such it provides an important, if often overlooked, indication of the way in which the supernatural would later be deployed by authors such as William Peter Blatty, Stephen King and Peter Straub.

The supernatural tale of terror was also lent a new-found sense of psychological realism and symbolic complexity in the short fiction of British author Robert Aickman. Like Jackson, he had a strong interest in the uncanny possibilities of psychosexual repression. In collections such as *Dark Entries: Curious and Macabre Ghost Stories* (1964) and *Sub Rosa: Strange Tales* (1968), Aickman re-invented the traditional English ghost story by imbuing his fiction with richly symbolic landscapes and thematic resonances that highlighted his familiarity with contemporary Freudian and Jungian thought.

Between the mid-1930s and the early 1970s, however, British horror fiction in the more obviously commercial sense was dominated by the novels of Dennis Wheatley. His oeuvre included bestselling tales of black magic and the occult such as *The Devil Rides Out* (1933), *The Haunting of Toby Jugg* (1948) and *To the Devil, A Daughter* (1953), as well as countless other horror novels and thrillers and a typically idiosyncratic 'non-fiction' guide to the occult, *The Devil and All His Works* (1971). Wheatley's interest in the occult was also present in the work of John Blackburn, another significant British author of the period. Blackburn's novels include *A Scent of New Mown Hay* (1958), which combined Cold War tensions with a hideous fungus-related plague, *For Fear of Little Men* (1972), which is about the revival of a pagan cult, and *Our Lady of Pain* (1974), a modern-day take on the legend of the 'vampire countess' Elisabeth Bathory.

Whereas Wheatley's fiction tended to have the devil's acolytes face off against morally upstanding aristocratic gentlemen in exotic or stately locales, on the other side of the Atlantic, in the work of authors such as Ray Russell, Ira Levin, and Charles Beaumont, the Prince of Darkness and his acolytes were more likely to show themselves in decidedly mundane settings. In Beaumont's 1953 story 'The New People', for instance, a family who have just moved to a seemingly welcoming suburb soon discover that the neighbours have started their own coven as a means of combatting middle-class ennui. Though the clergy do not feature in Beaumont's tale, in Russell's *The Case against Satan* (1962) an alcoholic priest battles to save the soul of a wayward teenage girl who appears to

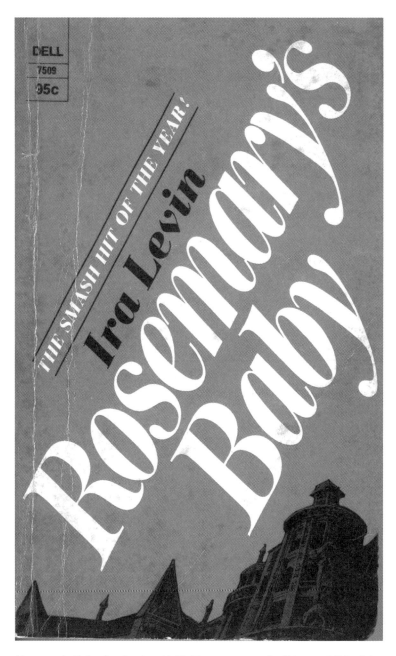

Rosemary's Baby, Ira Levin, 1967. Front cover of edition published by Dell, 1968.

have been possessed by the devil. The premise, of course, anticipated that of Blatty's *The Exorcist* (1971) by almost a decade. Russell also deserves a mention for his baroque, stylish short fiction, written somewhat in the style of Edgar Allan Poe. Recent reprints of his most significant work by Penguin suggest that his undeservedly obscure place in the post-war horror writer's pantheon, like that of John Blackburn, whose novels have recently been reprinted by Valancourt Books, is in the process of being re-evaluated.

Writing of the increasing prominence of Satanic themes in popular culture more generally during that period, W. Scott Poole observes that it was part of the 'Spiritual Warfare' (2009: 161) trope that would be revived as part of the emerging culture wars. As he puts it, 'in *Rosemary's Baby*, *The Exorcist*, and *The Omen*, the devil took over the American box office' (161). Before Satan became a staple of the big screen, however, there was Ira Levin's 1967 novel *Rosemary's Baby*. Levin began his career as a writer for television and was also a very successful playwright, his theatrical hits including *Death Trap* (1977). He had already published one genre novel in which a trusting young woman discovers that her man is up to no good (his 1952 thriller *A Kiss before Dying)*, and would reprise the same theme, this time in a suburban setting, in *The Stepford Wives* (1972).

Though much overshadowed by Polanski's acclaimed 1968 film adaptation, *Rosemary's Baby* helped to create the climate in which, in the next decade, mass-market horror fiction would begin to take off. Its protagonist is a young woman named Rosemary Woodhouse, a lapsed Catholic from the Midwest who has just moved into an extremely desirable New York apartment building, the Bramford, with her husband Guy, an actor teetering on the verge of his big break. After discovering that she is pregnant, she gradually becomes convinced that the meddlesome older couple in the apartment adjoining her own, Roman and Minnie Castevet, are involved in a conspiracy to harm her unborn child. Levin's novel works because, from the very beginning, he grounds Rosemary's paranoia-inducing predicament in the solid details of everyday life. In a technique also employed by Stephen King and many others belonging to the next generation of horror writers, Levin repeatedly mentions real people, actual locations, real events (Rosemary regrets missing the Pope's 1966 visit to New York, for instance) and media stories (such as the famous issue of *Time* headlined 'Is God Dead?', which Rosemary glimpses in her obstetrician's waiting room). The narrative is also lent an extra sense of urgency by frequent reminders of the date, and by the progress of Rosemary's horrendously unpleasant pregnancy.

The novel also establishes the personalities of Rosemary and the people around her in such an effectively economical way that, when the final, outlandish revelations begin to emerge, they seem entirely in line with what we have seen of these characters so far. For instance Guy's self-regard and seething professional ambition, established early on, play a crucial role in the coven's plot. Levin's Satanists are nothing like the evil sorcerers who often featured in Wheatley, or even the bile-spewing demon in *The Exorcist*. They are much closer to home than that. Indeed, throughout the novel, Rosemary's domestic space is repeatedly violated, both literally and metaphorically. Yet, even in the closing pages of the novel, this rickety crew of true believers, who have been waiting decades for the right womb to come along so they can inaugurate 'The Year One', would seem more pathetic than menacing, were it not for their monstrous ill-treatment of Rosemary – which gradually results in the loss of her physical, psychological and maternal agency.

The novel's final scene, in which Rosemary finally gets to meet her son, showcases Levin's unrivalled ability to combine horror, poignancy and mordant black wit. The Antichrist not only 'has His Father's eyes' (Levin 1967: 220), but the cutest little claws. At this point, like Rosemary, we finally realise why one of his elderly disciples was so intent on knitting booties 'shaped all wrong' (Levin 1967: 154). As Roman says, 'they're very tiny and pearly. The mitts are only so that He doesn't scratch Himself, not because His hands aren't attractive' (Levin 1967: 227). Little wonder, perhaps, that mother love conquers Rosemary's initial desire to rid the world of the 'God-knows-what' (222) to which she has unwittingly given birth.

The Evil Child Trope in Post-War Horror Fiction

As well as situating the coming of the Antichrist in late 1960s Manhattan, *Rosemary's Baby* was notable for helping to underline further one of post-war horror fiction's most pervasive themes: that of the evil, possessed, mutated or 'alien' child. Levin's depiction of an expectant mother-to-be who begins to suspect that something is terribly wrong with her unborn child tapped into particularly resonant anxieties about a woman's right to control her own body. As Skal notes, the contraceptive pill had been introduced in the US in 1960, heralding the beginning of the so-called 'sexual revolution' (1993: 288). Only two years later came the revelation that Thalidomide, a supposedly 'safe' sleeping pill often prescribed to pregnant women as a remedy for nausea, had caused thousands of miscarriages and absolutely horrific defects in many of the babies who survived until birth. The US Supreme Court decision legally to sanction abortion was also made in 1973. It was perhaps not surprising that a particularly timely depiction of a young mother, impregnated against her will with a foetus who eventually turns out to be something much more than human, struck such a chord.

Having said that, as early as 1942 Ray Bradbury had dealt with similar themes in his 'The Small Assassin'. In this story Alice, an anxious and paranoid mother-to-be, tries to convince her sceptical husband that she is in danger of being murdered by her unborn child. After all, she reasons, 'a baby is so new, so amoral, so conscience free' (Bradbury 1987: 11). Sure enough, not long after the baby's exceptionally difficult birth, Alice is found dead at the bottom of the stairs, and her husband begins to suspect that she may have been on to something after all. What if, he reasons, 'one child in a billion is – strange?' (22). And what if that child bitterly resented being torn away from the warmth and security of the womb and was determined to punish its parents?

The mutant child also takes centre stage in Richard Matheson's first published story, 'Born of Man and Woman' (1950), which is told from the poignant perspective of a deformed, green-blooded child who has been chained in a basement by its abusive parents since birth. Similar themes were explored in Judith Merril's 'That Only a Mother' (1948), which explores the relationship between a mother and her little girl. The daughter has been irrevocably damaged by nuclear radiation, her appearance symptomatic of a wider epidemic of birth defects (and an accompanying one of infanticide). Even more unnerving was the monstrously precious youngster featured in Jerome Bixby's 'It's a *Good Life*' (1953). Little Anthony Fremont has both a 'wet, purple gaze' and god-like powers that he freely exerts over the few family members and neighbours who have so far survived his reign over the small town of Peaksville (population 46, and dropping fast).

Although he is certainly no mutant, Robert, the little boy who is warped and abused by his monstrous mother in Charles Beaumont's 1957 story 'Miss Gentilbelle', like Matheson's tragically mistreated child, also eventually lashes out violently against those who have harmed him. What all of these children have in common is that they have been rendered 'monstrous' – either psychologically or physically – in a way that suggests that their behaviour is symptomatic of something very wrong in the world around them. Society at large, and the family unit itself, has helped to create these little monsters, and now it must pay the price.

The most famous evil child to come out of 1950s America was another eerily advanced aberration whose chilling behaviour is the result of biological destiny rather than radioactivity, family dysfunction or abuse. Like many of the most significant evil-child narratives, William March's 1954 novel *The Bad Seed*, which also spawned a play

The Bad Seed, still from film version, 1956. Warner Bros./Kobal collection.

and two film adaptations, focuses on the dilemma that faces a mother when she finally admits to herself that her child is deeply and irrevocably *wrong*. Much of the novel is told from the perspective of budding psychopath Rhoda Penmark's mother Christine, a cultured and gentle woman who is left alone with her eerily mature daughter while her husband is off at sea. Although Rhoda has always been extremely popular with adults who fall for her perfect-little-girl shtick – such as the Penmark's neighbour, bustling amateur psychoanalyst Mrs Breedlove – other children have always feared and disliked her. Following the suspicious death of a classmate who was awarded the penmanship medal Rhoda fiercely coveted, Christine finally begins to admit to herself that Rhoda is not, and indeed has never been, 'normal'. In the book's major (and completely unscientific) twist, it is revealed that Christine is in fact the daughter of a notorious female serial killer, Bessie Denker. Grandma's psychopathic inclinations have skipped a generation, resurfacing in full force in her pigtail-sporting grandchild. Like Rosemary Woodhouse, Christine must then decide what to do about the child that she simultaneously loves and fears more than anyone else in the world.

Another notably disturbing novel published the same year as *The Bad Seed* also focuses on the potential for evil contained within the suggestive figure of the child. William Golding's *Lord of the Flies* (1954) depicted the rapid descent of well-bred English public schoolboys into primitivism while marooned on a desert island. In an interesting indication of the more contemporary resonances of the novel, the boys' plane crashes while they are being evacuated during a nuclear conflict. Golding's schoolboys ultimately come to embody the universal battle between savagery and (supposed) civilisation: revealingly, some of the boys take much more easily to sadism, cruelty and even murder, than do their more principled peers.

In another classic British novel from the same era, science fiction author John Wyndham's *The Midwich Cuckoos* (1957), the adults who populate a previously idyllic rural village find themselves decidedly outmatched by alien offspring. The 'cuckoos' of the title appear to be superior to their human 'parents' in every conceivable way, due to their accelerated growth and hive-mind intelligence. As in several of the narratives just cited, Wyndham's hybrid interlopers take every advantage of the fact that their adult antagonists find it almost unthinkable to consider harming a child.

The substantial cultural impact of Blatty's seminal possessed-child novel *The Exorcist* meant that many of the tropes mentioned in this section would be resurrected over and over again during the 1970s horror boom. Blatty's depiction of a sweet-natured, innocent young girl who is ravaged by the demonic forces that possess her still retains the power to shock. Even the assumed re-imposition of order by the end of the novel does not erase the fact that the perfect daughter had been, albeit briefly, transformed into the perfect parental nightmare. However, by far the most horrific 'evil child' novel of the early 1970s is

Let's Go Play at the Adams', Mendal Johnson, 1974. Front cover of edition published by Panther Books, 1976.

one so disturbing that, unlike Blatty's bestseller, it has never made it to the big screen; indeed it has yet to be reprinted and remains something of a cult read. Mendal Johnson's *Let's Go Play at the Adams'* (1974) is loosely based upon the real-life case of Indiana teenager Sylvia Likens, who was horrifically abused and then murdered by her foster mother and a group of neighbourhood boys in 1965 (the story also inspired Jack Ketchum's 1989 suburban horror novel *The Girl Next Door*, as well as feminist writer Kate Millett's 1979 study *The Basement: Meditations on a Human Sacrifice*). Johnson's work was initially promoted as a Nixon-era variation on *Lord of the Flies* and *The Exorcist*.

When Barbara, a pretty, ultra-respectable and excessively *nice* babysitter (not long an adult herself) is chloroformed and tied to a bed by her young charges and a couple of their older friends, it all seems like a wearying, but silly prank that will soon lose its appeal. What happens, in fact, is that her captors, who call themselves 'The Freedom Five', discover that once they have violated this initial rule, anything is possible: '[a]ll right, here they were, out in the open, breaking the law between children and adults, and nothing was happening. They ignored the taboo, and no lightning fell' (1974: 32).

Johnson's sinister youngsters are not mentally ill; nor are they radio-active mutants, possessed by evil spirits or the offspring of alien invaders. They are, apart from their crime, supposed to be resolutely *ordinary*: well-spoken, well-educated, upper-middle-class kids who, to the adults around them, epitomise the very flower of American youth. Yet they are also profoundly, and mysteriously, *empty*, and the horrific 'game' they play with their increasingly resigned captive is a vivid expression of that chilling moral vacuum.

In a world that appears to have no meaning, clinically torturing an entirely innocent young woman who seems to epitomise goodness may be their crude way of seeking genuine emotional catharsis or deeper philosophical significance in life. However, it is also made terribly clear that Barbara's captivity presents them with an opportunity to wield the ultimate power over a representative of the adult world. *Let's Go Play at the Adams'* therefore foreshadows films such as *Funny Games* (Michael Haneke, 1997), *Goodnight Mommy / Ich Seh, Ich Seh* (Veronika Franz and Severin Fiala, 2014) and, in particular, Lionel Shriver's controversial bestseller *We Need to Talk About Kevin* (2003). Despite its current obscurity, Johnson's first and only published novel remains the most profoundly unsettling depiction of the post-war 'Generation Gap' in American horror fiction.

The Rise of the Psycho Killer

The turn towards horrors of an everyday and human nature that characterised post-war horror fiction meant that, from the late 1940s onwards, the genre often featured protagonists whose disturbing behaviour was the result of psychological aberration. The use of mental illness as a plot device was, first of all, an indication of the move away from overtly supernatural plot elements during the period: reflecting a tendency already present from Henry James's *The Turn of the Screw* (1898) onwards, it would become increasingly difficult to distinguish between what was 'real' and what was taking place in the protagonist's head.

However, such a trend also reflected the fact that attitudes towards mental illness had undergone a decisive shift in the post-war era. Thanks to increasing cultural awareness of psychoanalysis, as well as the arrival of a revolutionary new class of neuroleptic drugs, which facilitated the release of psychiatric patients who would, in previous years, have been deemed absolutely 'incurable,' so-called 'insanity' was no longer seen as a life-long affliction. The late 1940s also saw a spate of extremely high-profile scandals surrounding the overcrowded, underfunded and understaffed state asylum system. Alfred Deutsch's *The Shame of the States* (1948) and various newspaper and magazine exposés compared the conditions in some state institutions to those found in Nazi concentration camps, and did much to make the way in which the mentally ill were treated a national issue. In 1959 readers would have understood exactly where Norman Bates was coming from when he declares that he would never send his mother to one of those 'awful holes' (Bloch 1959: 38). Combined with Norman's obvious familiarity with pop psychology, it suggests that his inability to recognise that he is himself seriously unwell may be partially due to the fact that he cannot countenance institutionalisation.

Bloch was by no means the only horror writer of the period to replace the supernatural with the psychological as a source of terror, although, as we shall see, he was one of the most significant. Richard Matheson's short fiction displayed a recurrent concern with mental breakdown, usually that of a put-upon white-collar male for whom the American dream has been transformed into the stuff of nightmares; indeed, it displays a recurrent preoccupation with 'paranoia, alienation and estrangement' (Jancovich 1996: 141). Representative of this tendency was his 1953 story 'Legion of Plotters', in which the easily irritated protagonist comes to believe that the numerous petty annoyances of ordinary life are part of a conspiracy designed to drive him insane. He ultimately embarks upon a murderous rampage that anticipates the now tragically common phenomenon of spree-killings.

Another narrator whose sanity is in doubt from the start can be found in one of Matheson's most famous stories, 'Nightmare at 20,000 feet' (1961). In the story, a chronically nervous airplane passenger thinks that he can see a hideous creature scuttling along the wing, but cannot convince anyone else to believe him. Matheson also contributed to the then ever-expanding number of stories about multiple personality disorder in his 1969 story 'Therese', as did Shirley Jackson in her 1954 novel *The Bird's Nest*. Furthermore, a supposedly 'real-life' case of multiple personality disorder was also dramatised in the bestselling psychiatric case study *The Three Faces of Eve* (1957) by Corbett H. Thigpen and Hervey M. Cleckley; it was soon adapted for the screen.

From the early 1950s onwards Jackson's novels and short stories consistently depict troubled young women whose chronic inability to 'fit in' manifests itself in a wide range of psychological and emotional symptoms. This tendency reached its apotheosis in her final finished novel, *We Have Always Lived in the Castle*, in which one of the main characters is a psychotic mass-murderer.

Charles Beaumont, a gifted novelist, screenwriter and short story writer, never quite achieved the same public profile as his contemporaries due to his early death, but he also had a knack for writing stories of psychological breakdown and outright madness. As well as 'Miss Gentilbelle', stories such as 'The Hunger' (1955), 'Dark Music' (1956) and 'Fair Lady' (1957) all feature isolated and disturbed female protagonists for whom the consolations of fantasy have erased the lines between reality and imagination. The 2013 Valancourt Books reprint

Psycho, still from film version, showing Anthony Perkins as Norman Bates, 1960. Kobal collection/Paramount.

of Beaumont's most acclaimed collection, *The Hunger and Other Stories*, as well as the recent publication of his selected stories in the Penguin Classics anthology *Perchance to Dream* (2016), indicate that this important author's reputation is on the brink of a well-deserved reappraisal.

The most notable chronicler of the disturbed mind in American horror fiction during this period was, as noted earlier, Robert Bloch. In his typically lurid 1957 potboiler *Psycho* he helped to establish the 'deranged, mother-fixated serial killer' template that would shape the psychological thriller (which now so often overlaps with the horror novel) for decades to come. Bloch had been preoccupied with unstable identities and murderous impulses since the very beginning of his career. Starting out as a writer of Lovecraft-inspired weird fiction, he soon discovered his true métier. In his 1943 story 'Yours Truly, Jack the Ripper', a young man's search for the murderer of his mother climaxes with the revelation that the legendary killer has transcended time and continued his activities in the present day. Another work, 'Lucy Comes to Stay' (1952), anticipates the final revelations of *Psycho*, while an earlier novel, *The Scarf* (1947), features a protagonist who has an unshakable compulsion to murder young women with the eponymous accessory – thanks in part to the mother-issues resulting from his inappropriate boyhood relationship with a much older woman.

The apotheosis of Bloch's career-long fascination with split personalities and compulsively murderous behaviour was, of course, *Psycho*. *Psycho* was important because it represented the first and most influential fictionalisation of a true-crime case that rapidly came to be considered one of the decade's most lurid and upsetting true crimes. As has been well documented, Ed Gein had been, up until November 1957, considered an eccentric but completely harmless local character in the small rural community of Plainfield, Wisconsin. At least, that was the case until Bernice Worden went missing and blood was found on the floor of her hardware store. It was soon discovered that the last customer she had served was none other than Ed and so, justifiably suspicious, local law enforcement officers headed for Gein's farm. They discovered that not only had Gein shot and killed Worden, but that he had strung her headless body up like a deer carcass. What is more, his squalid house was full of spectacularly macabre relics crafted from the female corpses he had been stealing from local cemeteries for years, as well as body parts from a then unknown number of female murder victims.

Gein's alleged cannibalism, necrophilia and desire to make himself 'a woman suit' from human skin would have a seminal impact upon the development of American horror in the decades to come. Here was a man who had, like Ray Bradbury's 'Handler', lived undetected in the kind of place that was supposed to epitomise the 'real' America. As Bloch later put it, '[w]hat interested me was the notion that a ghoulish killer with perverted appetites could flourish almost openly in a small rural community where everyone prides himself [*sic*] on knowing everyone else's business' (Bloch, in Schechter 2008: 556).

In loosely adapting elements of the Gein case for his novel, Bloch made many significant changes. The most notable was that in this version of the story the Gein figure, Norman Bates, runs a small, out-of-the-way motel. The reason for the change was simple: Bloch knew that a motel manager would have easier access to victims than a farmer. For those who have only seen Hitchcock's 1960 film adaptation, the version of Norman Bates depicted in the source text may come as something of a surprise. Bloch's Norman is a seedy, alcoholic 40-year-old, very unlike the clean-cut, personable young man played by Anthony Perkins. Hitchcock may have started his film with Marion's impulsive theft of 40,000 dollars, but in the original version Norman's distorted, compulsive perspective takes centre stage from the first page. He is a profoundly repressed, self-pitying mother's boy who prefers reading true-life accounts of Incan torture rituals to engaging with the outside world. His life is in a decades-long state of arrested development, and he is completely incapable of coping with the reality of his own sexual impulses and severe mental illness. Now that they have moved away from the highway, he does not even have the distraction of work to keep his mind in check. Norman may not consciously be aware of what 'mother' is doing during his alcoholic blackouts, but the fact that he is unable to look at himself in the mirror does suggest that he recognises his personality is a profoundly unstable one. He even ponders whether he might have some form of mild schizophrenia.

It is clear that, like several of the other fictional characters referenced in this chapter (among them Robert Neville in *I Am Legend* and Monica Breedlove in *The Bad Seed*), Norman has been keeping up with current developments in psychiatry (Bloch 1959: 57). Although the novel's central twist has been referenced and imitated so many times that it is no longer remotely surprising, it remains a seminal point in twentieth-century horror fiction. Bloch established the blueprint that almost every other 'psycho killer' horror novel would either have to imitate or better (it is obviously no coincidence that the deranged narrator of the 1990 novel *American Psycho* is named Patrick *Bate*man). By the end of the 1950s, therefore, psychological instability had become firmly established as one of the major thematic concerns of American horror fiction. Fittingly, Bloch let nascent 'Final Girl' Lila Crane sum up one of his novel's most unsettling conclusions: '[w]e're all not quite as sane as we pretend to be' (1959: 125).

As well as forming the basis for the hugely successful film adaptation, Bloch's novel (and the Gein case itself), helped to inspire two of American horror cinema's most important films: *The Texas Chain Saw Massacre* (Tobe Hooper, 1974) and *The Silence of the Lambs* (Jonathan Demme, 1991). It is worth briefly mentioning that Thomas Harris's 1988 novel – which, along with his previous effort *Red Dragon* (1984), combined the Bloch-style deranged killer story with the police procedural – was also indebted to John Fowles's 1963 debut *The Collector*. *The Collector* contains two elements that would make their way into *The Silence of the Lambs*. The first is the idea of a deluded fantasist who decides to kidnap a young woman and keep her prisoner in his homemade 'dungeon' (although *The Collector*'s *nouveau riche* monster Fred Clegg claims that he wants to convince his captive to fall in love with him, not to murder her). The second lies in the villain's obsession with winged insects and the thematic resonances associated with the idea of 'collecting', and therefore with killing something that one finds 'beautiful'. Although butterflies feature in Fowles, it is famously the 'death's head moth' that plays a crucial role in Harris.

While Fowles's status as a 'literary' rather than a genre author means that the novel is seldom considered within the context of the horror genre, *The Collector*, like *Psycho*, played its part in ensuring that the most significant horror icon of the past 40 years would be what is often crudely called the 'psycho killer'. This tendency, as we have seen, was already present in short horror fiction from the late 1940s onwards. It accelerated appreciably from the late 1970s onwards, however, once the concept of the 'serial killer' entered the mainstream cultural consciousness. Harris helped to make the hybrid police procedural/Gothic horror novel one of the major forms of popular fiction in the late twentieth and early twenty-first centuries.

As will be outlined in the next chapter, the unprecedented surge in popularity experienced by the horror genre from the early 1970s onwards was particularly influenced by the work of American authors producing novels, short stories, screenplays and teleplays from the mid-1940s onwards. Stephen King, the most notable beneficiary of the boom and still the most famous horror writer in the world, has noted on many occasions the debt that he owes to writers such as Jackson, Bloch, Matheson and Bradbury. And in his immensely readable 1981 survey of the genre, *Danse Macabre*, King pays lengthy homage to his predecessors.

Horror fiction began to enter the literary and publishing mainstream during the post-war era because it had increasingly begun to reflect the myriad anxieties found in everyday life. Authors such as King, Barker, Campbell, Straub, Herbert, Blatty, Ketchum, Thomas Tryon, Joan Samson, Kathe Koja and many others would build upon this tendency in ways that added further depth, sophistication, frank sexuality and outright gore to the genre. They would do this by variously utilising the four major characteristics of the genre, as established a generation earlier. These are, as we have seen: a tendency to deal with horrors arising from the conditions of everyday life; an accompanying preference for mundane, contemporary settings; a movement away from the supernatural and towards the depiction of aberrant psychology as a source of terror (as epitomised by the soon-to-become iconic figure of the serial killer Hannibal Lecter); and a tendency to depict the supernatural in a much more 'grounded', naturalistic manner. When Tom Neville, the protagonist of *A Stir of Echoes*, despairingly wondered whether '[m]aybe we're all monsters underneath' (Matheson 1958: 39), he was doing more than simply highlighting the novel's most resonant theme. Neville was asking a question that would inform horror fiction for decades to come.

References:

Bloch, Robert, 'The Shambles of Ed Gein', in *True Crime: An American Anthology,* ed. by Harold Schechter (New York: The Library of America, 2008), pp. 549–56.

——, *Psycho* (London: Corgi, 1959).

Bradbury, Ray, *The Small Assassin* (London: Grafton Books, 1987).

Carson, Rachel, *Silent Spring* (Boston, MA: Houghton Mifflin, 1962).

Dziemianowicz, Stefan, 'Contemporary Horror Fiction 1950–1998,' in *Fantasy and Horror*, ed. by Neil Barron (Lanham, MD: Scarecrow Press, 1999).

Jackson, Shirley, *The Haunting of Hill House* (New York: Penguin, 1959).

Jancovich, Mark, *Rational Fears: American Horror in the 1950s* (Manchester: Manchester University Press, 1996).

Johnson, Mendal, *Let's Go Play at the Adams'* (London: Panther, 1974).

King, Stephen, *Danse Macabre* (London and New York: Hodder, 2012).

Levin, Ira, *Rosemary's Baby* (London: Corsair, 1967).

Matheson, Richard, *I Am Legend* (London: Millennium, 1954).

——, *A Stir of Echoes* (London: Boxtree, 1958).

Poole, W. Scott, *Satan in America: The Devil We Know* (Lanham, MD: Rowman and Littlefield, 2009).

Punter, David, *The Literature of Terror: A History of Gothic Fictions from 1765 to the Present Day, Volume 2: The Modern Gothic* (London: Longman, 1996).

Rigby, Jonathan, *American Gothic: Sixty Years of Horror Cinema* (London: Reynolds and Hearn, 2007).

Skal, David J., *The Monster Show: A Cultural History of Horror* (London: Plexus, 1993).

What to Read Next:

Robert Bloch, *Psycho* (1959; London: Robert Hale Ltd., 2013).

Shirley Jackson, *The Haunting of Hill House* (1959; London and New York: Penguin, 2009).

Ira Levin, *Rosemary's Baby* (1967; London: Corsair, 2011).

Richard Matheson, *I Am Legend* (1954; London: Gollancz, 2010).

Robert Aickman, *Dark Entries* (1964; London: Faber and Faber, 2014).

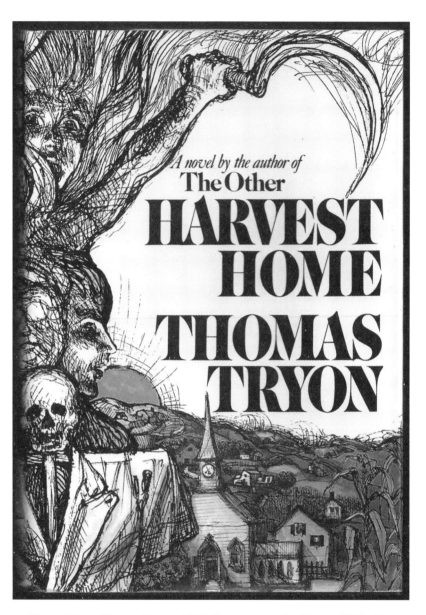

Harvest Home, Thomas Tryon, 1973. Front cover of edition published by Alfred Knopf, 1973.

Chapter 6

The Rise of Popular Horror, 1971–2000

Steffen Hantke

STARTING IN THE EARLY 1970s, horror fiction began to experience a boom that would last throughout the following decade and remain, to the present day, unrivalled in the genre's history. During this boom, horror would command its own ever-expanding section in bookshops, edging out fantasy and science fiction in volume, though perhaps less so in variety. Time and again, horror appeared at the top of the *New York Times* bestseller list. In fact, as was mentioned in the previous chapter, there had been a few previous runaway bestsellers, such as Ira Levin's *Rosemary's Baby* (1967), Tom Tryon's *The Other* (1971) and William Peter Blatty's *The Exorcist* (1971). These novels about Satan reborn, evil twins and demonic possession would convince the publishing industry that there was money to be made if only horror writers could be elevated to the status of stars. A decade later, the industry had accomplished precisely this with Stephen King, Peter Straub, Dean Koontz and Anne Rice, who deserves special credit as the single yet formidable female presence in an otherwise all-male canonical group. As the tide rising around these bestselling juggernauts began to lift a fleet of smaller boats around them, a vast array of mid-list writers saw their work accepted, advertised and published with unusual alacrity and enthusiasm. Writers who had worked in other genres were encouraged to switch to horror, while even books with arguable genre credentials would be packaged and marketed as horror. Commercially horror did well, commanding a mass audience.

But then, as the inevitable logic of boom and bust would have it, the genre started to slump. Readers grew weary with the recycling of the same old tropes, the increasingly worn-out promise of chills and thrills. Indulged by a generous audience, horror fiction had overstayed its welcome. Scores of derivative, second-rate hacks took down with them the talented, idiosyncratic and innovative writers who had never made the A-list. Sales dropped. Publishers cancelled imprints. Many abandoned the sinking ship and switched to more lucrative genres. The brand name writers survived, some of them are still going strong today, but the mid-list shrank.

A few internal permutations later, from garishly brute splatterpunk to self-consciously experimental horror, the genre had lost its grip on the market. Where once rows and rows of horror shelves had been, bookshops brought in thrillers, fantasy and science fiction. Horror would still be around, would linger and last – but as a clearly defined presence in the marketplace, it had vanished. And yet, in its commercial implosion, horror had passed on creative impulses to other genres. Detective fiction and police procedurals, for example, would never be the same again. Romance writers had tuned in to the enduring appeal of slightly darker, more brooding, more dangerous strangers. And here and there even mainstream fiction had tasted blood. With a mournful lament for the bright, creative work produced during this cycle of boom and bust, this chapter looks at the best and the brightest in horror fiction during the long 1980s.

Preparing the Way: Horror in the 1970s

Any search for a climate friendly to horror might begin with the tremors, instabilities, fractures and anxieties that run through a culture as it tunes in to imaginary monsters. Although every decade has its dark side, and is thus open to a grim, pessimistic reading, the 1970s provided a particularly rich array of things for Americans to worry about. By the turn of the decade the progressive, even utopian hopes of the 1960s had imploded. The implosion had left the countercultural cultivation of the self stripped of its socially conscious and beneficial components. In the public imagination the horror at Altamont had replaced the idyll at Woodstock, the sinister cult of the Manson Family had edged out the hippies that made up Ken Kesey's Merry Pranksters and White Flight had turned American cities into rigidly divided and tightly policed exclusionary zones. A disintegrating Nixon presidency would leave in its wake a climate of paranoia, just as the Vietnam War, after a series of increasingly horrid escalations, would leave God's own country with a lasting hangover. After a brief period with well-intentioned, bumbling Gerald Ford in the Oval Office, the nation would enter a decade of stag-flation under Jimmy Carter, exacerbated by the OPEC oil embargo and rising tensions in the Middle East. When Carter, in his famous 'malaise speech' in 1979, diagnosed the nation's current crisis of confidence, he effectively handed over the presidency to Ronald Reagan a year later – reason enough to think that a turning point had been reached.

Reagan's 'It's morning in America' campaign appeared to drain the swamp of 1970s malaise. What better antidote to bleakness than the new president's blend of patriotic sentimentality and conservative, Hollywood-infused nostalgia? Here was an optimistic nation regaining its footing; it was forward looking and confident – and yet horror boomed. Turning away from the vague sense of dread that had been its bread and butter during the preceding decade, 1980s horror would be driven by a desire to uncover the dark underbelly of this new self-confidence, to diagnose a stridency bordering on hysteria in the tone the nation would adopt in talking to itself and the rest of the world. Horror fiction would keep a close watch on the price that had to be paid in exchange for Reagan's neoliberal makeover – a price measured in 'greed and economic mate-rialism, military waste and jingoistic belligerence, growing inequality, a lack of concern for the poor, and a rolling back of gains for the rights of minorities and women' (Cannato 2009: 71). As much as 1980s America was telling itself that things were looking up, all was not well. Not by coincidence did the American small town, the epitome of the conserva-tive vision of the nation, become the prime setting for 1980s horror fic-tion: a sunny, cheerful place of white picket fences and apple pie where something would always be really, really wrong.

Against this historical background, the publishing market under-
went a change that was to prove fortuitous to horror as well. Ringing
in the 1980s horror fiction boom was a series of massive bestsellers
that appeared during the late 1960s and 1970s. These novels alerted
the publishing industry, not to mention a large mainstream audience,
to the potential and the pleasures of horror. One crucial aspect of this
transition of horror to the mainstream was the new prominence that
the novel was to enjoy within the genre. Of course, there have always
been successful horror novels; when horror began to define itself as a
distinct genre, it had notable novels such as *Frankenstein* and *Dracula* to
look back on, as previous chapters in this book have shown. Pulp fiction magazines, the single major outlet for horror fiction before the
paperbacks that appeared after the Second World War, had dealt with
stories that exceeded the word count of the short story or novella by
breaking them up into chapters and serialising them. Alongside such

The Books of Blood: Volume I: The Highway, Clive Barker, 1984. Illustration
by Clive Barker. Courtesy of the Clive Barker Archive.

serialised novels, however, the format of the pulp magazine was clearly more predisposed toward the short story.

In a similar move, the newly dominant post-war medium would no longer be the cinema but television. Unlike the self-contained story told in the hour-and-a-half commonly allotted to the feature film, television would be predisposed toward the small instalment of the episode within the series. This, in turn, accommodated the length and structure of the short story more seamlessly than those of the novel. Hence the magazine market and the television industry combined to produce a generation of canonical horror writers whose medium was the short story rather than the novel. While writers such as Richard Matheson, Robert Bloch, Ray Bradbury and Charles Beaumont would occasionally stray into the territory of the cinema and the novel – in the case of Matheson, with *The Incredible Shrinking Man* (Jack Arnold, 1957) and *I Am Legend* (Ubaldo Ragona and Sidney Salkow, 1964) and of Bloch, with *Psycho* (Alfred Hitchcock, 1960) spectacularly so – their strongest work would be on television and in the form of the short story. Yet short story collections, as the publishing industry was well aware, do not a bestseller make. For decades the standard advice to aspiring horror writers would be to break into the market with a novel, then, maybe, follow it with a story collection. The only exception to this rule, so noticeable that it has been repeated in all histories of horror fiction, is the case of Clive Barker. He established a reputation in the horror field with a series of short story collections, the *Books of Blood*, long before he published his first novel. Invariably, however, bestsellers were novels and so bestselling writers must, first and foremost, be novelists. As slicks and pulps would gradually yield to the mass-market paperback, with publishers Signet, Tor, Zebra and Ballantine in the lead when it came to horror, 1970s horror fiction would take its first steps into the mainstream when writers switched from short stories to novels.

First among these bestselling horror novelists was Ira Levin with *Rosemary's Baby*, a supernatural thriller about a young woman manipulated by a satanic cult into bearing what may be the devil's child. Like Levin's *The Stepford Wives*, *Rosemary's Baby* was keenly attuned to the women's movement of the 1960s and the scepticism it had engendered toward traditionally feminine domains such as mothering and home-making. To the present day, *Rosemary's Baby* still reads as a psychologically cogent analysis of the social pressures that come with pregnancy. In the novel, pregnancy is portrayed as exactly that gruelling mental and physical ordeal about which no young mother, infused with pregnancy's mandatory sentimental glow demanded by mainstream culture, is permitted to complain. In a scene in which Rosemary imagines 'whatever-its-name-was coming inch by inch out of her' body, Levin's language cleverly undercuts the mainstream culture's insistence that Rosemary is in full control of herself and that this must surely be a 'triumphant moment' for her (1967: 148). Meanwhile the supernatural elements in *Rosemary's Baby* also link the novel to the changing religious climate of the 1960s, when the Second Vatican Council (1962–5) marked the Catholic Church's attempts at repositioning itself within a rapidly changing social environment.

If Levin's work was characterised by a smart undertone that would allow readers to dismiss the supernatural elements as packaging for the political and social satire, then William Peter Blatty's *The Exorcist* would revisit Levin's examination of late twentieth-century Catholicism with deadly seriousness. In a similar way to *Rosemary's Baby*, Blatty's novel revolves around the dichotomy of science and religion. Even today, readers of Blatty's work might be struck by how serious and unironic is its engagement with the tabloid theme of demonic possession. If there is a subtext to Blatty's novel that is handled tongue-in-cheek, it is that of the generational conflict that had been brewing since the 1960s. The transformation of the serene teenager Regan into the foul-mouthed (literally and figuratively speaking) host of the demon Pazuzu rings true for all those 1970s parents 'who felt, in a kind of agony and terror, that they were losing their children and could not understand why and how it was happening' (King 1981: 169).

To understand the 1980s boom in horror fiction, the outstanding cinematic adaptations of *Rosemary's Baby* (Roman Polanski, 1968) and *The Exorcist* (William Friedkin, 1973) serve as potent reminders of how crucial the interaction with cinema would turn out to be for the fiction market. Early in the 1970s Stephen Spielberg's blockbuster version of Peter Benchley's novel *Jaws* (1974) had demonstrated that a generously budgeted, vigorously and creatively promoted and competently directed adaptation of a cheesy 1950s 'creature feature' had the potential to break out of the ghetto of horror and reach a vast mainstream audience. One might argue that Levin, Blatty and Benchley were simply lucky to have their novels passed on to particularly competent directors; in the case of *Rosemary's Baby*, this meant that William Castle was to produce but not, as he had initially hoped, to direct the film. Nonetheless, neither Polanski nor Friedkin nor Spielberg had earned his standing in the industry at the time they made these three films. Although, given the chance, they would prove to be brilliant directors, they all posed risks for the studios entrusting them with prestigious properties. Something else was happening that energised the interaction between horror fiction and horror film, between genre and mainstream.

Enriching these interactions was the elevation of horror film by so-called 'neo-horror' films from adolescent fare to adult seriousness. The best indication of this turning-point is perhaps Roger Ebert's famous 1969 review of George Romero's *Night of the Living Dead*. In the review Ebert recounts his visit to a screening of the film attended largely by a raucous teenage audience. As the film progresses, Ebert reports that there 'wasn't a lot of screaming anymore; the place was pretty quiet' (1969). The audience was growing increasingly alarmed and, ultimately, distressed. 'I don't think the younger kids really knew what hit them', Ebert concludes, '[t]hey were used to going to movies, sure, and they'd seen some horror movies before, sure, but this was something else' (1969). Because of the graphic violence and explicit sexuality that silenced Ebert's teenage audience so efficiently, neo-horror films would never be able to compete with the likes of *Jaws* or *The Exorcist* at the box office (though given their small budgets, they would still make a profit). However, mainstream horror films would learn their lesson from neo-horror. Gore and graphic violence could be part of a new seriousness and maturity; packaged appropriately, they could elevate the horror film's profile and open it up to a larger audience. The success of films such as *Alien* (Ridley Scott, 1979), a mainstream blockbuster with neo-horror sex and gore, would prove this theory correct.

While the nexus between the mass-market bestseller and the cinema laid the commercial groundwork for horror to emerge as a dominant genre during the 1980s, it is also important to look for precursors to its emergent themes. Prime among the bestselling authors was actor-turned-author Tom Tryon with his two novels *The Other* (1971) and *Harvest Home* (1973). While Levin and Blatty had told stories about urban settings – New York City in Levin, the Georgetown section of Washington D.C. in Blatty – Tryon placed his novels in idyllic rural locations. In *The Other* the story about identical twins, one of them murderous, takes place on a farm and is set in the distant past of the 1930s, while *Harvest Home* moves the action to a small Connecticut community in thrall to a matriarchal pagan religion. Tryon's lavish prose with literary aspiration, differing sharply from the sober, pragmatic styles of Levin and Blatty, helps to tint this rural environment in a glow of such rich nostalgia that regional specificity pretty much disappears. There is a bit of stylistic overcompensation here, reminiscent of Ray Bradbury's flights of verbal fancy, but, thanks to these deft touches, rural life in Tryon has little of the hardship, monotony and claustrophobia that motivated Marx's famous dictum about the 'idiocy of rural life' (2015: 4).

Where Levin and Blatty depend on a hard-edged realism to evoke a normality then shattered by the eruption of the supernatural, Tryon's golden-tinged countryside is not the stuff of pure idealisation. When violence erupts, it destroys paradise, not normal life. Still, there is a sense even in Tryon that white flight – the massive exodus to the suburbs in the wake of the 1960s race riots, followed by the decline of American inner cities during the 1970s – came at the expense of a profound sense of disorientation among those city dwellers who found themselves out in the boonies. The black inner city of the 1970s might not be home to the white middle-class family Tryon writes about, but neither were the suburbs. The same sense of being out of place also features in Levin's *The Stepford Wives* where, just as in *Harvest Home*, it reflects white and formerly urban anxieties about the displacement to an unfamiliar environment seen as a form of social and cultural regression. In the end, the escape from the snares and slings of urban life would come with few consolations in 1970s horror fiction. In *The Stepford Wives* it is imagined as a woman's confrontation with pre-feminist knuckle-draggers; in *Harvest Home* as a man's sacrifice of his prerogatives to a functioning pre-Christian matriarchy; in *The Other* as the psychological regression of a twin boy on a remote farm.

The Height of the Boom: The 1980s

With the ground prepared by the bestselling horror novels of the 1970s, the floodgates were opened for a host of writers whose work saw publication usually in paperback originals, occasionally even in hardback. There are too many writers, and too many good ones, to discuss them all, but their names deserve honorary mention: Chet Williamson, John Saul, Dean Koontz, Robert McCammon, Richard Laymon, Brian Lumley, Whitley Strieber, John Farris, Gary Brandner, Joseph Citro, Charles L. Grant, Les Daniels, Hugh B. Cave, Guy N. Smith, Dennis Etchison, Owl Goingback, Elisabeth Massie, S. P. Somtow, Karl Edward Wagner, Robert Weinberg, Thomas Tessier, Kathryn Ptacek, Thomas Monteleone, Lisa Tuttle, William Schoell, John Tigges, William W. Johnstone, S. K. Epperson, Douglas Clegg, Rick Hautala and Ruby Jean Jensen. This is not an exhaustive list, but its length gives a clue as to the sheer scope of the horror boom. Added to the list should also be writers whose main body of work would be in other genres, but who would transition into horror while the going was good (for instance Lucius Shepard with *The Golden* in 1993 or Dan Simmons with *Song of Kali* in 1985), or whose work precedes the 1980s boom, for example Hugh B. Cave and Robert Bloch. Through reprints and anthologies, pulp writers from the 1940s and 1950s would also gain new momentum thanks to the increased commercial potential. The list also features writers whose work drew upon a sense of American regionalism, carrying on an older tradition in which horror fiction had been associating itself with the landscape and history of a particular American region or local culture. Regardless of its own geographic roots, the mainstream audience would embrace Michael McDowell's Alabama, Stephen King's Maine, Peter Straub's Wisconsin, S. K. Epperson's Kansas, Joseph Citro's Vermont and Anne Rice's Louisiana.

This close association between horror fiction and place would also manifest itself in the 1980s obsession with the American small town. Among the brand name writers, it is perhaps Stephen King whose work has remained most closely associated with what one might call 'setting as theme'. Whereas King's first novel, *Carrie* (1974), the one that brought him into the spotlight with one bucket of pig's blood,

Stephen King signing copies of *Cujo, Salem's Lot, Christine* and other titles, Truth or Consequences, New Mexico, *c.* 1976. Photo Buddy Mays/Alamy Stock Photo

was not yet as concerned with its small town setting as it was with its scorned teenage protagonist and her psychokinetic revenge on her high school bullies, his second novel set the tone for much 1980s horror fiction to come. A deft update on Bram Stoker's archetypal vampire, *Salem's Lot* (1975) would paint its eponymous Maine small town as a microcosm of American life around the time of the nation's bicentennial. At the same time, King also succeeded in creating a highly specific regional, anthropological and sociological study of the region in which he himself had grown up (in later novels, Castle Rock would serve that same function). The novel would also turn that richly detailed and generously universal description of the American small town into the foundation of what was to become King's transformation of his native Maine into a mythical realm to equal Faulkner's Yoknapatawpha

County. The creative and commercial impact of King's fictional small town would resonate through 1980s horror fiction; the cover of the Popular Library edition of Charles L. Grant's novel *The Hour of the Oxrun Dead* (1977), for example, features this advertising blurb, '[t]he most terrifying town since *Salem's Lot*. [...] Horror at its finest [...]. [G]uaranteed!', attributed to the *Hartford Courant*. If Grant were to show himself mildly annoyed with King's massive success in a roundtable discussion in 1983 (Anon. 1983), it was King who had prepared the reading audience for Grant's lighter, more lyrical, touch in handling small town settings. Many other writers were to follow suit.

There is another aspect to King's work that was to prove programmatic for the 1980s horror boom. He was swift to perfect a stylistic hyper-realism with an attention to pop cultural references, the casual use of brand names and the exploration of American slang and vernacular. To be clear, this was not an update intending to bring horror fiction out of the Gothic past and into the modern urban and technological world of the twentieth century. Pulp writers such as Charles Beaumont and Richard Matheson had already cleared the path, as the previous chapter has shown. Fritz Leiber's work alone, culminating in *Our Lady of Darkness* (1977), had infused the modern city with a sense of doom and dread (Goho 2014: 181). King's achievement was to update horror fiction *stylistically*. Casually conversational and very American, his style cuts down on the florid excesses of horror's Gothic predecessors – excesses that still plagued Tom Tryon's prose – and expands upon the journalistic terseness, often stripped of the lived-in feel and specifi-city of late twentieth-century American life, of writers from Matheson to Levin. King's prose occupies a carefully calibrated middle ground between these two extremes, and it succeeds beautifully in evoking a highly realistic Middle America. Only King's obvious pleasure in blasting this idyll apart (in 1978, in *The Stand*) he would gleefully wipe out almost all of humanity) redeems him from the charge that, in the end, his vision of the world is rather conservative, no matter if the world returns to safety at the end of his novels or not. The golden rule of his fiction has always been that the more ordinary the world appears, the more shocking its disruption.

While one might argue about the merits of King's advice to other writers, his early foray into non-fiction in the form of *Danse Macabre* (1981), as well as many of his forewords, introductions and interviews, made a cogent and sympathetic sales pitch for horror to its growing audience throughout the 1980s. King would not be the only writer commenting on the genre and the craft. Unlike the reticence of, or the lack of publishing outlets for, earlier horror writers, much horror fiction in the 1980s would be accompanied by a running commentary from its creators. Steven Jones and Kim Newman, for example, would publish *Horror: 100 Best Books* (1988), a collection of short essays introducing classic and contemporary horror fiction. The hook of having horror writers themselves pick their favourite books by other writers worked so well that a second volume, *Horror: Another 100 Best Books*, was released in 2005. As King's gregariousness rubbed off on other authors, all of them happy to explain themselves and their chosen genre to the audience, horror extended itself from a small fan community into the mainstream. In the case of, for example, *Cut: Horror Writers on Horror Film* (1992), edited by Christopher Golden, this meant that horror writers would be granted an opportunity to praise or criticise their favourite directors, while in *Dreamers: Conversations with the Masters of Horror* (1990), edited by Stanley Wiater, fans were able to conduct interviews with their favourite writers. Years later, in *On Writing: A Memoir of the Craft* (2000), King would discuss the tradition and the actual writing of horror. From critics and fans such as Golden and Wiater to established writers such as King, horror fiction was coming to terms with its sudden mainstream success.

In the hands of capable editors, anthologies would serve the same ends, introducing a new audience to the historical and stylistic range of horror fiction and rallying them around the expanding canon. By way of editorial selection, many of these collections would provide an inventory of the genre; they served to grant it legitimacy by placing pulp alongside respectable literary fiction. More than any other anthology, *Dark Forces* (1980), edited by Stephen King's first agent, Kirby McCauley, would perform this task admirably. Like the eclectic reading list at the end of King's own *Danse Macabre* and *On Writing*, McCauley's selections for *Dark Forces* brought together literary greats such as Isaac Bashevis

Singer and Joyce Carol Oates with genre writers such as Karl Edward Wagner and Charles L. Grant (both of them outstanding editors in their own right). In the introduction McCauley expressed his admiration for August Derleth's Arkham House, a small press dedicated to horror in the Lovecraftian tradition, and to Harlan Ellison's *Dangerous Visions*, famous for stretching the boundaries of its own genre, science fiction (McCauley 1980: xi–xvi). *Dark Forces* would set its sights on Derleth's canonical purity and combine it with Ellison's brash innovation. Other successful anthologies were to follow throughout the 1980s (for example, David Hartwell's *The Dark Descent* in 1987), but even as the horror genre would continue to explain itself to that mainstream audience, the terrain of the bestseller remained firmly in the hands of the novel.

Although Stephen King would publish three collections of short stories during the 1980s – *Night Shift* (1978), *Different Seasons* (1982) and *Skeleton Crew* (1985) – the reputation he had established with *Carrie*, *Salem's Lot* and *The Shining* (1977) would be cemented by a string of novels written quickly and published steadily: *The Stand* (1978), *The Dead Zone* (1979), *Firestarter* (1980), *Cujo* (1982), *Christine* (1983), *Pet Sematary* (1983), *It* (1986) and *Misery* (1987). While the first half of King's output during the 1980s continues his updating of horror tropes (*The Stand*, for example, as a massive follow-up to 1950s and 1960s post-apocalyptic survival stories, or *Cujo* as a late entry in the 1960s and 1970s cycle of 'animals-gone-berserk' novels and films), the last two novels return to King's impulse to inventory and canonise the horror genre that had been so good to him for the past decade. In its portrayal of a small town in Maine troubled by centuries of alien occupation, *It* revolves around a monster, aptly referred to with little specificity. The creature runs through a series of monstrous permutations – famously epitomised by Pennywise the clown – which summarise the archetypes of the horror genre as King had originally laid them out in *Danse Macabre*. In *Misery* (1987), this impulse to justify horror as a legitimate literary tradition is cast in a more personal framework; the novel shores up its own gruesome tale of the author held captive by an obsessive fan with a narrative of live entombment in the vernacular of the Gothic bodice ripper.

King's interest in the horror genre as a validating historical and cultural tradition is also shared by the other hugely successful, bestselling author of the 1980s, Peter Straub. Not by coincidence did the two authors collaborate on an early novel, *The Talisman* (1984), capitalising on their celebrity status. After a few lacklustre mainstream novels, Straub's first massive bestseller, *Ghost Story* (1979), anticipated King's amorphous monster in *It* by casting the creature as a female entity that presents itself, in turn, as a werewolf, a Native American nature spirit and a vampire. Straub was to follow up this success with novels that chart a more complicated course through supernatural horror, magical realism and uncanny thrillers: *Shadowland* (1980), *Floating Dragon* (1983), *Koko* (1988) and *Mystery* (1990). With King and Straub as the most visible horror writers, the long novel with epic aspirations seemed for a while to become industry standard.

King's novels tended to be massive. *It* is well over 1000 pages, while *The Stand* appeared originally in a 823-page hardcover and then, in 1990, in a complete and unabridged version with an impressive (or excessive) 1472 pages for the mass-market paperback edition. From *Ghost Story* onwards, Straub's novels would routinely cross the 500-page mark, while Robert McCammon's post-apocalyptic *Swan Song* (1987) clocks in at over 800 pages. Splitting such a long novel into discrete pieces, Michael McDowell became the first to try his hand at serial publication with the *Blackwater* series (1983), long before Stephen King embarked upon a similar experiment in 1996 with the serialised publication of *The Green Mile*. Always a steady workhorse of the genre, John Saul would eventually join in with *The Blackstone Chronicles* (1996–7). After the turn of the millennium, digital publishing would render such experiments with the mass-market paperback format obsolete.

One novel that beautifully combines that 1980s impulse to survey and inventory the genre with massive length is T. E. D. Klein's *The Ceremonies* (1984). Extrapolated from a short story, 'The Events at Poroth Farm' (1972), Klein's elaborate Lovecraftian fantasy about the calling up of the Elder Gods features a literary scholar who spends the summer at a New Jersey farm to work on a book on horror fiction. While signs of the supernatural begin to accrue around him, Klein has his readers look over the scholar's shoulder as he goes through the history of horror fiction that makes up his academic project. A former editor of *Twilight Zone Magazine* (1981–5), Klein shows off his impressive expertise in running through canonical names and titles, interspersed with brief summaries and critical commentary, to introduce less well-known, obscure and forgotten writers and books to the mainstream audience that launched *The Ceremonies* on to the *New York Times* bestseller list. Like King's *Danse Macabre*, *The Ceremonies* is both a love letter to the genre and a reading list for all the new fans-in-the-making. An exceptionally gifted writer, Klein would follow up *The Ceremonies* with a volume of remarkable stories, *Dark Gods* (1985). Unfortunately, however, his inability to produce a second novel, one he has been rumoured to have worked on for decades, would deprive the genre of one of its strongest voices.

Not by coincidence does the small town setting, which was to play such an important role in 1980s horror fiction, trace its ancestry back through a primarily female tradition – from New England regionalists such as Sarah Orne Jewett and Mary Wilkins Freeman around the turn of the century to Shirley Jackson and Grace Metalious in the 1950s. If 1980s novels about American small towns were primarily written by men, as would be much of the fiction during the boom in general, female writers would move on to other things. Among the brand-name authors, Anne Rice entered the fray with *Interview with the Vampire* (1976) before going on to dominate bestseller lists throughout the 1980s with a string of vampire novels. Carefully negotiating the boundaries between horror and, respectively, softcore erotica and historical romance, Rice substituted an immortal cast of characters for a consistent setting in order to impose coherence onto what was to develop into a growing fictional universe. The mannered sexual fluidity of her vampiric characters garnered her a devoted following with a large female and a sizeable queer component. Aside from the occasional indignant flutter on the right by which the 1980s Culture Wars would begin to announce themselves, Rice operated within relatively safe boundaries. While a later group of predominantly female authors were to push the sexual envelope past the line of softcore, Rice's own pornographic writing would tastefully be labelled 'erotica' and published separately under two pseudonyms, Anne Rampling and A. N. Roquelaure. Still, Rice was a trailblazer in standing up to the male stars of the genre and expanding the tonal and thematic range of 1980s horror.

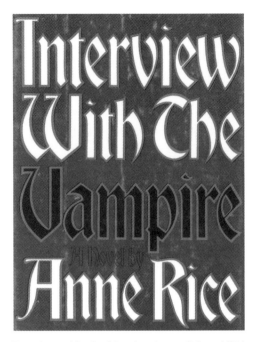

Interview with the Vampire, Anne Rice, 1976. Front cover of first edition, published by Alfred Knopf.

While the boom in horror fiction was primarily a US phenomenon, a few British writers were also to profit from the sudden popularity of their chosen genre. For one thing, political and social conditions in both countries had certain similarities, enabling British horror fiction to fit into some of the American paradigms. The US developed its own social, economic and cultural pathologies under the neoliberal regime of the Reagan administration, while in the UK the Thatcher government, which had taken the reins a year earlier, produced conditions similarly favourable to horror fiction. Starting with the early novels, Ramsey Campbell would be a keen and devoted chronicler of the urban blight afflicting his native Liverpool and the industrial north, hit hard by Thatcher's opening salvo against the coal miners' union at the start of her political tenure. Campbell affectionately reminisces about watching horror films in 'the decaying Liverpool cinemas in the midst of blitzed streets that became [his] personal gothic landscape' (Campbell 2001: 4).

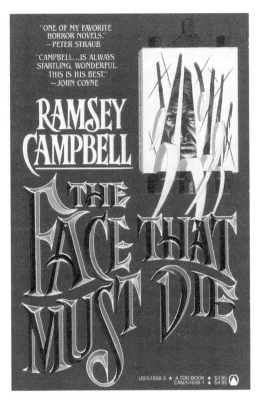

The Face That Must Die, Ramsey Campbell, 1979.
Front cover of paperback edition published by
Tor Books, 1985.

Similarly James Herbert's novels from the same period seem to place
Britain under a perpetually dark cloud, with titles such as *The Fog* (1975)
and *The Dark* (1980). While the author Shaun Hutson was to remain an
exclusively British phenomenon, and writers such as Stephen Gallagher
or Guy N. Smith would only have a minor impact on the American
audience, King's *Danse Macabre* helped Herbert and Campbell to gain a
sizeable audience in the US as well.

Praised by King for their unpretentious immediacy, James Herbert's
The Rats (1974) and *The Fog* helped to dispel popular American notions
about British horror lagging behind the times (mired, one would pre-
sume, in the genteel tradition of well-mannered ghost stories). More
stylistically demanding than Herbert, Ramsey Campbell also found

an ardent promoter in King. An early novel of Campbell's, *The Doll Who Ate His Mother* (1976), received a detailed endorsement in *Danse Macabre*, bringing its author to the attention of a US audience. After a few years' delay, another British author also entered the fray. With the *Books of Blood* (published in America in 1986), Clive Barker would bridge the gap between Campbell's more lyrical language and Herbert's blunt physical horror. Throughout the final phase of the 1980s boom, Barker served to broaden the spectrum of horror tropes toward the more exquisitely garish and grotesque – preparing the ground for what was to become known as 'splatterpunk'.

The Decline of the Late 1980s and Early 1990s

In a brief history of the Horror Writers Association (HWA), Stanley Wiater recalls that it was Robert McCammon who, in 1984, 'first publicly expressed his desire for a professional organisation specifically geared to the needs of fellow writers of fear' (1996). What was then called HOWL ('Horror/Occult Writers League') and was later to become the HWA, was duly founded in 1985. It incorporated in 1987 and a year later began handing out its own award, the Bram Stoker Award. The World Horror Convention would start in 1991. Motivated by the same mainstream success as the HWA, another professional organisation, the International Horror Critics Guild, later to rename itself the International Horror Guild, was founded in 1995. Unlike the HWA, however, this organisation appears to have been largely defunct since 2008.

The first founding of a professional association for horror writers in the mid-1980s, based on the models of crime and mystery writers as well as science fiction writers, might be seen as a sign of the genre's substantial standing in the marketplace. It might also signal the genre's arrival at a point of commercial and cultural respectability possibly at odds with horror's disreputable content of blood and guts. Mainstream success has a way of undercutting the cool of pretty much anything. For a younger generation of writers who had watched the brand name giants of King, Straub, Koontz and Rice (none of whom, incidentally, would play a major part in the HWA) dominate the bestseller lists with their bloated, lumbering tomes, the creation of a professional association may have nudged horror just a bit too far toward the corporate assembly line. Younger, edgier writers such as John Skipp and Craig Spector, who would choose the title 'On Going Too Far' as a programmatic statement for their own work, might have seen mainstream acceptance as a sign of the genre selling out. For McCammon the HWA would be a sign of horror's success; for Skipp and Spector it would foretell the genre's impending decline.

Anyone trying to read 1980s horror fiction as a cyclical story of economic boom and bust might be tempted to consider the rise of splatterpunk as an indication of exactly this dynamic. Although horror writers throughout the 1980s had been writing more graphic violence (Ray Garton, Edward Lee, Jack Ketchum and Richard Laymon come to mind), the movement would have its key texts with two collections of short stories, Skipp and Spector's *Book of the Dead* (1989) and Paul M. Sammon's *Splatterpunks: Extreme Horror* (1990). Recurring names in both collections would be Joe R. Lansdale, David Schow, Phil Nutman and the dynamic duo of Skipp and Spector themselves. As a subgenre of horror, splatterpunk seemed dedicated primarily to depictions of graphic violence and bodily injury, degradation and decay – a thematic and affective agenda that suggested to many a desperate attempt at holding on to an increasingly jaded audience by escalating the thrills of sex and violence. An editorial in the *New York Times* – the place of publication alone confirming horror's place in the cultural mainstream of the time – proposed a more objective explanation. Even though critic Ken Tucker describes splatterpunk as 'an aggressively grubby underground movement [which] now seeks to compete with more conventional horror writers like [Stephen] King, Peter Straub and Dean R. Koontz' (Tucker 1991), he goes on to qualify the process of competition and escalation in terms of media technologies as

> the print medium's latest attempt to compete with ever more sophisticated visual images and if you take comfort from nothing else about this fiction, it is a measure of print's enduring vividness and power that violence seems even more punishingly assaultive and nasty in splatterpunk than it does in other media. (Tucker 1991)

This would have suggested not so much a baroque phase of horror fiction's development, but rather a phase of radical simplification. Splatterpunk was stripping down the genre to what fans and practitioners might consider its essential qualities, much as punk sought to put an end to the lumbering dinosaurs of 1970s stadium rock with its aggressive musical austerity.

When David Schow had coined the term in 1986, he had taken the lead from the previous rise of cyberpunk in science fiction. Despite its digital euphoria, cyberpunk already pointed to the radical demystified vision of the human body that splatterpunk would articulate in the vernacular of horror. Like cyberpunk, splatterpunk was all about what William Gibson had called 'the meat' (1984: 6): the filthy, soiled, emaciated, neglected body of the hacker that remained in material space while the mind was gloriously and transcendently jacked into the matrix of digital space. The radical demotion of the human body might very well have been the point of splatterpunk, as it harnessed the genre to the questioning of the human body as a privileged object in the material hierarchy of the world. Historically speaking, this philosophical argument registers all the more at the end of the two presidential terms of Ronald Reagan. As Reagan's delimited, accelerated form of capitalism had created entire classes of dehumanised bodies – a vast army of the homeless, the drug-addicted, those left behind and maimed by the neoliberal measures of economic recovery after a decade of stagflation – splatterpunk reacted by putting these bodies and the violence done to them on gruesome display. While King, Koontz and Rice were big business, splatterpunk felt dangerous – which may or may not have been the reason why writers such as Joe R. Lansdale would change style with every novel, while others, for example Clive Barker, would reject the label altogether. Still, by bringing a fresh biopolitical perspective to horror's cosy co-existence of supernatural forces with social realism, splatterpunk effectively launched the most radical assault on American culture during the Reagan years.

However, as with the horror mainstream against which splatterpunk had ostensibly rallied itself, the movement remained largely male-dominated. Next to the few female writers (such as Poppy Z. Brite, Kathe Koja and Lucy Taylor), male writers dominated the key splatterpunk anthologies. Skipp and Spector's *Book of the Dead*, for example, failed to include a single female writer. This is not to say that male writers did not take on gender issues with 'feminist' verve. Edward Bryant's story 'While She Was Out'

(1990), for example, traces the transformation of a suburban housewife into a competent killer by way of her escape from male violence. But, as in the case of splatterpunk-inspired fiction, for instance Bret Easton Ellis's *American Psycho* (1991), a problematic preoccupation with sexualised violence specifically against female bodies remained troublesome whenever the movement sought to leak into the mainstream. It would be up to the few exceptional female writers to add thematic nuance to the movement.

Although she would favour male protagonists, Kathe Koja had a way of exploring physical vulnerability in ways that challenged the gender line. In foregoing graphic violence in favour of an uncomfortably heightened body awareness, her early novels, *The Cipher* (1991), *Bad Brains* (1992) and *Skin* (1993), are keenly attuned to the rising prominence of new tribalism, tattooing and body modification – an agenda that would find itself reflected in bands such as Nine Inch Nails and their use of photographer Joel-Peter Witkin. Katherine Dunn's *Geek Love* (1989) had already started moving the literary mainstream in the same direction. With *The Flesh Artist* (1994) and *The Safety of Unknown Cities* (1995), Lucy Taylor would invent forms of eroticism revolving around freakish, non-normative bodies in violation of strict gender norms, providing a female equivalent to similar thematic concerns in the work of a queer horror writer like Clive Barker. With Taylor working more self-consciously in relation to pornography than the milder-mannered Anne Rice, and Koja examining countercultural communities and identities estranged from the mainstream, the market expansion of the 1980s now provided speciality niches for these writers. Work hitherto limited to independent small publishers could now appear in mass-market paperback.

While Lucy Taylor would never find an audience outside of the small press market, Kathe Koja's entrance into the market followed a different path – one that could be read as a sign of horror's decline around the turn of the decade. Since writers such as King and Straub, who represented horror as a commercial mainstream, became increasingly associated with massive 'doorstop' novels, the corrective counter-move to keep horror from growing stale and repetitive was to slim volumes down. Even as amplified splatter and gore had promised to return horror to its essentials, brevity promised a new leanness and meanness for

The Cipher, Kathe Koja, 1991. Front cover of kindle edition, published by Roadswell editions, 2012.

the novel. This did not have to mean that the horror novel would lose its ability to envelop the reader in a fully realised imaginary world. What it did mean, however, was that this immersiveness would be re-defined from its social to its psychological aspects. A new breed of horror would shrink down King's and Straub's large casts of characters to a small, intensely explored configuration. Kathe Koja, for example, expressed a strong preference for the triangle as her favourite character configuration, 'playing two characters against the remaining one, subtly shifting and re-shifting the balance of power among them' (Hantke 2003: 542). Writers like Koja also rejected the kitchen sink realism that had made King and Straub such meticulous chroniclers of American everyday life. Instead, Koja's novels explored the intensely inward psychological landscapes of their characters, sketching in settings with a few lurid, expressionistic brush strokes. As a result of this tight focus on psychological interiority, horror fiction of the late 1980s and early 1990s lost the spatial and regional specificity which had rendered many novels and short stories such faithful reflections of ordinary American life.

Kathe Koja appears, not by accident, as a representative of this shift around the end of the decade and the beginning of the next. Her first novel, *The Cipher*, opened a new imprint of paperback originals by Delacorte called Abyss. Under the competent editorship of Jeanne Cavelos, Dell's Abyss series provided a home to horror writers who had been popular during the 1980s (Melanie Tem, Brian Hodge and Michael McDowell) but were trying to reinvent themselves creatively, as well as to new writers such as Mike Arnzen and Michael Blumlein, both eager to break new ground. The advertising copy printed on the inside cover of Abyss titles announced this claim to originality as clearly as, by the same token, it indicted 1980s horror for having outlived its relevance:

> The Abyss line of cutting-edge psychological horror is committed to publishing the best, most innovative works of dark fiction available. Abyss is horror unlike anything you've ever read before. It's not about haunted houses or evil children or ancient Indian burial grounds. We've all read those books and we all know their plots by heart. Abyss is for the seeker of truth, no matter how disturbing or twisted it may be. It's about people and the darkness we all carry within us. Abyss is the new horror from the dark frontier. (Quoted in Hantke 2008: 63)

As if to cast doubts on the confidence with which the blurb announced its genre revolution, it was immediately followed by a promotional blurb of roughly equal length from Stephen King praising the entire series for its innovative character and consistency in 'terms of quality, production and plain old storytelling reliability (that's the bottom line, isn't it?)' (King, quoted in Hantke 2008: 63).

While Abyss saw itself as injecting fresh blood into horror, most of the fiction it published abandoned the self-awareness that had driven so much of early 1980s fiction to explain and account for itself. For the duration of its existence Abyss would cultivate tight, claustrophobic novels in which little of the larger world – the social world or the vast universe of horror itself – would impinge upon the mad minds of its protagonists. In this regard Abyss failed to transform the self-reflexive impulse of horror into a new source of creativity. With the exception of an aptly titled collection called *Metahorror* (1992), edited by Dennis Etchison, the self-conscious exploration of horror's traditions and aesthetics would remain a challenge to be met elsewhere.

As a critic and historian with an encyclopedic grasp of horror, Kim Newman would deconstruct the genre's familiar horror tropes in his short fiction ('Further Developments in the Strange Case of Dr Jekyll and Mr Hyde', published in 1999) and his novels (for example, the *Anno Dracula* series of 1992–2013). Similarly idiosyncratic is the work of Thomas Ligotti, which stands out as a self-conscious departure from the hyperrealism that had dominated the 1980s boom. With the short story collections *Songs of a Dead Dreamer* (1986), *Grimscribe* (1991) and *Noctuary* (1994), Ligotti established a rhetorically self-conscious voice in which he would rework Lewis Carroll's Alice, the less familiar satirical writings of Edgar Allan Poe and Lovecraftian regionalism into a highly self-conscious philosophical mix. Limiting himself to short stories only and not being a prolific writer, Ligotti has remained somewhat of an insider tip within the genre. Alongside such oddly idiosyncratic figures a late generation of strong yet more conventional writers, ranging from Robert Deveraux, Charlee Jacobs, Gary Braunbeck, Thomas Picirilli, Tim Lebbon and Norman Partridge to Sarah Langan, Sarah Pinborough, Glen Hirshberg and Brian Keene, has been holding up the flag of the horror paperback original. This has happened largely under the auspices of the Leisure Horror imprint, the last recognisable paperback horror line to survive the 1990s.

Despite all this talent, the market still crashed. In the October 1990 issue *Locus* magazine ran an article entitled 'Tor Drops Horror Line', which reported: '[f]ive years ago [1985], Tor was the first company to start a separate horror line' (Anon. 1990: 5). Horror's decrease of market shares in the late 1980s, however, led to the company's decision to market each month's lead title no longer as genre but as mainstream fiction (Hantke 2008: 56). In March 1996 Pulphouse Publishing was shut down after publishing a total of 230 books and magazines. In November 1996 Zebra, 'the last existing genre horror line in US publishing', was also discontinued, its horror titles 'still being published, but mostly as general fiction, romance (!) or suspense' (Anon. 1996: 8). Simultaneously in Britain 'the Creed horror imprint from Signet was also dropped' (Anon. 1996: 8). Summarising all these developments, Edward Bryant would conclude, '[o]kay, okay, so horror is still dead. Or dying. . .' (Bryant, quoted in Anon. 1996: 38). Yet Bryant's deadpan comment contains a glimmer of hope – 'dying', not dead – and this would be reflected in the fact that horror's loss of mainstream appeal did not signal the end of the genre. To the present day the HWA continues to conduct its annual meetings, Bram Stoker Awards are still given out each year and great horror fiction keeps getting written. But the cultural spotlight that had shone so brightly on horror for about a decade had moved elsewhere.

Impacts and Traces

Mystery fiction would emerge as the genre profiting the most from horror's loss of the cultural spotlight. Not only did writers such as Joe R. Lansdale, Norman Partridge and John Skipp switch gears, but one relatively new variant of the murder mystery absorbed most of horror's more grisly impulses: the serial killer novel. Prefigured brilliantly by Shane Stevens' *By Reason of Insanity* (1979), which never amounted to more than a cult sleeper, the serial killer novel came into its own as early as Thomas Harris's *Red Dragon* (1981) and

The Silence of the Lambs (1988). With strong cinematic adaptations, Harris's creation of aristocratic madman Hannibal Lecter picked up two elements of splatterpunk. One would be the focus on excessive violence, perpetrated by the killer; the other the focus on bodily abjection, put on display by meticulously researched scenes showing the work of forensic science. As noted in chapter 5, Harris's immense commercial success created the serial killer novel as a subgenre of the murder mystery, spicing up the police procedural with the gore borrowed from horror. Some writers, for example Michael Slade, would close the gap between the two genres more from the side of horror; others operated more soberly within the conventions of the mystery, for instance John Sandford or David Wiltse. With its eponymous monsters often operating at superhuman levels of cunning and elusiveness, even a hint of the supernatural – the hallmark of so much 1980s horror fiction – managed to survive in the serial killer novel, despite its emphatic commitment to the empirical.

As a close relative to the serial killer novel, the forensic police procedural would eventually come to correct one imbalance typical of mainstream horror during its heyday. If 1980s horror produced only Anne Rice as a notable author, with a limited number of female mid-list writers, in the forensic thriller the gore of the autopsy and the gruesome murder scene became almost entirely the domain of female writers. Initiated by Patricia Cornwell's immensely popular Kay Scarpetta novels, first published in 1990, the work of Kay Hooper, Tess Gerritsen and Kathy Reichs is enjoying a long afterlife in prolific television franchises, from *CSI* (2000–present) and *Bones* (2005–present) to *The Fall* (2013–present) and *Fortitude* (2015–present). All of these get away with putting more gruesome sights on television than horror ever did. Similarly the realm of the supernatural, in a publishing cycle starting a decade later, would be dominated by female writers. Taking their cue from Anne Rice in blending romance and horror, writers of the so-called paranormal romance such as Kelley Armstrong, Charlaine Harris, J. R. Ward and Sherrilyn Kenyon would redress the gender imbalance typical of the 1980s horror cycle.

Closing another gap, that between splatterpunk and the literary mainstream, was Bret Easton Ellis with his novel *American Psycho*.

Published to considerable public controversy in 1991, Ellis's novel charts similar territory as Tom Wolfe's *The Bonfire of the Vanities* (1987), satirising 1980s yuppie greed and the excesses of Reaganomics by following the murder spree and mental decline of Wall Street operator Patrick Bateman. While Wolfe had gone for broad satire, Ellis took his clue from splatterpunk, making his hero Patrick Bateman a serial killer in the vein of Harris's Hannibal Lecter (with a nod to Robert Bloch's Norman Bates). *American Psycho* would hark back to genre fiction by Rex Miller and Michael Slade, ramping up the levels of violence and gore to degrees past those of Harris, whose work had already entered the mainstream. Given Ellis's literary credentials, the publication of *American Psycho* packaged as mainstream and not genre fiction dropped the novel into an audience unfamiliar with horror; the shock and outrage produced by this calculated mismatch propelled the novel to its massive success.

Under the guise of various labels (more the tools of marketing than of critical and historical assessment), horror has remained a reference point for fiction with serious literary aspirations to the present day. When horror is subsumed under the umbrella term of 'the Gothic', the result are high-profile anthologies such as Brad Morrow's and Patrick McGrath's *The New Gothic* (1993) and Joyce Carol Oates's *American Gothic Tales* (1996), both projects notable for the sterling literary credentials of their respective editors. Under the rubric of 'the supernatural', horror is now the stuff of the most mainstream of publishers; Penguin, for example, recently published S. T. Joshi's *American Supernatural Tales* (2009) and a series of collections reviving interest in twentieth-century pulp fiction (by writers like Ray Russell, Charles Beaumont and Thomas Ligotti). Labelled as a version of 'the fantastic', horror fiction has even made inroads into the prestigious Library of America series with the two-volume collection *American Fantastic Tales* (2009), edited by Peter Straub. None of these books is likely to rise to the top of the *New York Times* bestseller list, but their existence testifies to the fact that horror has survived its plunge from the heights of mainstream popularity. Like many of its entertaining monsters, it is simply not that easy to kill.

References

Anonymous, *Locus*, 37.5 (1996), 8.

——, *Locus*, 32.1 (1994), 6.

——, 'Tor Drops Horror Line', *Locus*, 24.4 (1990), 5.

——, 'Dell to Launch New Horror Line', *Locus*, 24.5 (1990), 5.

——, *The State of Modern Horror Fiction* (1983) <https://www.youtube.com/watch?v=PYqK4gIq5Sw> [accessed 16 January 2015].

Bryant, Edward, '1996: The Year in Review', *Locus*, 38.2 (1997), 38.

Campbell, Ramsey, 'My Roots Exhumed', in *Ramsey Campbell and Modern Horror Fiction*, ed. by S. T. Joshi (Liverpool: Liverpool University Press, 2001), pp. 1–5.

Cannato, Vincent J., 'Bright Lights, Doomed Cities: The Rise or Fall of New York City in the 1980s?', in *Living in the Eighties*, ed. by Gil Troy and Vincent J. Cannato (Oxford and New York: Oxford University Press, 2009), pp. 70–84.

Ebert, Roger, 'Review of *Night of the Living Dead*' (1969) <http://www.rogerebert.com/reviews/the-night-of-the-living-dead-1968> [accessed 18 May 2015].

Gibson, William, *Neuromancer* (New York: Ace, 1984).

Goho, James, *Journeys into Darkness: Critical Essays on Gothic Horror* (Lanham, MD: Rowman and Littlefield, 2014).

Hantke, Steffen, 'Kathe Koja', in *Supernatural Fiction Writers: Contemporary Fantasy and Horror*, ed. by Richard Bleiler, vol. II (New York: Thomson & Gale, 2003), pp. 541–9.

——, 'The Decline of the Literary Horror Market in the 1990s and Dell's Abyss Series', *The Journal of Popular Culture*, 41.1 (2008), 56–70.

Joshi, S. T., *The Modern Weird Tale* (London and Jefferson, NC: McFarland, 2001).

King, Stephen, *Danse Macabre* (New York: Berkeley, 1981).

Levin, Ira, *Rosemary's Baby* (New York: Dell, 1967).

Marx, Karl, and Friedrich Engels, *The Communist Manifesto* (1848; London: Penguin, 2015).

McCauley, Kirby, 'Introduction', in *Dark Forces: New Stories of Suspense and Supernatural Horror*, ed. by Kirby McCauley (New York: Bantam, 1980), pp. xi–xvi.

Tucker, Ken, 'The Splatterpunk Trend and Welcome to It', *The New York Times Archive* (1991) <http://www.nytimes.com/1991/03/24/ books/the-splatterpunk-trend-and-welcome-to-it.html> [accessed 16 January 2015].

Wiater, Stanley, 'A Shockingly Brief and Informal History of the Horror Writers Association', *Horror Writers Association* (1996) <http://horror.org/aboutus.htm> [accessed 16 January 2015].

What to Read Next

Clive Barker, *Books of Blood, vols 1–3* (1984; London: Sphere, 1988).

Fritz Leiber, *Our Lady of Darkness* (1977; New York: Orb Books, 2010).

Thomas Ligotti, *Songs of a Dead Dreamer* and *Grimscribe* (1986, 1991; London: Penguin, 2015).

Stephen King, *It* (1986; London: Hodder and Stoughton, 2011).

Anne Rice, *Interview with the Vampire* (1976; London: Sphere, 2008).

Peter Straub, *Ghost Story* (1979; London: Gollancz, 2008).

Pride and Prejudice and Zombies, Jane Austen and Seth Grahame-Smith, 2009. Front cover of first edition, published by Quirk Books, 2009.

Chapter 7

Post-Millennial Horror, 2000–16

Xavier Aldana Reyes

AFTER A RELATIVELY QUIET PERIOD in the 1990s, horror is, once again, popular; it could indeed be said to be undergoing a second golden age in the twenty-first century. Although the monthly volume of published works is nowhere near that of the 1980s the genre is in good health, with sales steady and a clear shelf presence in bookshops and online retailers. Well-known writers such as Stephen King, Dean Koontz and Clive Barker are part of the catalogue of mainstream publishing houses and their imprints, for example Hodder and Stoughton, Macmillan or HarperCollins, while a plethora of magazines and journals, such as *Black Static*, *Nightmare* or *Cemetery Dance*, publish a consistent stream of horror short stories. Even *Granta*, the prestigious literary magazine, dedicated an entire issue to horror writing in 2011.

On the one hand, this ubiquity is a result of the gradual acceptance of horror as a 'worthy' genre – propelled no doubt by the long establishment of popular authors, especially Stephen King, who began their careers in the 1970s and 1980s and continue to be successful. A number of playfully metatextual and postmodernist novels and short story collections by cult writers, such as Mark Z. Danielewski's *House of Leaves* (2000), Chuck Palahniuk's *Haunted* (2005), Bret Easton Ellis's *Lunar Park* (2005) or David Mitchell's *Slade House* (2015), have, naturally, contributed to the restitution of horror as a serious genre capable of housing visceral scares alongside more evidently intellectual pursuits. As other more mainstream and canonic writers have delved into the Gothic and the ghost story, most notably, Sarah Waters with *The Little Stranger* (2009), Jeanette Winterson with *The Daylight Gate* (2013) and Kate Mosse with *The Winter Ghosts* (2009), *The Mistletoe Bride and Other Haunting Tales* (2013) and *The Taxidermist's Daughter* (2014), horror could be said to have escaped the confines of the pulpy, cheap presses and become a respectable genre.

And yet, on the other hand, a clearly specialist market for horror has developed to suit the needs of the most dedicated readers. Centipede Press, for example, prints lavish, often signed short runs (generally limited to 100 copies) of out-of-print horror novels. These are special editions, often featuring additional material for the hardcore fan or collector. In this way the work of once popular and influential writers, such as John Farris, has been made available for a very specific type of nostalgic and dedicated reader. Another press, PS Publishing, specialises in novella-length works which also receive rather limited and exclusive print runs and normally appear in hardback format. Ramsey Campbell and Conrad Williams, among others, have worked with them in recent years. Deadite Press, an imprint of Eraserhead Press, is perhaps the most extreme and gory of the specialist presses. Home to works by the likes of Edward Lee or Wrath James White, it focuses on producing much more affordable paperbacks with lurid covers, marketed to a very particular readership in search of extreme literary experiences. The digital age, especially the advent of Kindles and other e-book readers, has meant that a number of texts previously only available second-hand, say a few of the novels by Jack Ketchum or Joe R. Lansdale, are now readily obtainable at affordable prices. The splatterpunks, especially John Skipp, have also resurfaced in the 2000s and published a new stream of novels and edited collections. This literary market is very compatible with similar products in other media, where horror has also flourished.

Most significantly, horror has had a strong purchase on graphic novels and comics, especially through the series *The Walking Dead* (2003–), and in survival horror video games such as the *Dead Space* (2008–13) trilogy and the found footage-influenced *Outlast* (2013). Horror now also transcends ages – or rather can be found across a varied demographic. From R. L. Stine, whose revolutionary 1990s *Goosebumps* series for young

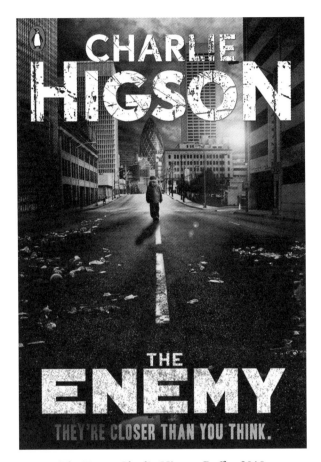

The Enemy, Charlie Higson, Puffin, 2010.

readers returned in the form of the spin-off series *Goosebumps Horror-Land* (2008–12), to the successful careers of Darren Shan as new polyvalent 'horror-meister' and the publishing sensation that has been Charlie Higson's young adult zombie series *The Enemy* (2009–15), it is clear that the genre is no longer the exclusive province of grown-ups. More significantly, it is now tolerated by the parents of the children who crave it.

The Cult of the Established Horror Auteur

One of the key differences between the post-millennial period and previous ones is, as I have noted, the establishment and canonisation of a series of writers who have led very successful lives as horror auteurs. Many writers who started in the 1970s and 1980s, or even before then, such as Thomas Ligotti, John Farris, John Saul, Steve Rasnic Tem, Jack Ketchum, Joe R. Lansdale and Kim Newman (whose *Anno Dracula* series has been recently reprinted), as well as the now-deceased Richard Matheson, Tanith Lee and James Herbert, continued to produce novels in the twenty-first century, however irregularly. Although they are well known, their work is still relatively niche, with their names not necessarily recognisable to readers outside the horror and dark fantasy circuits. Other writers, however, have by now had long and prolific careers, spawning a number of texts considered classics and often adapted to the screen. Stephen King, Clive Barker, Ramsey Campbell, Dean Koontz, Peter Straub, Dan Simmons and Anne Rice have all paved the way for new authors and gone some way towards establishing horror as a profitable, fun and literary artistic pursuit. Of course, this has been aided by various forms of public and institutional recognition, such as awards not strictly connected to the genre. For example, Stephen King was the recipient of the 2003 National Book Foundation Medal for Distinguished Contribution to American Letters and, in 2015, of the National Medal of Arts. Proof of this canonisation beyond the exclusive remit of the horror convention includes the invitation of these writers to universities, where they give advice to new and upcoming writers, the running of conferences in and around their work and, ultimately, the publication of monographs or collections exploring their respective oeuvres. In a sense, then, these writers have been responsible for carrying the horror torch, even during periods where it has proven less fashionable, and, in spite of other major trends, their outputs have continued to be of interest to loyal fan bases. They have, in other words, aided in the nurturing of the cult of the established horror auteur – one who specialises in a certain type of product and has his or her own distinctive and recognisable style, interests and motivations.

Of these key genre masters, the most well-known is, undoubtedly, Stephen King. His name has become synonymous with the genre – and of a very specific type of sprawling, psychologically and supernaturally-oriented work – and he actively engages in the promotion of new writers. Not only is he the world's bestselling horror writer of all time, with more than 350 million copies of his books sold, but he is also the most widely translated and adapted. His praise and endorsements are often enough to put writers in the critical and readerly spotlight. Despite initial fears that a car accident in 1999 might have affected his capacity to write, King has gone on to publish new fiction at an incredible rate in the twenty-first century. His bibliography, which now includes over 50 books and 200 short stories, has conjured up a series of complex communities (especially around the fictional Castle Rock location) of some scope that have provoked comparisons to classic social realists like Charles Dickens. A devoted reviewer, he has carved himself a niche as king of the genre whilst remaining an always humble and affable presence. Aware of his role as entertainer, King has also been happy to concede that horror fiction can do more than simply thrill. As Steffen Hantke mentions in the previous chapter, King has even published a biographical guidebook, *On Writing* (2000), for those wishing to practise the craft.

Despite this, King's work has taken a critical dip since the turn of the century – partly as a result of the perception that some of his writing is either treading old ground or showing signs of creative exhaustion. Good cases in point are the return to aliens in *Dreamcatcher* (2001), dangerous cars in *From a Buick Eight* (2002) and the female melodrama of *Dolores Claiborne* (1992) and *Rose Madder* (1995) in *Lisey's Story* (2006). Other good examples are the divisive sequel to *The Shining* (1977), *Doctor Sleep* (2013), which some felt could have been written outside of its intertextual context, and the last three volumes of the *The Dark Tower* series, published in quick succession between 2003 and 2004, with an additional, non-chronological eighth volume appearing in 2012. Arguably the best work King has produced in the twenty-first century, apart from the effective zombie novel *Cell* (2006) and the hefty throwback tome *Under the Dome* (2009), has come in the short story format. The collections *Just after Sunset* (2008) and *Full Dark, No Stars* (2010), made out of four novellas, were both Bram Stoker Award winners and highly praised by critics. The other interesting area King has recently explored, although he was never a stranger to it, is the hard-boiled detective fiction or crime thriller. *The Colorado Kid* (2005), *Blaze* (2007), written as

Under the Dome, still from television series, final episode, 2015. CBS Photo Archives/Getty Images.

Richard Bachman, *Joyland* (2013) and the Detective Bill Hodges trilogy, which includes *Mr. Mercedes* (2014), *Finders Keepers* (2015) and *End of Watch* (2016), have more vividly showcased King's vibrant voice and proved that, above all, he is a talented psychological writer.

Another giant of the genre, Clive Barker, whose *Books of Blood* changed the landscape of horror and got him tipped as its future, has, like King, evolved and moved on to other connected projects. Not fully comfortable with the 'horror writer' label, preferring that of dark imaginer – especially after the publication of ambitious fantastic and imaginative works such as *Weaveworld* (1987) and *Imajica* (1991), which only contained some horrific elements – Barker has spent a good part of the twenty-first century working on a mammoth series of young adult books called the *Abarat* quintet (2002–present). Set on the 25 islands that give the name to the book and accompanied by hundreds of oil paintings made by himself, the series is a testament not just to Barker's prodigious imagination, but also to his, by now perfected, art of creating monsters that challenge Manichean notions of good and evil. The most notable example is that of the tragic and tormented primary antagonist, Christopher Carrion. Lord of Midnight on the Island of Gorgossium, his mouth was once sewn shut by his grandmother,

Mater Motley, after he dared to utter the word 'love'. Bent on plunging the Abarat into eternal darkness, his appearance is as elaborate as that of any of the monsters in *Cabal* (1988): he wears a collar full of a fluid hosting the physical incarnations of his nightmares, which flow from his skull and, when they rub against his face, make him relive his fears.

However, even if this project has taken up great time and effort, Barker has never truly left horror behind. He has collaborated on horror films as producer and writer, as well as on the acclaimed video games *Undying* (2001) and *Jericho* (2007) and the comics *Seduth* (2009) and *Next Testament* (2013), and continued to work on his particular brand of multi-dimensional, supernatural horror fiction. 2001 saw the publication of the Hollywood-set *Coldheart Canyon*, the closest thing Barker has ever come to writing to a ghost story, while his novella *Tortured Souls*, which chronicles the fall of the fictional city of Primordium, features cenobite-style figures and was, initially, written to accompany a line of McFarlane toys. *Mister B. Gone*, a short comedy horror novel set in hell and, later, the fourteenth century, was published in 2007. 2015 saw the much-awaited return (and final and definitive annihilation) of one of his most celebrated creations, the Hell priest better known as Pinhead, in *The Scarlet Gospels*.

Ramsey Campbell has been deemed 'Britain's most respected living writer of the mode' (Birch 2009: 499) by *The Oxford Companion to English Literature* and compared to respected figures such as H. P. Lovecraft, his biggest influence, and Algernon Blackwood. The recipient of an endless stream of awards, a number of them for his work in weird fiction, he has given countless interviews and made many appearances in the media. A charismatic auteur who actively champions and reviews horror fiction and film, Campbell has been invited on numerous occasions to share his expertise in documentaries, magazines, horror encyclopaedias and even DVD liner notes. Most importantly, he has written more than 30 horror novels and a prodigious number of short stories, gathered together in more than 10 collections and horror anthologies.

The twenty-first century has seen Campbell as active and prolific as ever, and returning to old concerns as well as developing new ones.

For example, the cinematic investigations of *Ancient Images* (1989) make a comeback in *The Grin of the Dark* (2007), the leafy weird is the central character in *The Darkest Part of the Woods* (2003) and his novella *The Last Revelation of Gla'aki* (2013) returns to a Lovecraft-inspired creature which appeared in Campbell's first short story collection, *The Inhabitant of the Lake and Less Welcome Tenants* (1964). The digital world has also made it into his work, with emails becoming a source of threat in *The Seven Days of Cain* (2010) and an online murder blog in *Think Yourself Lucky* (2014). His oeuvre has received the moniker 'the fiction of paranoia' (Joshi 2001: 133), a term that gestures towards Campbell's focus upon cities and modern life as the catalysts of fear. This preoccupation has made him an important 'poet of urban squalor and despair' (Joshi 2014: 664). Campbell's work is, at the same time, characteristic for its use of humour, especially evident in his novel *The Overnight* (2004), which describes a bookshop besieged by supernatural phenomena. However, in spite of overwhelming critical acclaim, his fiction is still less popular than that of other mainstream horror writers and shows that there might be more than one horror market. Campbell's writings are sophisticated and referential, and do not necessarily follow the plotting of more generic fare. For this reason, his work might appeal to a different type of horror reader – one better versed in the history of the genre and less concerned with specific popular trends.

Focusing on King, Barker and Campbell is useful in determining the role of continuity – that is, how twenty-first-century horror is partly driven by 'old blood'. Although the gradual dying-off of a number of previously key writers – the aforementioned Matheson, Herbert or Lee – may be an indication that the 'boom' generation is coming to the end of its natural life cycle, King, Barker and Campbell are powerful examples of how these writers have explored personal areas of interest, pushed the genre in different directions, helped to keep its momentum and, most significantly, been influential in the development, and even marketing, of younger writers. Their establishment as auteurs who do not need to legitimise what they do for a living has been foundational to the growing cachet of horror as literary, resourceful and polymorphic.

New Voices

If the twenty-first century has seen a number of well-known, successful and popular writers canonised, it has also seen the emergence and rise of some strong new voices. Although some are popular in their native countries – Patrick Senécal, Edo van Belkom, Tony Burgess and Nancy Kilpatrick in Canada; José María Latorre and Pilar Pedraza in Spain – only a few have managed to break through into the international market, generally with a novel or series. A few significant examples include the South African S. L. Grey (Sarah Lotz and Louis Greenberg) and their *Downside* series (2010–13), their compatriot Lauren Beukes and her works *The Shining Girls* (2013) and *Broken Monsters* (2014), the Spanish Albert Sánchez Piñol with *Cold Skin* (2002) and *Pandora in the Congo* (2005) and the Irish Peter Connolly with his *Nocturnes* anthologies (2004; 2015) and some of his Charlie Parker thrillers (1999–present).

Nevertheless, the large majority of active, popular and successful horror writers continue to be American and British, no doubt a result of the nature of the publishing market and far reach of English as a language, as well as of particular individual talents. Whether unfairly or not, names such as Max Brooks, John Ajvide Lindqvist, Justin Cronin, Joe Hill, Adam Nevill, Gillian Flynn, Jonathan Maberry, Sarah Pinborough, David Moody, Glen Duncan, Conrad Williams, Joseph D'Lacey, John Shirley, Alison Littlewood, Graham Joyce, Joel Lane, Guillermo del Toro and Chuck Hogan, Sarah Langan, Brian Keene, Tom Fletcher or Tim Lebbon, among others, are still the most widely connected to horror. Of these new voices I want to discuss two in particular: Hill and Ajvide Lindqvist, both of whom have stuck out due to their personal styles, particular success and promising futures.

Joe Hill, perhaps one of the most famous new horror writers in America, once attempted to hide the fact that he is Stephen King's son, choosing, instead, to carve out a name for himself through the publication of a number of short stories. His parentage did not remain a mystery for very long, however, and he has now embraced his connections by co-authoring work with King – the short stories 'Throttle' (2009) and 'In the Tall Grass' (2012). His first book was a collection of the stories he published between 1999 and 2005, the misleadingly titled *20th*

Century Ghosts (2005), which does not focus on spectrality (only two of the stories, '20th Century Ghost' and the superbly eerie 'The Black Phone', feature actual ghosts) and is not particularly wedded to the twentieth century. This collection already pointed to some of the motifs and themes Hill would later develop in his novels and which are eminently Christian in their nature: the fight between good and evil, the pervasive nature of sin (especially when connected to perceived sexual perversions), the possibility of an afterlife and the purity of children. The latter is perhaps the most significant, and Hill's interest in child psychology belies his main writing influence, that of his own father. Traces of Stephen King's work can be found in certain quirks and turns of phrase, and even in the occasional use of striking typesets or in the arrangement of chapters. Hill has gone as far as to reference novels by King – *The Stand* (1978), *The Dark Tower* (1982) and *It* (1986) – in his later work, perhaps as a form of acknowledgement of the influence his father's fictional universe has had on his own. His new novel, *The Fireman* (2016), was, in fact, presented as Hill's version of King's *The Stand*.

Hill's first novel, *Heart-Shaped Box* (2007), updated the ghost story for the twenty-first century: in it Jude, an ageing rock star interested in creepy memorabilia, deliberately buys a ghost over the internet. Attached to a suit, the deadly spirit is soon revealed to be intimately connected to his buyer and, unlike other vengeful apparitions, is capable of following Jude around and of controlling people via mesmerism. Although the premise is interesting, and there was much pomp around its publication, with Subterranean Press selling out of two limited editions of the book, *Heart-Shaped Box* is a good deal less accomplished and interesting than Hill's later offerings. Its potential as a new ghost tale soon descends into a long and drawn-out horror road movie that would have worked better as a shorter piece. By contrast *Horns* (2010), which was adapted into a 2013 film directed by Alexandre Aja and featuring Daniel Radcliffe, makes for a relatively simple, but effective, narrative. Ig, a man accused of murdering his girlfriend and who suddenly wakes up with the eponymous horns, finds his life crumbling as those around him find it impossible to lie and feel compelled to talk about their darkest urges. An interesting writing exercise that blends magic realism, gory horror and satanic iconography with more traditional romance, *Horns* can be read as an allegory for the need to repent and accept destiny.

However, Hill's most satisfying work to date has to be *NOS4R2* (2013), or *NOS4A2* in his native America. The work features his most interesting villain to date, Charles Manx – a supernatural child kidnapper who takes his victims to the 'inscape' or thought land, known as Christmasland, by luring them into his 1938 Rolls-Royce Wraith, an 'extension of [his] thoughts' (Hill 2014: 379). Fashioned, self-avowedly, after Count Orlok in F. W. Murnau's *Nosferatu* (1922), Manx 'drains unhappiness from [. . .] children just like a B-movie v-v-vampire suck[s] blood' (Hill 2014: 553). In the same process, however, he turns them into monsters stuck in a macabre, twisted recreation of an infinite Christmas. So vivid and imaginatively rich is this fictional world that it experienced a return in the prequel standalone graphic novel *Wraith: Welcome to Christmasland* (2014). This creative incursion is not a rarity, as Hill, like Neil Gaiman, has shown a keen interest to work in this sister narrative medium. Not only did Hill co-write an adaptation of his short story 'The Cape' (2010), he is also the writer of the popular comic series *Locke & Key* (2008–13). Taken as a whole, Hill's writing easily embodies the less nihilistic and most creative side of new horror, mixing the supernatural and dark fantasy with a more traditional religious morality that rewards innocence, perseverance and hard work, and punishes incest, the very prevalent abuse of women or the mistreatment of children.

As I began by suggesting, it is notoriously difficult for genre writers whose first language is not English to achieve literary success outside their home countries. Aside from authors who have had some moderate success, whether commercial or critical, with one novel or series, such as the Flemish writer Stefan Brijs with *The Angel Maker* (2008), the Swede Stefan Spjut with *Stallo / The Shapeshifters* (2015) or the later novels of the Japanese Koji Suzuki – catapulted to fame after his *Ring* (1991) was made into the classic film *Ringu* (Hideo Nakata, 1998) and its American remake, *The Ring* (Gore Verbinski, 2002) – the market is largely dominated by American and British writers. Others, such as the Russian Sergei Lukyanenko, with the popular hexalogy that started with *Night Watch* (1999–2014), only use some horror elements; their novels are more accurately, and generally, classed as fantasy or supernatural fiction. The notable exception is, of course, that of John Ajvide Lindqvist, whose personal brand of literary horror is as intrinsically Swedish as

Let the Right One In, John Ajvide Lindqvist, Quercus, 2007.

it is heir to the established Western horror tradition (James Herbert, Stephen King and video nasties are all mentioned in his novels), and has received a warm welcome in many countries.

Since the translation of his *Let the Right One In* (2007), but especially after the critically acclaimed 2008 Swedish film adaptation by Tomas Alfredson and the American remake *Let Me In* (Matt Reeves, 2010), Ajvide Lindqvist's works have been systematically, if slowly, appearing in English; his persona has been compared to that of Stephen King (Ajvide Lindqvist 2012: 512–13). The truth is that his style does feel fresh, and his reluctance to offer final answers or rounded resolutions – most notably in *Harbour* (2010) and *Little Star* (2011) – imbues his novels with an allegorical power that, although it can feel somewhat vague in places, shows the work of a truly ambitious writer interested in exploring themes such as the turmoil of adolescence, loneliness, death and mourning or the possibility of overcoming trauma. Like King, Ajvide Lindqvist is interested in child psychology, especially where the children are damaged or social outsiders. Unlike other horror writers, he focuses almost exclusively on working-class characters or otherwise downbeat figures who manage to escape simple social typecasting. His is the world of failed hopes and dreams, of bullied children, of drunkards who just get by and of families destroyed by sudden and unexpected death. And yet, in all his novels, there is a clear sense of hope and the possibility of a bright and promising future. His main message seems to be that life is gruelling and difficult, but that it can also be rewarding and fruitful for those who persevere and accept the prevalence of pain.

Ajvide Lindqvist's first novel, *Let the Right One In*, is the best retelling of the vampire narrative of the twenty-first century: a true masterpiece of literary horror that expertly blends complex character psychology, vampire myth and gore. At a time when vampires have become desirable lovers, the novel's lonely, jaded and brittle-looking Eli, a vampire boy castrated over 200 years before the story begins, embodies all the social exclusion and sordidness usually ascribed to that supernatural figure. For some, Eli is '[p]ure Horror. Everything you were supposed to watch out for. Heights, fire, shards of glass, snakes' (Ajvide Lindqvist 2008: 246). The novel's real triumph, however, is the pairing of this character with Oskar, a 12-year-old outcast who uses a 'pissball' in order to hide his incontinence and who is the subject of constant bullying from his classmates. His friendship with Eli, whom he initially mistakes for a girl, helps him develop into someone strong enough to fight back and to accept being loved. Tragic, elegantly written and rich in memorable characters, the novel received a species of sequel in the form of the short story 'Let the Old Dreams Die' (2012), which recounts, at a remove, Oskar's apparent turning into a vampire and subsequent move to Barcelona with Eli.

Ajvide Lindqvist's second novel, *Handling the Undead* (2009), is an equally mesmerising take on the zombie outbreak narrative. In this work the undead, or rather, the 'unliving', are not presented as threatening, brain-eating figures, but rather as empty, decaying vessels who decide to return home. As such, the novel does not focus on survival. Instead it explores loss and grief, and it speculates on the potential governmental procedures that would necessarily develop as a consequence of such a major social disruption. Similarly *Harbour* is not an ordinary ghost story, even though a father is terrorised by the spirit of his disappeared daughter. The novel offers a complex study of the overcoming of pain and acceptance of the past, where the ghost literally comes to possess the body of the haunted. It is perhaps Ajvide Lindqvist's most Swedish novel, too, focusing on the country's connection to the sea, which becomes the ultimate source of evil in it and, in a turn of events reminiscent of *The Wicker Man* (Robin Hardy, 1973), a force to be appeased via sacrifice for the good of the community. His work is highly allegorical, and it seems that Ajvide Lindqvist's interest lies in making readers 'think the unthinkable' (Ajvide Lindqvist 2011: 2) – an effect he achieves through sheer accumulation of inordinate and shocking events. These, rather than require a direct investment in a belief in the supernatural or in horrific powers, force us to consider our search for meaning more generally, as well as the metaphorical significance they may have in Ajvide Lindqvist's work. This alone makes this author one of the most interesting new voices in the genre.

The Contemporary Weird and the New Weird

Of horror's many subgenres, the weird has been one of its most popular in the twenty-first century. Although several writers, most notably August Derleth, Robert Bloch and Ramsey Campbell, kept the flame of the Cthulhu mythos alive throughout the twentieth century, H. P.

Lovecraft's reappraisal in the twenty-first century as master of the weird tale and as a key writer in the Gothic horror tradition has been as unexpected as it has been welcome. In 2005 the inclusion of a collection of his short stories in the Library of America, *Tales*, raised a few conservative eyebrows, but his canonisation as a classic in American literature was not news to readers of horror and science fiction, nor indeed to the numerous writers who have been influenced by his works. The Lovecraft craze has been truly phenomenal in scope and effect: the twenty-first century has seen countless editions of his short stories and novellas published around the world, including editions by highly reputed presses such as Oxford University Press – *The Classic Horror Stories* (2013), edited by Roger Luckhurst – and three volumes in Penguin's Modern Classics series – *The Call of Cthulhu and Other Weird Stories* (1999), *The Thing on the Doorstep and Other Weird Stories* (2001) and *The Dreams in the Witch House and Other Weird Stories* (2005), all edited by weird expert S. T. Joshi. Academic editions such as *The New Annotated H. P. Lovecraft* (2014), edited by Leslie S. Klinger and introduced by Alan Moore, have happily co-habited with paperback editions of selected stories by presses such as Vintage or Wordsworth Classics, a testament to the diverse audiences his writings currently attract.

Lovecraft's works are both the subject of specialist academic conferences *and* part of a wide network of cultural adaptation and appropriation that ranges from video games and Lovecraft-themed role-playing weekends to craft patterns for knitted Cthulhus and tentacular balaclavas. The current cult of Lovecraft may, of course, be connected to a recuperation of genre fiction in the twenty-first century, following the deconstructive disruptions of the canon of poststructuralism and the various challenges that the Leavisite understanding of literature has received since the 1970s. It may also be linked, as has been suggested, to the materialist specificity of Lovecraft's view of the world (Joshi 2004: 77–97), a materialism that develops from his hodgepodge brand of 'cosmic horror' – or even to the perceived spiritual void of the new century which, for some, renders figures such as Cthulhu 'the only accessible bridge to the transcendental' (Nelson 2012: 71). The rise of philosophical work influenced by Lovecraft's oeuvre, namely the New Horror best represented by philosopher Eugene Thacker, as well as studies by Ben Woodward or Dylan Trigg, show just how far Lovecraft's influence has spread.

Whatever the possible motives for its current appeal, the consequences of Lovecraft's return have reached further than a sudden interest in, and attention to, his fictional creations. It has, for example, sparked numerous works by other artists seeking to expand his universe, as well as tributes, and even a mash-up collection, *Shadows over Baker Street* (2003), edited by Michael Reaves and John Pelan, which brings Lovecraftian beings into contact with the celebrated detective Sherlock Holmes. It has also led to the critical recuperation of other forgotten and under-read weird writers, for example William Hope Hodgson, Arthur Machen, Algernon Blackwood, M. P. Shiel or Clark Ashton Smith, all of whom have had their work reprinted and collected in new editions by Penguin. Taken together, their fiction, and that of others, constitutes a weird canon (see VanderMeer and VanderMeer 2011). It has certainly influenced contemporary writers, who have drawn from, and developed, this legacy in new and interesting ways.

Since the weird has now become a recognisable subgenre or genre hybrid belonging, depending on whom one asks, to science fiction, speculative fiction or horror (or all of them), the anxiety of influence has become less problematic. Writers in this vein can be understood to be working within a subgenre, or to have a set of specific aesthetic or philosophical concerns, rather than operating as Lovecraft imitators. It is also important to note that the label 'new weird', often used in journalism and reviews to refer to this type of fiction, defines a related yet intrinsically different subgenre explored below. The contemporary weird is marked out by the influence of the Lovecraftian tradition, is more readily aligned with horror (and especially, but not exclusively, concerned with cosmic horror) and has proliferated mostly in the short story format. Arguably genre ascription may be less important than literary quality, but significant works by the likes of Laird Barron, Jonathan Thomas, Ramsey Campbell, Caitlín R. Kiernan, Dennis Etchison, Tanith Lee, John Shirley, Norman Partridge and Thomas Ligotti have ensured that this is not an issue.

Of these writers, perhaps the most singular, especially given he is still a relative newcomer, is Laird Barron. Winner of three Shirley Jackson awards, two for his short story collections *The Imago Sequence and Other Stories* (2007) and *Occultation* (2010), he has also been nominated for numerous others, including the prestigious Bram Stoker, the World Fantasy and the International Horror Guild awards. Barron has very quickly built up a sizeable and critically acclaimed oeuvre that has even led to a tribute collection by Ross E. Lockhart and Justin Steele, *The Children of Leech: A Tribute to the Carnivorous Cosmos of Laird Barron* (2014). Although virtually every one of his stories is bursting with ideas (for some readers sometimes too many) and his three short story collections deserve the praise they have received, it is perhaps his development of the Old Leech mythos through a series of short stories and a novella – 'The Broadsword' (2010), *Mysterium Tremendum* (2010), 'The Siphon' (2011) and 'The Men from Porlock' (2011)' – culminating in his novel *The Croning* (2012), that has been most captivating and belies the most sustained debt to Lovecraft's work.

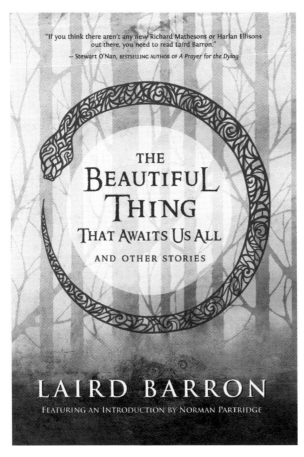

The Beautiful Thing That Awaits Us All, Laird Barron, 2013.
Front cover of edition published by Nightshade Books, 2014.

Certainly Barron's preoccupation with dreams, occult sects, a mysterious book containing mystic lore, alien creatures that inhabit other parts of the universe and come into contact with Earthlings through portals, and the hallucinogenic horror that derives from, among other things, the non-Euclidean physiognomies of some of these beings or their capacity to pass for humans, have clear antecedents in previous weird work. However, Barron's imagination is also original and impressive: his linear concept of time, encapsulated by the recurring broken ring or Ouroboros symbol, as well as the announcement of The Great Dark that is to fall upon Earth as it is dragged from its orbit around the sun or the development of Old Leech, 'a deity that ate the fucking dinosaurs, several species of advanced hominids and the Mayans' by 'open[ing] a gate and slurp[ing] them through a funnel' (Barron 2012: 216), all provide good examples. Beyond his remarkable hallucinatory style, the other interesting facet about Barron's fiction is the resignation of his characters to a reality and future that they cannot hope to conquer or alter. This acceptance of the horror of reality and of human helplessness is not far, although essentially different, from the epicurean pessimism of Thomas Ligotti. His own concept of 'the darkness' in his 'The Shadow, The Darkness' (2006) as a vast nether space that lies beyond ordinary human experience can be seen as another influence on Barron's fiction.

The other main strand of the weird in the twenty-first century is not so much a continuation or expansion of ideas and notions raised by earlier weird writers as a re-imagining of its motifs and characters, via transplantation into a more obviously fictitious, more recognisably science fiction or fantastic environment. While the horrific weird tends to focus on the penetration of dark forces into the real world, generally the contemporary one, the new weird sets its stories in alternative pasts or futures. In one of the few pieces to tackle the nature and origins of the subgenre, Jeff VanderMeer sees the new weird as developing from the science fiction New Wave of the 1960s – in particular the work of M. John Harrison, Michael Moorcock, J. G. Ballard and Jack Vance, as well as from the then new 'transgressive horror' of Clive Barker's *Books of Blood*, which 'focus[es] on the monsters and grotesquery but not the "scare"' (VanderMeer 2008: x) and on corporeal transformation, decay or mutilation. This horrific component, essential but not overwhelming at the level of its impact on the reader, is what distinguishes the new weird from slipstream and interstitial fiction. Weird creatures may play a significant role in the action, but, if still uncanny, they are no longer receptacles for the unknown, the unknowable or the unnameable. VanderMeer's own work, perhaps also the best exponent of the fungal weird, offers a good case in point.

The various texts that take place in the cruel and dangerous city of Ambergris – namely the collection of novellas entitled *City of Saints and Madmen* (2001) and, after its second edition, an additional series of vignettes, the fictional biography *Shriek: An Afterword* (2006) and the science fiction noir *Finch* (2009) – are all haunted by the presence of the 'gray caps'. Thus named because of their use of fungi, lichen, mould and other forms of fruiting bodies as weapons and spies, their revenge on Ambergrisians is chronicled by different characters in interconnected narratives that take place over hundreds of years. The gray caps prove to be the original dwellers of Ambergris, before the city was conquered by Manziquert I, their race slaughtered and the survivors forced underground, left to roam the world beneath the city and its sewers. Of an enigmatic, nightmarish appearance, with 'green pupils and yellow where there should be white' and 'rows and rows of needle lines set into a face a little like a squished-in shark's snout' (Vander-Meer 2010: 4), they generally wrap themselves in robes and hide their heads in 'wide-brimmed gray felt hats' (VanderMeer 2014: 28) that make them resemble mushrooms.

Always present in the periphery, their ritualistic practices left vague and obscure at best, the gray caps encapsulate the weirdness of the Love-craftian Old Ones, but represent a different form of underlying threat. Their reverse colonisation of Ambergris via fungal processes and weapons, which includes the Silence (the sudden disappearance of 25,000 Ambergrisians) and, years later, the physical invasion of the city known as the Rising, disperses any sense that these creatures disturb the thin veil of reality. Rather they are a part of it, of the world of decay embodied by the fungi that have overtaken Ambergris. If direct sympathy may be precluded by the horrible pictures painted by characters under their attack and control, it is clear that the gray caps are as monstrous as they are human. In other words, they are driven by similar feelings and emotions to those of their human enemies. Similar ecological nightmares, including odd organisms that may produce death by assimilation or sporic infection, appear in VanderMeer's *Southern Reach* trilogy, composed of *Annihilation, Acceptance* and *Authority*, all published in 2014. In them forms of foreign threat, through their strange and life-changing qualities, constitute a source not only of dread and horror, but also of fascination.

Influential and ground-breaking as these novels, or those by China Miéville, K. J. Bishop or Steph Swainston, have been, they can only be partially called horror. For example *Finch* is much more obviously a noir novel with touches of fantasy and science fiction, and Miéville defines his work as science fiction or speculative fiction. It is precisely their decidedly label-resistant work, a conjunction of science fiction and fantasy scenarios populated with creatures that are clearly connected to, yet not derived directly from, the Lovecraftian weird tradition, that makes the work of these writers so rich and proves that horror can manifest effectively beyond strictly delineated generic boundaries. Beyond the literary accomplishment of individual texts, the new weird's mixing of genres is, no doubt, one of the reasons for its contemporary popularity.

The Zombie Boom

Aeons-old, interdimensional, unnameable creatures are not the only monsters to have blossomed in the twenty-first century. While the vampire has been very actively appropriated and assimilated by dark romance, a genre that gained mainstream appeal in the 2000s – especially after the rise to popularity of the *Twilight* books (2005–8) and Charlaine Harris's *The Southern Vampire Mysteries* (2001–13) – the zombie has stayed resolutely within the realm of visceral horror. Although a few exceptions have mixed horror with romance, such as Isaac Marion's *Warm Bodies* (2010), which follows zombie protagonist R on his way to becoming human through love, or with dark humour and melodrama, as in the zombie comedy *Breathers: A Zombie's Lament* (2009), by S. G. Browne, Diana Rowland's series *White Trash Zombie* (2011–15) or the literary melodrama *The Reapers Are the Angels* (2010) by Alden Bell, the majority of zombie novels have expounded on the inescapable, post-apocalyptic nightmares familiar from the films of George A. Romero.

The success and prevalence of zombie fiction has been great, constituting a true publishing boom: over 70 notable zombie novels were published between 2000 and 2016, and dozens more are available to the insatiable reader via Kindle. Anthologies such as Christopher Golden's *The New Dead: A Zombie Anthology* (2010) and *Zombie: An Anthology of the Undead* (2012) or John Skipp's *Zombies: Encounters with the Hungry Dead* (2011) coexist with a new young adult market that includes Darren Shan's *Zom-B* series (2012–16), the aforementioned *The Enemy* (2009–15) series by Charlie Higson and Carrie Ryan's *The Forest of Hands and Teeth* series (2009–11). Since the publication of the first comic issue of *The Walking Dead* in 2003, itself a foundational and very influential literary piece, novels following the adventures and turmoils of groups of survivors routinely battle for attention among similar filmic offerings.

A writer who has done much to shape this fictional landscape is Max Brooks. His *The Zombie Survival Guide: Complete Protection from the Living Dead* (2003), which purported to have been written for civilians and in order to 'provide the knowledge necessary for survival against these subhuman beasts' (Brooks 2004: xiii), did much to establish some of the motifs of the contemporary zombie novel. The book is a compendium of zombie lore, refined and expanded. It covers anything from the weapons and combat techniques necessary to fight the dead to a chronological history of recorded attacks dating back to 60,000 BC. Brooks also takes the opportunity to dispel some zombie myths and, most significantly, to develop the viral nature of the creature, who is described as a 'new organism' (Brooks 2004: 2) born out of infection. The book dispenses with the Haitian zombie, the result of black magic and fictional supernatural occurrence, and makes a case for the existence of the real zombie, the factual one. *The Zombie Survival Guide* covers the symptoms, incubation period and transference of the virus; it even acknowledges that genetic research is being carried out to find a cure. Together with *The Walking Dead*, which similarly presented its human survivors as already-infected subjects who are, in a sense, already dead,

Brooks's book was responsible for firming up the global pandemic as the quintessential twenty-first-century zombie narrative. It reappeared in, among many others, Mira Grant's Newsflesh series (2010–16), Jonathan Maberry's Joe Ledger series (2009–present) and, in fungal form, in M. R. Carey's *The Girl with All the Gifts* (2014). The viral zombie has resonated with our microbiologically-aware present, and its affliction has spread to fellow monsters. For example, the vampires in novels such as *Let the Right One In* or Justin Cronin's *The Passage* (2010–16) have, themselves, become the result of viral contagion.

If *The Zombie Survival Guide* laid the ground for the contemporary zombie, Brooks's second book, the novel *World War Z: An Oral History of the Zombie War* (2006), would become a true literary sensation. Perhaps one of the best horror novels ever written, its beauty resides in its narrative framing. Composed of a collection of interviews with survivors of 'The Zombie War' (Brooks 2013: 1) during the gathering of data for the United Nation's Postwar Commission Report, the book is introduced as 'a book of memories' (3) published in order to preserve them from the passing of time. Thus the novel intends to highlight what its anonymous reporter terms the 'human factor' (2), distinguished from the cold data and timelines of the purged report, and establishes itself as an alternative history that will allow readers not to lose perspective of the real cost of the past. The novel, which runs chronologically from the first sightings and warnings of the infection to the process of regeneration undergone after its relative containment, is multi-voiced, massive in scale and as political as horror gets. Key characters from all over the world recount their personal experiences, and their arrangement and focus constitute a global narrative that is concerned with geopolitics, biopower (especially the role of the military in the regulation of civilian life) and the war histories of specific nations (albeit as perceived by a distinctly American narrator).

The true horror at the heart of *World War Z* does not, ultimately, rely on the abject nature of the undead or their incessant drive for fresh flesh, but on the psychological consequences of their relentless attacks on human beings and the delicate quality of the social structures thereby shaken. The return to a survival ethics is dictated by the encounter with a force that, at first, seems capable of extinguishing our civilisation. As one of the interviewees explains towards the end of the novel, in an answer that directly connects World War Z with the Holocaust, 'even those who managed to remain technically alive were so irreparably damaged, that their spirit, their soul, the person that they were supposed to be, was gone forever' (Brooks 2013: 340). Although Brooks's novel has a relatively 'happy' ending, with humanity conquering back the world, a decade-long war has had lasting effects likely to affect future generations. Praised upon release by critics and a true commercial hit, Brooks's novel further entrenched the zombie as a significant and appealing figure for horror fiction and managed, as did Colson Whitehead's later *Zone One* (2011), to overcome the survivor microcosm stories that proliferated after *The Walking Dead*.

However, not all horror fiction took the undead as seriously as Brooks did. In fact the other key text to emerge from the zombie boom could be considered the direct opposite of *World War Z*'s meticulous dystopian consideration of an infested world that is very eminently ours. Supplanting verisimilitude for grossness and laughs derived from the incongruence of setting and tone, Seth Grahame-Smith's trendsetting *Pride and Prejudice and Zombies* (2009) pitted the explicit, carnal pleasures of zombie trash against the literary, canonical fiction of Jane Austen. The novel, which names Austen as first co-author, is an effective mash-up of her famous classic with reworked passages and scenes that relate a zombie invasion. Although the events follow the original quite closely, the additions naturally lead to the telling of a very different story, one in which the heroine Elizabeth Bennet is fighting, in the same stride, both the abstract social pressures of Regency England and a very literal, flesh-eating horde. Thus the novel's famous opening line, '[i]t is a truth universally acknowledged, that a single man in possession of a good fortune must be in want of a wife' (Austen 2008: 1), becomes '[i]t is a truth universally acknowledged that a zombie in possession of brains must be in want of more brains' (Austen and Grahame-Smith 2009: 7). Although considered little more than a silly pulp experiment by some or, at worst, a sacrilegious cash-in appropriation of a classic of British literature, *Pride and Prejudice and Zombies* proved a novelty with bite.

Apart from being the source of a prequel, *Pride and Prejudice and Zombies: Dawn of the Dreadfuls* (2010), which follows Elizabeth Bennet's upbringing and training in the art of defeating the dead, and a sequel, *Pride and Prejudice and Zombies: Dreadfully Ever After* (2011), Quirk Books also published a number of other, less well-known parodies that continued to rewrite Austen (Ben H. Winters's *Sense and Sensibility and Sea Monsters* in 2009) alongside the work of Tolstoy (Ben H. Winters's *Android Karenina* of 2010) or Kafka (Coleridge Cook's *The Meowmorphosis* of 2011). The novel was also adapted into a major film by Burr Steers in 2016. Seth Grahame-Smith continued to develop this parodic subgenre by writing *Abraham Lincoln, Vampire Hunter* (2010), quite possibly the first biographical horror mash-up novel, and which, as its title suggests, imagines an alternative life for the 16th president of the United States. In it, Lincoln's abolitionist beliefs (and familial vampire-killing skills) are underscored by the revelation that bloodsuckers are also slave drivers.

More than any other monster, zombies have become the most pervading horror icon for the early twenty-first century. Their metaphorical value has allowed for readings that understand the shambling, endlessly replicable, empty-minded mass of the undead as negotiating pressing concerns related to economics (Quiggin 2012), public education or politics (Giroux 2010) or the terrible legacy of neoliberal capitalism on the contemporary subject (Harman 2010). The zombie is also the network monster par excellence, insofar as it channels preoccupations related to the role of the individual in an overpopulated world dominated by social media and information systems which, ironically, could be pushing us further and further away from each other. As Roger Luckhurst has put it, it is possible to see zombies as

> simply us reflected back, depersonalised, flat-lined by the alienating tedium of modern existence. They are the pressing problem of the modern world's sheer number of people, the population explosion, bodies crammed into super-cities and suburban sprawls, demanding satiation beyond any plan for sustainable living. Survival horror is the crisis of the last representatives of rugged Western individualism trying to wrest themselves from the unregarded life of the anonymized mass. (Luckhurst 2015: 10–1)

It is not surprising, then, that in Stephen King's *Cell*, it is precisely a signal – the Pulse – broadcast over the global phone network which corrupts the brains of its listeners and becomes the catalyst for the zombie apocalypse. A creature that both defines our contemporary, hyper-affected and forever mediated post-millennial condition and still, simultaneously, continues to embody the worst apocalyptic nightmare yet to come, the zombie serves to channel fears intimately connected to modern digital technologies and the pessimistic view that we are already living in the end times. Our embrace of and persistent fascination with this figure needs to be explained as more than a simple interest in visceral literature; the zombie also serves as a cautionary tale. Worryingly, our zombies are not just ourselves, but an image of what we might still become – should we persevere in mindlessly shuffling onwards, unwilling to come to terms with the horrors of the present.

References

Ajvide Lindqvist, John, *Let the Old Dreams Die* (London: Quercus, 2012).
——, *Little Star* (London: Quercus, 2011).
——, *Let the Right One In* (London: Quercus, 2008).
Austen, Jane, *Pride and Prejudice* (Oxford: Oxford University Press, 2008).
——, and Seth Grahame-Smith, *Pride and Prejudice and Zombies* (Philadelphia, PA: Quirk Books, 2009).
Birch, Dinah (ed.), *The Oxford Companion to English Literature*, 7th edn (Oxford: Oxford University Press, 2009).
Barron, Laird, *The Croning* (San Francisco, CA: Night Shade Books, 2012).
Brooks, Max, *World War Z: An Oral History of the Zombie War* (London: Duckworth Overlook, 2013).
——, *The Zombie Survival Guide: Complete Protection from the Living Dead* (London: Duckworth Overlook, 2004).
Giroux, Henry A., *Zombie Politics and Culture in the Age of Casino Capitalism* (New York: Peter Lang, 2010).
Harman, Chris, *Zombie Capitalism: Global Crisis and the Relevance of Marx* (Chicago, IL: Haymarket Books, 2010).
Hill, Joe, *NOS4R2* (London: Gollancz, 2014).
Joshi, S. T., *The Modern Weird Tale* (Jefferson, NC: McFarland, 2001).

——, *The Evolution of the Weird Tale* (New York: Hippocampus Press, 2004).

——, *Unutterable Horror: A History of Supernatural Fiction. Volume 2: The Twentieth and Twenty-First Centuries* (New York: Hippocampus Press, 2014).

Luckhurst, Roger, *Zombies: A Cultural History* (London: Reaktion, 2015).

Nelson, Victoria, *Gothicka: Vampire Heroes, Human Gods, and the New Supernatural* (London and Cambridge, MA: Harvard University Press, 2012).

Quiggin, John, *Zombie Economics: How Dead Ideas Still Walk among Us* (Princeton, NJ: Princeton University Press, 2012).

VanderMeer, Ann, and Jeff VanderMeer (eds), *The Weird: A Compendium of Dark and Strange Stories* (London: Corvus, 2011)

VanderMeer, Jeff, *City of Saints and Madmen* (London: Tor Books, 2014).

——, *Finch* (London: Corvus, 2010).

——, 'The New Weird: "It's Alive?"', in *The New Weird*, ed. by Ann and Jeff VanderMeer (San Francisco, CA: Tachyon Publications, 2008), pp. ix–xviii.

What to Read Next

John Ajvide Lindqvist, *Let the Right One In* (2007; London: Quercus, 2009).

Laird Barron, *The Beautiful Thing That Awaits Us All: Stories* (New York: Night Shade Books, 2013).

Max Brooks, *World War Z: An Oral History of the Zombie War* (2006; London: Duckworth Overlook, 2013).

Joe Hill, *NOS4R2* (2013; London: Gollancz, 2014).

Caitlín R. Kiernan, *The Red Tree* (2009; New York: ROC Books, 2010).

Jeff VanderMeer, *Area X: The Southern Reach Trilogy: Annihilation, Authority, Acceptance* (London: Fourth Estate, 2014).

Further Critical Reading

This list is intended for the interested reader who might want to find out more about the history of horror or key debates in this field. It includes a selection of critical works, both monographs and edited collections, and readers.

Aldana Reyes, Xavier, *Body Gothic: Corporeal Transgression in Contemporary Literature and Horror Film* (Cardiff: University of Wales Press, 2014).

Auerbach, Nina, *Our Vampires, Ourselves* (London and Chicago, IL: Chicago University Press, 1995).

Baldick, Chris, *In Frankenstein's Shadow: Myth, Monstrosity and Nineteenth-Century Writing* (Oxford: Clarendon Press, 1987).

Barker, Clive, *Clive Barker's A–Z of Horror*, compiled by Stephen Jones (New York: HarperCollins, 1997).

Barron, Neil, *Fantasy and Horror: A Critical and Historical Guide to Literature, Illustration, Film, Radio and the Internet* (London: Scarecrow Press, 1999).

Bell, Karl, *The Legend of Spring-Heeled Jack, Victorian Urban Folklore and Popular Cultures* (Woodbridge: The Boydell Press, 2012).

Berrutti, Massimo, S. T. Joshi and Sam Gafford (eds), *William Hope Hodgson: Voices from the Borderland* (New York: Hippocampus Press, 2014).

Birkhead, Edith, *The Tale of Terror: A Study of the Gothic Romance* (1921; Cirencester: Echo Library, 2005).

Bloom, Clive, *Gothic Horror: A Guide for Students and Readers*, rev. edn (1998; Basingstoke: Palgrave Macmillan, 2007).

—— (ed.), *Creepers: British Horror and Fantasy in the Twentieth Century* (London: Pluto Press, 1993).

Bown, Nicola, Carolyn Burdett and Pamela Thurschwell (eds), *The Victorian Supernatural* (Cambridge: Cambridge University Press, 2004).

Briggs, Julia, *Night Visitors: The Rise and Fall of the English Ghost Story* (London: Faber and Faber, 1977).

Byron, Glennis, and Dale Townshend (eds), *The Gothic World* (Abingdon: Routledge, 2014).

Carroll, Noël, *The Philosophy of Horror: Or, Paradoxes of the Heart* (London and New York: Routledge, 1990).

Crow, Charles, *American Gothic* (Cardiff : University of Wales Press, 2009).

Docherty, Brian, *American Horror Fiction: From Brockden Brown to Stephen King* (Basingstoke: Macmillan, 1990).

Drakakis, John, and Dale Townshend (eds), *Gothic Shakespeares* (London: Routledge, 2008).

Errickson, Will, *Too Much Horror Fiction: Horror of the 60s, 70s, 80s.* <http://toomuchhorrorfiction.blogspot.kr> [accessed 10 October 2015].

Frayling, Christopher, *Nightmare: The Birth of Horror* (London: BBC Books, 1996).

Gelder, Ken, *The Horror Reader* (London: Routledge, 2000).

——, *Reading the Vampire* (London: Routledge, 1994).

Gilbert, Pamela K. (ed.), *A Companion to Sensation Fiction* (Oxford: Blackwell, 2011).

Goddu, Teresa A., *Gothic America: Narrative, History and Nation* (New York: Columbia University Press, 1997).

Goho, James, *Journeys into Darkness: Critical Essays on Gothic Horror* (London:, MD: Rowman and Littlefield, 2014).

Golden, Christopher (ed.), *Cut: Horror Writers on Horror Film* (New York: Berkley, 1992).

Grixti, Joseph, *Terrors of Uncertainty: The Cultural Contexts of Horror Fiction* (London: Routledge, 1989).

Groom, Nick, *Gothic: A Very Short Introduction* (Oxford: Oxford University Press, 2012).

Halberstam, Judith, *Skin Shows: Gothic Horror and the Technology of Monsters* (London and Durham, NC: Duke University Press, 1995).

Hills, Matt, *The Pleasures of Horror* (London: Continuum, 2005).

Hogle, Jerrold E. (ed.), *The Cambridge Companion to Gothic Fiction* (Cambridge: Cambridge University Press, 2002).

Hurley, Kelly, *The Gothic Body: Sexuality, Materialism, and Degeneration at the Fin de Siècle* (Cambridge: Cambridge University Press, 2004).

Jackson, Rosemary, *Fantasy: The Literature of Subversion* (London and New York: Routledge, 1988).

Jancovich, Mark, *Rational Fears: American Horror in the 1950s* (Manchester: Manchester University Press, 1996).

——, *Horror* (London: B. T. Batsford, 1992).

Jones, Darryl, *Horror: A Thematic History in Fiction and Film* (London: Arnold, 2002).

Jones, Stephen, and Kim Newman, *Horror: 100 Best Books* (London: NEL, 1992).

Joshi, S. T., *Unutterable Horror: A History of Supernatural Fiction*, 2 vols (New York: Hippocampus Press, 2012).

——, *The Weird Tale* (Holicong, PA: Wildside Reference, 2003).

——, *The Modern Weird Tale* (Jefferson, NC: McFarland, 2001).

King, Stephen, *Danse Macabre* (London: Warner Books, 1981).

Lloyd-Smith, Allan, *American Gothic Fiction: An Introduction* (New York: Continuum, 2005).

Lovecraft, H. P., *Supernatural Horror in Literature* (1927; Mineola, NY: Dover, 1973).

Luckhurst, Roger, *Zombies: A Cultural History* (London: Reaktion, 2015).

Poole, W. Scott, *Monsters in America: Our Historical Obsession with the Hideous and the Haunting* (Waco, TX: Baylor University Press, 2011).

Punter, David, *The Literature of Terror: A History of Gothic Fiction from 1765 to the Edwardian Age, Vol. I, The Gothic Tradition* (1996; Abingdon: Routledge, 2013).

——, *The Literature of Terror: A History of Gothic Fiction from 1765 to the Edwardian Age, Vol. II, The Modern Gothic* (1996; Abingdon: Routledge, 2013).

Sage, Victor, *Horror Fiction in the Protestant Tradition* (Basingstoke: Macmillan, 1988).

Schmid, David, *Natural Born Celebrities: Serial Killers in American Culture* (Chicago, IL: University of Chicago Press, 2005).

Seltzer, Mark, *Serial Killers: Life and Death in America's Wound Culture* (New York: Routledge, 1998).

Showalter, Elaine, *Sexual Anarchy: Gender and Culture at the Fin de Siècle* (London: Bloomsbury, 1991).

Skal, David J., *The Monster Show: A Cultural History of Horror* (New York: Plexus, 1994).

Smith, Andrew, *The Ghost Story 1840–1920* (Manchester: Manchester University Press, 2010).

Soltysik Monnet, Agnieszka, *The Poetics and Politics of the American Gothic* (Farnham: Ashgate, 2010).

Springhall, John, *Youth, Popular Culture and Moral Panics: Penny Gaffs to Gangsta-Rap, 1830–1996* (Basingstoke: Macmillan, 1998).

Sullivan, Jack, *The Penguin Encyclopaedia of Supernatural Literature* (New York: Penguin, 1986).

Townshend, Dale (ed.), *Terror and Wonder: The Gothic Imagination* (London: British Library Publishing, 2014).

Twitchell, James B., *Dreadful Pleasures: An Anatomy of Modern Horror* (New York: Oxford University Press, 1985).

——, *The Living Dead: A Study of the Vampire in Romantic Literature* (Durham, NC: Duke University Press, 1981).

Tymn, Marshall B., *Horror Literature: A Core Collection and Reference Guide* (London and New York: R. R. Bowker Company, 1981).

Wisker, Gina, *Horror Fiction: An Introduction* (New York: Continuum, 2005).

Index

Italic page numbers refer to illustrations.